AGAINST THE BABYLONIAN CAPTIVITY

FISCHER.

Au Pontife Romain je temoigne mon Zele,
Aue depuis de celui que je dois a mon Roi,
Je meurs comme martir, ou bien comme rebelle,
Et je veux tout le monde ou pour ou contre moi.

Adr. vander Werff pinx.   G. Valck Sculp.

The Defense of the Royal Assertion
AGAINST MARTIN LUTHER'S THE BABYLONIAN CAPTIVITY OF THE CHURCH

By

St. John Fisher

Translated by
Jonathan Arrington

With a new foreword by
Joshua Charles

MEDIATRIX PRESS
MMXXIV

ISBN: 978-1-957066-47-9

Translated from *Assertionum Regis Angliæ De Fide Catholica Adversus Lutheri Babylonicam Captivitatem Defensio*, Opera Omnia; Würzburg, Germany, the house of George Fleischmann, 1597. All Rights Reserved.
Scripture quotations taken from the Douay Rheims Edition.

Cover art/Frontispiece: *St. John Fisher.*
Gerard Valck, 1697.

Mediatrix Press
607 6th Ave.
Post Falls, ID 83854
www.mediatrixpress.com

CONTENTS

FOREWORD
by Joshua Charles

T is a high honor to pen this introduction to a great work by a holy saint. For too long, St. John Fisher's *Confutation* of Luther's *The Babylonian Captivity of the Church* and *Response to Henry, King of England* has laid in obscurity, unavailable to the mass of Catholics unlearned in the ancient Roman tongue.

Thanks to this great labor of love, this obscurity has now been dispelled, and the glorious light of truth that laid hidden within this masterpiece has now been revealed.

St. John Fisher was one of the holiest men of his era. Admired throughout Europe, he was not only a champion of scholarship, but a man of great sanctity. Ordained at 22, he was appointed the bishop of Rochester at 35. This diocese was often seen as a stepping-stone to higher office in the Church in England, but Fisher would remain there the rest of his life. He rose to become Chancellor of Cambridge University, where he championed new scholarship, while remaining grounded in the ancient. He helped recover the works of the Church Fathers, as well as the Scriptures in their original Hebrew and Greek tongues.

The Controversy with Luther

But providence had even more in store for Fisher, whose great learning proved to be a powerful tool in defense of Catholic truth amidst the revolutionary tumult of the protestant revolt. He would be one of Martin Luther's greatest antagonists. His writings against perhaps the greatest of all heresiarchs are finally being recovered thanks to apostolates like Mediatrix Press.

As a convert from protestantism myself, it is remarkable to see Fisher argue based on the very facts which did so much to effect my conversion. The short version of the long story is this: throughout my late adolescence and 20's, I had a growing number of questions about how to square basic protestant doctrines (and their multiple variants) with Scripture. I read protestant authors, and discussed my struggles with learned mentors. The answers they gave me were quite unsatisfying—including those I read from Luther himself. I kept assuming someone had squared the round hole of "faith alone" and other protestant doctrines that simply made no sense to me from Scripture.

Such were the conclusions I had reached prior to reading a single Catholic.

Everything began to change when, in my late 20's, I began reading the ancient Church Fathers. Prior to that time, all I had read were small selections from St. Augustine's *City of God* and *Confessions*. But beginning in the summer of 2017, reading the Church Fathers literally became my full-time job.

What I discovered—initially to my great horror—was that protestantism was absolutely nowhere to be found in their writings. The ancient, supposedly biblical faith we declared we had restored against Catholic usurpation and apostasy was simply not there. Instead, from the times of the earliest Fathers who enjoyed the company of the Apostles through the first millennium and into the medieval era, I found the Catholic Faith and Church everywhere.

Why did this matter so much? Because I knew Christ had promised to remain with the Church and guide Her into all truth. If Luther's was the "true Gospel," what I was reading in the Fathers proved that the "true Gospel" had been unknown for 1,500 years.

But if that was true, all sorts of frightful conclusions followed in its wake. Why should Luther be believed over the consistent witness of 1,500 years of Christians? If 1,500 years of Christians were wrong, how could I have any confidence that Luther and his progeny were right? These and other questions led to a genuine crisis of faith. I did not cease trusting that Christ would guide me to where I should be. But I knew I had to get to the bottom of things. Eventually I did, and I am now Catholic. I trust my conclusions were obvious.

This is all worth mentioning because one of the biggest issues I struggled with for years was the problem of resolving theological controversy while maintaining the unity of the Church. Both seemed to be clearly exemplified in Scripture in places like the Jerusalem Council in Acts 15. But we protestants had nothing like what I saw in Acts 15—a Church that could consider a theological controversy and render judgment with God's authority.

These are among the points that Fisher repeatedly makes against Luther. While the bishop of Rochester was more than happy to dismantle his reading of Scripture on a purely exegetical basis, he also appeals to the consistent witness of the Fathers against Luther's novelties. Indeed, one of the ways I tried to *avoid* becoming Catholic was reading and re-reading even more works by Luther and the like, hoping they would convince me of their position. My hopes were bitterly disappointed, as I was astounded to see Luther so openly admit that he could not find his notion of "faith alone" and other doctrines in the Fathers. Meanwhile, he congratulated himself on supposedly restoring "pure" doctrine. As he was recorded saying in §530 of his *Table Talk*, closer to the end of his life:

> Behold what great darkness is in the books of the Fathers concerning faith...St Jerome, indeed, wrote upon [books in Scripture], but, alas! very coldly. Ambrose wrote six books upon the first book of Moses, but they are very poor. Augustin wrote nothing to the purpose concerning faith...I can find no exposition upon the Epistles to the Romans and Galatians, wherein anything is taught pure and right...We must read the Fathers cautiously, and lay them in the gold balance, for they often stumbled and went astray, and mingled in their books many monkish things...The more I read the books of the Fathers, the more I find myself offended...

Elsewhere, he mentions other Fathers who apparently missed

11

the heart of the gospel that he had recovered.

To get around the charge that he was inventing novelties, Luther would sometimes claim that all he was asserting was what was "ancient." But what he meant by "ancient" was Scripture itself, and his peculiar interpretation of it—an interpretation that, as he himself admitted, had been missed by millennia of Christendom's greatest saints. Fisher called Luther a "fox" for such intellectually dishonest behavior, which, with the powerful aids of gaseous oratory, he often weaponized to great effect.

Fisher exposed Luther's pretense of being "ancient" by appealing to the consistent witness of the Church Fathers—the very thing that did so much to help me and many other former protestants come Home to the Catholic Church:

> Therefore, it is not as Luther boasts, "My teachings are nothing other than Christ's teachings," given that he is at odds with the Fathers; Luther's teachings, you see, are nothing other than scriptural interpretations that are twisted to be against the true sense of Christ, and since Luther's teachings have still not been corroborated by any miracles, Christians are not at all bound to give assent to his teachings.

As Fisher explained elsewhere, in the absence of any patristic support, Luther's only recourse would have been miraculous signs, which he never claimed:

> This is why, if Luther wishes to introduce other things than that which the Church has hitherto believed and which are clearly different from what she has believed up to this point, then he must do so by a demonstration of the Spirit and of power; that is, he must prove it with signs and miracles, rather than by a twisted misinterpretation of Scripture that goes against the meaning that Christ and so many

and so very learned and holy Fathers gave as their unanimous decisions, those who have preceded us by many centuries.

"I do not deny that one or another of the Fathers might err," qualified Fisher, "but that all should err in a serious matter that pertains to the faith, and when they have unanimously agreed upon it? I am so far from believing such, that I should much rather die in this faith." His reasons were precisely the same as the ones that convinced me of Catholic claims—Christ's promises to His Church precluded such a possibility:

> I do not deny that one or another of the Fathers might err, for it is unbelievable that the same Holy Spirit whom Christ called the Spirit of Truth and promised to send for this purpose—that is, to remain within the Church to teach us all truth—should allow it to happen that so many of our leaders who went before us should have all erred, through such a long period of time, and with such great damage and disastrous death for souls. I should also add that whoever decides to despise these predecessors and disdains to hold these prior Fathers as the leaders of his path and progress, but rather remains confidently reliant on his own judgment and follows his own spirit, such a person invades Christ's flock, and the indication is quite evident: the gatekeeper did not open unto him, nor did he enter through the true door, but like a thief and robber, he came upon the gate and the gatekeeper from another location.

Luther's *Babylonian Captivity*, in particular, was truly astounding in both the breadth and falsity of its claims. Many protestants today claim Luther was simply trying to reform from within the Church, not fundamentally change its faith. That may have been true in 1517. But by the early 1520's, it most certainly was not.

By then, Luther had come to deny a majority of the sacraments; he excluded books like the epistle of James from the biblical canon; he denied the sacrificial nature of the Eucharist and the existence of the ministerial priesthood, both of which are unanimously attested across all generations of the Church Fathers. His *Babylonian Captivity* is full of countless errors such as these, accompanied by his ersatz religion to replace them.

Luther was not reforming anything—he was revolting. Despite his many promises of obedience to various authorities—to the Pope, yes, but others as well—his theology continued to grow increasingly radical. Between 1518 and his finalized excommunication in 1521, Luther repeatedly dug in his heels. He had promised obedience; he instead rebelled. He famously declared at the *Diet of Worms* that his conscience was captive to the "word of God." But if indeed that was true, then as Fisher noted, countless generations of saints and martyrs of the highest standing in both east and west were simply unaware of, and indeed often unanimously contradicted Luther's "word of God." Either Luther was right, and they were wrong; or Luther's "word of God" was actually just the word of Luther, devilishly disguised by appeals to Christ and the Bible.

Such is the general outline of Fisher's refutation of Luther. The details are rich and engrossing. Fisher's pen is not only erudite, but clever and delightful to read.

Be assured of an intellectual and spiritual feast within these pages whose reappearance in the English language we have cause to celebrate in an age of often false and deceptive ecumenism.

The King's Great Matter

Given his reputation for both scholarship and holiness—both abundantly exhibited in his confrontation with Luther—Fisher was called upon by King Henry VIII in 1527 to assist in the resolution of "the King's great matter." The "great matter" was the issue of his marriage to Queen Catherine of Aragon. Henry asserted their marriage was invalid. Catherine disputed this. Judgment in the case rested with the Holy See.

Fisher represented the Queen in the controversy. From the beginning, he was clear as crystal, and bold as a lion in his defense of the both the sanctity of marriage, its indissolubility, and the authority of the Pope to decide in the matter. Henry, of course, would come to dispute each of these points. But Fisher remained unmoved. His conduct throughout would exemplify the same zeal for truth as he showed against Luther when the King was on his side. The world was tossed about with the wind. The saint was not.

Henry's ultimate break with Rome would not come until 1534, when the "Act of Supremacy" declared him head of the Church in England. But in the decade or so prior, many Englishmen of high estate in both sacred and secular orders began the protracted process of caving to this tragic outcome, quite literally affirming "That is truth if it pleases your highness." Fisher went on record in dissent: "No, sir, not I. Ye have not my consent thereto."

Throughout the entire affair, he was threatened both implicitly and explicitly—first with glances and whispers, then with clenched fists and shouts—with loss of goods, office, and reputation. In his defense of the validity of Henry and Catherine's marriage, he even cited the example of St. John the Baptist dying at the hand of King Herod, another lecherous monarch. As the secretary of the Cardinal who was managing the case observed, Fisher "has kept everyone in wonder."

Martyrdom and Glorification

Fisher's stalwart courage in defense of matrimony and the papacy would ultimately cost him his life.

When he was arrested and imprisoned in the Tower of London, his goods were confiscated. His estate was exceptionally modest. Instead of pomp and riches, the royal officers found his hair shirt and whip—tools by which the holy man submitted himself to the ascetical training so frequent among the saints.

Before his execution, he was named a Cardinal, making him the only Cardinal to this day who has suffered martyrdom.

We are thus struck by a most ironic but cathartic parallelism between the lives of Luther and Fisher.

The German monk abandoned his vows of fidelity, obedience, chastity, and poverty, declaring the voluntary inhibitions of the flesh in which he once believed to be evidence of the "captivity" of the Church. The once thin monk ended his life voluptuously. He thought himself fit and able to invent a new faith, and his grotesque pride has been begrudgingly recognized even by protestants. His obstinacy often relied on continuous royal support of one kind or another. He declared himself "liberated" from the Catholic Faith as it had always been believed. He claimed that his manic depression was caused by a supposed Catholic focus on "works" at the expense of grace, and that it was cured by his newfound "freedom of a Christian" based on "faith alone." In reality, the rest of his life up to his death was as full of manic swings between elation and despair as it had always been. He lived long enough to witness many others take up the same "freedom of a Christian" he had, and in the process inventing countless new errors and effecting endless schisms, often contradicting him as much as they contradicted the Pope.

Fisher, on the other hand, was virtually the opposite in every regard. He remained faithful to all his vows until the end. He lived the life of an ascetic, pounding his body into submission, as St. Paul had, lest after preaching to others he himself be disqualified. His body expired thin and gaunt. He defended the ancient faith against novel heresies seeking to supplant it. He was famous not for his pride, but for his humility and virtue. His tenacity never wavered, regardless of royal support. He did not presume to liberate himself from the ancient Faith, but considered himself captive to it, even while championing new forms of scholarship. He ended his life as he had begun and lived it: a faithful son of the Church.

He was the St. Athanasius of England insofar as he was opposed by almost all. He was a greater than Athanasius insofar as it cost him the shedding of his own blood.

It is thus of monumental significance that this work has been translated into his own native tongue, and ours, for the first time in 500 years.

May it validate, confirm, and encourage Catholics in their fidelity to the one true Faith.

May it help unite the scattered remnants of the elect deceived by the errors inherited from their protestant ancestors.

May it cause our hearts to burn with charity unto the attainment of that heavenly glory in which God is all in all.

St. John Fisher—pray for us!

PUBLISHER'S PREFACE
TO THE 1ST ENGLISH EDITION

MOST Catholics have heard of St. John Fisher, but usually in association with his fellow martyr, St. Thomas More. Many know few other details than that he refused to accept Henry VIII's break from Rome, and was thus executed. Few know that Fisher was famous in the first half of the 16th century, not only as a holy reforming bishop, but also as one of the greatest theologians in Europe.

Fisher was a major figure at the University of Cambridge, eventually rising to be its chancellor. He was an incredibly gifted academic, whose fidelity to the Church did not prevent him from embracing what was called the "new learning," the theological track of Renaissance Humanism focusing on a recovery of the Church Fathers, as well as the Greek and Hebrew Languages. Yet, Fisher's embrace of the new did not cause him to throw out the old, as it did with his friend Erasmus. Both the Fathers and Scholastics formed one tradition and one faith for Fisher, together with the Councils and teaching authority of the Church. His masterful theological acumen made him the right man to oppose the ill wind blowing in from Germany.

Luther had begun, to all appearances, from the fairly modest position of reform of abuses. But he quickly moved to deny several Catholic doctrines, and assert many other teachings which were false on Justification, the Papacy, the Sacraments, etc. In 1520 he was condemned by Pope Leo X in his bull *Exsurge Domine*, and Luther, far from recanting, reasserted his forty articles, and burned the entire corpus of Canon Law.

As the crisis continued, Henry VIII of England sensed an opportunity to win prestige in letters which had been denied to him in war. He assembled numerous theologians, including St. John Fisher, who aided him in writing a defense of the Church's sacraments against Luther's treatise *De Babylonica Captivitate*, or, *The Babylonian Captivity of the Church.* Henry's work was titled *Assertio Septem Sacramentorum* or, the *Assertion of the Seven Sacraments: Against the Doctrine of Martin Luther.* It contained a dedicatory epistle to Pope Leo X, with a robust defense of Papal Supremacy. The occasion of the public unveiling of this book in England also became Fisher's first foray into the defense against Luther. Cardinal Wolsey had prepared a splendid ceremony at St. Paul's Cross, where Fisher was appointed to preach against Luther's heresies. His sermon, on the assistance provided to the Church by the Holy Spirit, was printed numerous times. During a pre-arranged point in the sermon, Fisher paused, and made reference to the King's book (the *Assertio*), which Wolsey held up to the crowd for great applause and cheering. The ceremony concluded with the burning of Lutheran books and tracts. At the same time, Fisher was already hard at work on a refutation of Luther's Articles, which would eventually be published in 1523 and to which he refers the reader several times. As of the time of this publication, it is yet to be rendered into English.

Just the same, the 1521 publication of Henry's *Assertio* did not escape Luther's notice. The next year, he vigourously replied with his work *Contra Henricum regem Angliæ,* or *Against Henry, King of England.* Throughout, Luther mocks Henry, and resorts to name-calling worse than what had hitherto been seen in print, while only giving limited response to the arguments. Henry would not respond—indeed, royal protocol would not allow him to acknowledge such insults against the royal person. Instead, he tapped More and Fisher to write responses. More's response, the *Responsio ad Convitia Martini Lutheri,* was published in 1523 under the pen name of Guilielmus Rosseus (William Ross). Since a William Ross had died on pilgrimage in Rome, it was supposed for a while that he must have written it (see Stapleton, *Tres Thomæ*). The work uses foul language at least as bad, if not worse than Luther's response to the King, but More's point in employing such language was not to justify the use of rude language per se, but rather, to show he could use Latin cuss words more eloquently, more intelligently, and with better puns and turns of a phrase than Luther could. *Quasi dicere,* More would have it that Luther is such a dunce, he can't even swear like an educated man.

At any rate, Fisher took a different approach. As we mentioned, his magnum opus against Luther, the *Assertionis Lutheranæ Confutatio* was published in January of the same year as More's response. The text weighs in at over 800 pages in Latin, quoting Luther verbatim in each article, and taking exhaustive pains to attack the foundation of Luther's thought, especially the doctrine of faith alone. Even more than his English sermon at St. Paul's cross, the *Confutatio* would go through countless editions, and would go on to be influential at the Council of Trent.

The present volume, *The Defense of the Royal Assertion*, however, is a work that is more on the defensive, and would have to take a different tone from that of the *Confutatio*. Fisher could not quote the scurrilous things said about Henry, so he widens the work to address not only Luther's response, but Luther's work *On the Babylonian Captivity*. Fisher's tone is more aggressive than in his other works, aggrieved by Luther's sheer impudence in not answering his king but hurling abuse at him instead. The extent to which Fisher defers to Henry and takes pains to defend him might surprise the reader, who has the benefit of history to know the poor reward Fisher was to receive for his efforts a mere 10 years later.

It is with great pleasure that we are able to present the first English translation of Fisher's work against Luther since the late Fr. Hallett began the work in the 1930s with Fisher's *Defence of the Priesthood*. Moreover, we are happy to compliment Angelus Press' 2023 publication of Fisher's defence of the Holy Eucharist against Oecolampadius. We can only hope that all of Fisher's Latin treatises may find their way into print so as to give the glory due to Fisher in letters, which he has enjoyed for his holy martyrdom.

Ryan Grant
Post Falls, ID
January 2024

PROLOGUE

IN this prologue the author reckons with and reproaches Luther, whom he depicts precisely, as he gives the rationale, substance, and order of what will follow.

It is Christ's voice in the Canticle of Canticles: "Capture for us the little foxes that destroy the vineyards" (Song of Solomon 2). Thereby he clearly warns that heretics are to be taken before their kindling grows up, because these same men seek by vulpine fraud to raze the vineyards, that is, Christ's Church. So, I should have hoped that those whose duty it is to round up heretics while they are still small had heard that voice: then there would not be such a serious storm in the Church and upheaval of everything, had Luther been repressed while he was still a little fox. Now, however, he has turned into a pretty well grown-up fox, full of years, inveterate, armed with so many tricks and wiles so that it is extremely difficult to hold this crafty character in place. But why did I call him a fox? That is not sufficient: I should have said "a rabid dog," or rather the greediest wolf or a most brutal mother-bear that grabs her young and rages about with them. Or, more like all these things simultaneously: this monster feeds many beasts within — but he is proud of this list of names. He actually calls himself a mother bear and lioness, because he promises to be such towards Catholics: "You will encounter Luther as a mother bear along the way, a lioness on the path."

From a little fox, Luther finally turned into this sort of monster. For some time he played the fox, you see, by his deceitfulness and subterfuge; then he became a dog by his lack of shame, bark, and bite; he later showed himself to be a wolf by his rapaciousness, feral nature, and mangling; finally he has betrayed that he is lioness and bear by his fury and cruel severity. He is a monstrous wild beast for sure, such that not even those which Daniel saw in the sea sufficiently show his uniquely horrendous unnaturalness in evil. He has the eyes of a man because he sees nothing above man and yet from that fact, even if at some point he had been taken up to the third heaven, his mouth speaks immoderate things. He is fashioned with a tongue that is most virulent. He is armed with teeth that are harder than iron and with which he insatiably devours men's flesh; he mixes up all things and trounces with his feet whatever is left over. Yes, Luther has turned from a little fox into this sort of monster, and he got for himself such a den in which to safely hide that he securely exhales into the whole world a stinking breath from his putrid chest: the lethal virus of his heresies. If anyone should dare to contradict him there is none whom he would not pursue with such bitter and biting insults and abusive invective such as can hardly be dreamed up, so that this beast takes no mind even of the most potent kings.

For lately, the king of England, who is renowned for his military and literary exploits, set about to admonish him and to go through some of his errors, thus exhorting him to come to his senses. When Luther should have given thanks to his devout admonisher, he nevertheless spared no expense in the verbal abuse which he very cynically aimed at the king. You see, he had no respect either for the sacred learning which he himself professes or for the reverence due to such royalty, but rather like an insane and rabid person he poured all his soul's fury onto the most illustrious king, so that I marvel how anyone should trust such a man's teachings when he might clearly note how openly such a man contravenes Christ's mandates.

Yet he drew the poor people as he proudly threw about assertions and empty promises, and so did he attach them to himself such that they venerate him as a sort of prophet; for one so shamelessly and arrogantly can boast of himself as this Luther does in the beginning of his little book which he wrote against the most erudite king. Here is how he speaks: "I am certain that I have my teachings from heaven because they have triumphed against him who in his little finger has more power and craftiness than do all the popes, kings and Doctors." What incredible arrogance! What a horrifying monster! What a shameless face! Who has ever heard a beast that spoke such open lies about himself? His books are full of tons of errors, and yet he doesn't shy from calling himself certain that he got his dogmas from heaven. From sanity he has been cast down to such reproaches and he has lost his self-mastery and yet he brags that he has overcome the demons. As we shall soon show, he will try to cover up, lest certain very patent vices of his haughtiness should dissuade trust in him, and he will try to craftily cover up such things by a violently contorted use of the Scriptures. Therefore, we will give our manly best that this beast's fraud, lies, dogged voracity, and shameless selling of himself — which he used in his little book against the unconquerable king — be unearthed, as succinctly as we can manage. But so that this coming disquisition can proceed most clearly we will arrange it in 12 chapters, according to the order that he followed in his own booklet.

CHAPTER I
Luther's Agitated Arrogance Is Openly Deceitful

T this foundational point, let us ponder Luther's boast by which he claims to have certainly received his dogmas from heaven. I know not what dogmas Luther wishes to be held as his, because if he happened to call them the counsels and commands of Christ, I in no way object that such are from heaven. Just the same, for those things that are beyond the meaning of Christ's words, Luther erroneously added such from his own brain, and such are in no way from heaven, yet these alone can be called Lutheran dogmas. They are indisputably of that sort whenever he introduces his own heresies, rather than the diametrically opposed institutes of the Most Holy Fathers, or when he interprets Scripture by his insane mind's musings, or then when, with habitual heedlessness, he condemns the Scriptures that had hitherto been received by the Church if they happen not to fit with his inventions, or he casts aside those Scriptures as if they were condemned. He condemns the Epistle of James, as it is clearly adverse to his heresies. He therefore rails that it is not at all apostolic, although it is approved by the Fathers all over the place, and is counted among the Catholic Epistles (or General Letters) by the universal Church. Please take note of the scoffing, dear reader.

This is the way he writes in his commentary on St. Peter's First Letter: "One can easily learn from this that the letter that is ascribed to James is no wise Apostolic, since it has no element of these things: most important is this article of faith, for unless there were the resurrection, we would have no consolation or hope, and Christ's work and passion would be in vain."

So you see why Luther denies that this letter is Apostolic: of course because James did not mention "Christ's resurrection." But if on this stingy account the letter of James is not apostolic, then neither are some of Paul's — especially the one written to Philemon, and both to Timothy — since therein the word "resurrection" does not appear.

Additionally, neither would Second Peter, of which Luther approves, be Apostolic, since Peter does not speak of the resurrection in it. If such a mock trial were admitted, we would reject many of the letters which the Church receives.

On the other hand, even if James does not expressly make mention of the resurrection, he does however mention both Christ's passion and his future coming — the two of which cannot be understood without an intervening resurrection. He likewise mentions in Chapter 5 the powerful word whereby we were regenerated, and that in the same words that Peter uses on the same subject in regard to God, "who regenerated us unto living hope." James speaks in this way: "Of his own will hath he begotten us by the word of truth, that we might be some beginning of his creature." St. Paul says something similar in his letter to the Hebrews: "We are made partakers of Christ: yet so, if we hold the beginning of his substance firm unto the end." Certainly the fact that we are regenerated by Christ and made partakers through the beginning of his substance refers to the power of his resurrection, birth, and passion, as well as anything else of worth which Christ took on for our sake, wherefore Luther's teaching here is not sound, nor is it credible that it emanated from heaven.

Other of Luther's dogmas is that Peter, Paul, and even the Most Blessed Virgin Mother of God enjoy no greater honor or dignity than does any other Christian, for he says this explicitly in his commentaries: "But since we are God's born again sons and inheritors, we are equal in honor and dignity to Sts. Peter and Paul, the Holy Virgin Deipara and all the saints, because we have the same treasure from God and all the same goods as fully as they, since they, too, had to be reborn, as do we. For that reason, they have nothing more than all other Christians." Those are Luther's claims.

Yet such words are plainly against the Scriptures, because they received a greater abundance of faith and grace than others, as is doubtless to be believed, and to that extent they are esteemed as worthier and more honorable than other Christians, such as they obtained a greater faith and grace. And although all of us have received from Christ's fullness, as John tells us, yet this was not imparted in equal measure to each person, since Paul says in Rom. 12, "We have diverse gifts according to the grace given to us," and again to the Ephesians in Ch. 4, "To each of us is grace given, according to the measure of Christ's gift." About faith, too, Paul says that the same measure has not been given to all (Rom 12), and he thus stipulates that none should esteem himself haughtily, but as God has given to each the measure of faith. Indeed if faith were not more meager in some and more copious in others, the Apostles would not have said to Christ: "Lord, increase our faith!"

On top of that, Christ praised Peter's faith but then elsewhere calls him a man of little faith. And if all have been born again, yet not all have received the same equal gift. It is clear, too, that the Blessed Virgin, before being born again of water, was filled with grace — and more than all others with a particular grace that she enjoyed before God, who filled her much more than any other besides Christ. There is no doubt that if there could have been any additional grace, she would have accepted it by her soul's more complete consent. Who needs to hear any more? This dogma — unless there is some additional explanation — is so patently insane that it needs no further refutation.

In addition, he made away with freedom of the will in his teaching, and he preaches that God is in us as the author of the good and bad, and that is most clearly against the Scriptures. So that I can bypass innumerable other points: in the First Epistle of Peter it is said, "You call Him Father, who is no respecter of persons as He judges the work of one and all." There you have it: God judges all impartially and according to each's works. But how can there be an impartial respect for persons with God when God would move me to sin and would produce in me nothing but evil? If he is the author of evil works towards me and the author of good works for another, how would he not be more kindly respecting that other person than me? And how would he justly judge me according to my works — which are not really mine — which I would have never completed by force of my own free will. Similarly the same

Peter notes this in Acts 10: "In very deed I perceive that God is not a respecter of persons. But in every nation, he that feareth him and worketh justice is acceptable to him." Now see here, if I am not working justice of my own accord, then I hope in vain to be accepted by God and on the other hand, if I am doing justly I will be accepted, since there is no respect of persons in his judgment; rather, of those works which are good or evil as they were carried out by those persons, there will be a just examination and for each, according to the measure of his strict judgment, the judgment will proceed rightly.

He also teaches that the judgment of whether or not a gospel is a gospel or something apostolic in Scripture or not is something that belongs equally to all Christians and that thus nothing can be held as definitive outside the time of the Apostles, even of that which our predecessors determined, be they of greatest erudition or exemplary sanctity. Anyone who is somewhat sane can see how much impiety that dogma contains. If there was ever in the church correct, precise, and solid judgment, then it was certainly in those days that were proximate to the Apostles, who are illustrious on account of their great and pure faith, as well as for the splendid abundance of their divine gifts. For this reason if it is permissible for modern Christians to call into doubt which our betters had approved in their prior judgments, what then inside the church can we hope to ever be certain, firm, and stable? We will discuss this more elsewhere, but I don't want this in the meanwhile to be left untouched: let us hear what Luther says, or does he believe that our betters — I'm speaking here of those ancient ones — had the true faith or not? If he does not believe so, then who at this point does not understand how he should justly be cursed by all. On the other hand, if he does believe that they had the true faith, then it should not escape us that their judgment must be confessed by all to be true and solid, for he writes thus in his commentaries on Peter's epistle: "Faith is a thing so lofty and wonderful that by it we may have a certain and clear knowledge of all the things that pertain to salvation, and we are then able to judge and pronounce freely on all those things which are upon the Earth. This doctrine is sound, that other is false. This life is good, that one is reprobate. This was done well, that was done otherwise. And whatever this sort that man defines, it is true and thus, for he cannot be deceived but is preserved and guarded by God's power and he remains thus: a judge of every doctrine."

In these words you see, reader, that the one who has faith has the power to judge each matter, and, moreover, that his judgment is true and cannot be deceived. For this reason, since our betters had the true faith, it also follows from Luther's own statement that they could not have been deceived in their judgment, because if their judgment was right and established how would the judgments of others who judged differently not also be completely judged beforehand? Now since Luther has pronounced a judgment against all of these, it is clear that his judgment is worthless, false, and erroneous.

Therefore it follows from what has been said that whatsoever Luther taught about the sacraments, contrition, Confession, and satisfaction, the Mass, The Testament, communion under both species, the priesthood, vows, the primacy of the Roman pontiff, the precepts, sin, good works, purgatory, excommunication, the power of absolving, and about whatever else likewise against the unanimous decision of our betters, must be judged to be completely alien to the truth. And so far from Heaven should it be believed to have come, that there is no doubt that it was rather inspired from hell and from the prince of darkness, Satan.

Furthermore, that his mouth was born for nothing but lies we shall clearly show from his own words, found at the bottom of his commentaries in an appendix written to Conrad Pelicanus, where the reader will see how he confesses three things: first that he erred greatly on the 11th psalm, and these are his words: "If Psalm 11 has not been printed I would like you to delete at the end of the final page B, verse 12, with the three following verses of letter C, for you can see how pitifully I erred in regard to the Hebrew word there." That is one error which not even he could deny. He would once again confess an error from the 13th psalm, as he writes in that same letter: "Having now forgotten what I dreamed up in regard to the Hebrew verb in verse 26 of Psalm 13, please delete that." There: these errors are so clear that no lying obfuscation was left for Luther to gloss over them. And yet he preached these from on high publicly.

You will see this from that same letter which we just read above: "There is much grace and Light that comes to hearers of something said live, which the chaos of books neither has nor contains." Now who will still say that these teachings came from Heaven? But hear, oh reader, this third admission in that same letter: Pelicanus seems to have warned him about his ferocious cursing and immoderate nature towards everyone, and Luther responded to him: "You correctly warn me about modesty and I myself note it, but I'm not in control of myself. I am taken by some spirit which I know not, since I am conscious that I will no ill to anyone. These people also urge most madly that but I do not sufficiently take note of Satan." Those are Luther's words.

Here the reader learns that Luther is not in control of himself, to wit that he is enraptured by a satanic spirit, and although he says it first that he does not know by what spirit, he later adds that he did not sufficiently make note of Satan, because there is hardly a doubt that it was his spirit that incited him and led him to such mad insanity. Yet note how openly he lies, for he says that he does not wish ill to anyone, although he nevertheless seeks to take away a person's good name — that thing which is most precious of all — by the insults and railing abuse against anyone who contradicts him. For the rest, I have noted these things thus far so that the candid reader may understand what Luther's teachings are like, how he claims to have certainly received them from heaven. I for sure, were I to want to force Scripture after the manner of Luther, might also show that Luther had received these teachings from heaven, since Christ said: "I saw Satan fall from Heaven like lightning." Perhaps he brought with him from heaven the teachings which he then passed on to Luther. To be sure, I can find no other manner by which Luther could have drawn up such pestilential teachings, since Satan is the very one against whom Luther boasts to have triumphed: "I have triumphed against him who in his pinkie finger has more power and craftiness than have all popes, kings, and Doctors." Now who else can be met here than Satan who — Luther claims — has such power and craftiness in his pinkie? Because if Luther triumphed over Satan then would he not have likewise despoiled him? That is, taken from him all his diabolic mysteries? Without a doubt unless he were full of the spirit of Satan he would have never been able to vomit forth against the great king and cultivator of the true faith such venomous bile and cantankerous anger.

But there is no doubt that Luther pretends that such is the case so that he can obtain for himself a greater authority with the common people, or else he is terribly mistaken, because how else can he be certain about all his dogmas, that they came from heaven, unless it had been plainly revealed to him? What is more, if it had been revealed to him then still such revelations most often deceive, because whatever is thought to have emanated from God is for the most part discovered to have come forth from a malign spirit. Or does Paul not say, "For Satan himself is transformed into an angel of light (2 Cor. 11:14)"? And in 3rd Kings[1] do we not read that a certain spirit said to the Lord, "I will go out and be a lying spirit in the mouths of all Ahab's prophets"? Even in our day there was a rather learned Girolamo of Florence (Jerome Savonarola) who persistently predicted what would happen to the people of Florence, and for that reason he gained for himself great fame both among the people and the princes. Notwithstanding, nothing of those things which he had predicted came about after his death, and by that meager means of discernment, it is clear (if we trust the Prophet Jeremiah) that his predictions did in no way come from God. For in Chapter 28 Jeremiah spoke this way to Ananiah who was prophesying falsely: "A prophet who foretells peace and then his word comes to pass will then be known as the prophet whom the Lord has truly sent." This same Savonarola therefore, as is clear, was deluded, although he was an ingenious man, and as much as can be discerned from human judgment, he was venerable both in word and in deed, nor did he ever establish anything in his own teaching that departed in the least from the orthodox Fathers, save that he thought nothing of the excommunication leveled against him and taught others to likewise despise that excommunication. So if that man who was so great and so Catholic could be seduced by revelations, what sort of certainty could we possibly have regarding Luther's revelations? That Florentine seems to have received serious affronts from Alexander, who was

---

[1] 1st Kings 22:22 in some Bibles.

then the sovereign pontiff, but he never spoke against the pope's authority but only against the abuse of that authority because he was possessed of great modesty, humility, patience, and charity. He never used invective against the pontifical dignity but against certain morals and ways of life, nor did he ever presume that something should be taught that was against the commonly held faith of the Catholic Church; but Luther is hardly ashamed to rail against the church's dogmas, to belittle the consensus of the fathers, to call even great and holy pontiffs "impostors", to consider naught that authority which Christ bestowed upon Peter, to attach the worst insults and invective to the loftiest kings, to infest the people with the most pernicious heresies, and to fill Heaven and Earth with lies. So shame-faced is he that he boasts that he received all of his teachings from heaven.

But let us see first what that fox has to cover his own cursing speech. He says that the king went after him first: but the king, as we shall soon see, did so in full justice: "But he pursued with utmost bitterness, although Paul says: 'speak well of those who pursue you.' Yet he followed up with the most bitter words. And what then? Does not Paul forbid us to render evil for evil and cursing for cursing? Yet I could not bear this insult nor did there lay bare another manner of vindication. "Yet you ought to have rather hearkened to Paul who admonished in this way: "Do not seek vengeance for yourselves, beloved, but give place to wrath" (Romans). Surely no one will ever persuade me that he overcame Satan unless he first overcame himself: for whoever is overcome by anger is a slave of anger and of sin, and a servant of Satan, yet he stupidly boasts that he has overcome Satan. You see, Luther cannot protest lest wrath should be a grave sin and especially since he openly declares elsewhere that in any and every work — no matter how good — there is sin. So, wrath cannot *not* be a grave sin, since even Christ holds liable to the fire of hell the one who is guilty of wrath against his brother. Because if the one who, due to anger, calls his brother a fool is thus held by Christ to be liable of hell-fire, then how much more the one who curses with innumerable blasphemies the same great prince and most devout cultivator of the Christian faith? This is hardly redolent of the spirit of Christ, rather it is plainly diabolical, because Christ's spirit in Paul commands that every soul should be submissive to the higher powers. He commands likewise that honor should be rendered to the same powers, since it is not without cause that they bear the sword. Luther, however, considers no king or prince to be in any respect greater than the most contemptible of poor men, for who — except the most insane and mindless — would so furiously go after the most base men, and spill upon them so many and so great angry abuses, as Luther drunkenly does against this most illustrious king? It would have gone much further had he been wholly ignorant of sacred Scripture rather than openly contradicting it. But why am I speaking of princes and kings? He belittles even the commands of the emperor nor does he judge the Sovereign Pontiff worthy of any respect. Rather, he levels him with insults, assaults him with taunts, and pursues him with invective. Paul once upon a time in ignorance of the one who was then the chief priest, cursed him because he had commanded for Paul to be struck against the law, but then as soon as it was made known that this man was the chief priest he offered his ignorance as an excuse and immediately added, "Brethren, I did not know that this man was the chief priest."

"Thou shalt not curse the prince of thy people" (Exodus 22). Paul showed this reverence to the prince of the past priesthood, which he otherwise considered to have passed away. Yet Luther sullies with all offensive cursing the prince — not of the old — but of the new and everlasting priesthood, to wit Christ's vicar, the sure successor to the prince of the Apostles. Paul humbly complied when he was admonished, by showing deferential honor to that priesthood, but Luther contends that it is permissible for him to acknowledge no superior, to reverence no one's power, to consider himself bound in the end by no laws, certain as he says he is that he received this from heaven and that he has fully triumphed over Satan. What an incredibly great and impudent arrogance in one man. How completely insane. Who does not clearly see these to be pure lies? Yet Luther is so blinded by his ill will, that he has been persuaded to impose himself, in full arrogance, over the entire world.

I don't think that anyone is so light minded as to easily trust these crass lies, because it is no small thing to triumph against

Satan, when Job can say that there is no power upon Earth that could be compared to Satan's. It is a great thing if someone should resist Satan, much more so if he should conquer, but the greatest of all would be to triumph. Such a phrase is barely attributed to Christ in the Scriptures, except after that greatest victory of the cross, when Paul says that Christ plundered the principalities and powers and thus clearly shows that he triumphed over them by himself. And although he battled with Satan elsewhere and confounded him three times, what does Luke still write in Chapter 4? To be sure it's not that Christ triumphed over Satan but that once the temptation was finished, the devil departed from him for a while: what an incredible thing! It was only once Christ had died that he triumphed over Satan, and yet Luther is already triumphing while he still lives in the flesh and in sin?

Yet even if one should resist any demon, this must not be ascribed to his own powers, but rather to God's grace, because even when St. Paul could justly and rightly say some great things about himself, he nevertheless added: "Not I, but the grace of God in me" (1 Cor. 15).

But Luther boasts that he has so magnificently triumphed against Satan that he makes not one mention of God's grace. Paul speaks this way to those who have overcome to inculcate a fear of relapse: "Let the one who stands take heed lest he fall" (1 Cor. 10). Elsewhere, in Romans 11: "Do you stand in faith: do not be carried away in spirit, but rather fear."

Luther has already obtained the triumph: He boasts that he is secure as if he could not fall again. Although St. Peter had visibly received the Holy Spirit, he was not so secure that he could not fall again, and as Luther himself authoritatively tells us, Peter did truly mortally sin afterwards. Yet Luther has so triumphed over Satan that he cannot once again be taken captive.

In other respects, maybe Luther gathers that he has conquered because he escaped despair, by which — according to his own insinuations — he was frequently besought. Yet despair does not happen to someone unless there are some horrible and abominable crimes, the like of which, were Luther to confess that he committed and continues along in those things which are hardly trivial, e.g., enmity and envy, anger and jealousy, contention and fights, seditions and sects, and such like (and in Galatians 5, Paul numbers these among the works of the flesh) wouldn't he be ashamed to boast that he has conquered Satan? Or how he could be certain that his own doctrines come from heaven? You see, the wisdom that is from heaven — if we trust Solomon's writing — implants itself in holy souls, and not in those who are unsettled by fury and disgraceful deeds. In James, Chapter 3, we are taught that Luther's wisdom is not from heaven: "Who is a wise man, and endued with knowledge among you? Let him shew, by a good conversation, his work in the meekness of wisdom. But if you have bitter zeal, and there is contention in your hearts, glory not and be not liars against the truth. For this is not the wisdom that descends from above, but earthly, sensual, devilish. For where there is envying and contention: there is inconstancy and every evil work. But the wisdom that is from above is first of all chaste, then peaceable, modest, easy to be persuaded." That is what James says.

So you see, dear reader, that if Luther had his wisdom from heaven, he would be chaste and meek in manner, peaceable and modest, persuadable. Likewise, he would not be full of bitterness, envy, and contention. It is for this reason that whenever he goes beyond all modesty and to the contrary become so furious, so mindless, and so debauched against all men whosoever should themselves be opposed to his most perverse heresies, it is manifest that he did not take these teachings from heaven but rather was inspired by Satan — against whom he claims to have triumphed.

CHAPTER II
His Apology That Attempts to Hide Notable Vices Is in Vain

I N the second place, Luther attempts to cover up some of his obvious vices, and first of all he tries to clear himself of the two for which the most illustrious king had at times censured him. First, that he contradicted himself; second, that he had inveighed against the pontiff with insults. Yet, let the reader beware of how much craftiness this transforming trickster makes use, since he is clearly in an ill way when these two objections were presented to him, given that they make it clear that Luther had been overcome by the demon rather than having overcome the demon. Thence as well is it solidified that his dogmas did not come from heaven, and so in his attempt to confront these two points, Luther spins a large web of verbose nonsense and grumbling — although it benefits him nothing, as will soon become clear.

You, dear reader, may nevertheless wonder why he has so studiously sought by argumentation to purge himself of his inconstancy: of course it's because this deceitful fox saw clearly that such advice would detract from his authority and no small amount among all men, because lack of constancy is shameful to any sort of teacher — and especially to one who boasts that he received his instruction from heaven. Not only is it shameful, but even ignominious and disgraceful, and it even deprives of any trustworthiness the rest of his teaching. You see, whoever claims to have his doctrine from heaven, as soon as he is seen in the least to have been guilty of a lie, such a one will no longer merit trustworthiness in other matters, and Luther was clearly imprudent when he leveled such a declaration against himself by objecting to the king in the following manner: "He should take pains to write against heresies, that he might not be found out in even the semblance of a lie. But now that he has covered himself with lies, who on this account will believe any part whatsoever of his writing?"

But we can throw this same claim back in Luther's face easily, because if one who writes against the heretic ought to take pains lest he be convicted of anything falsified, much more so should the one who claims to have his teachings from heaven take care, since if he were taken in even one lie that would be enough to reject all else that he taught. Besides, the most illustrious king is quite immune from any lying and Luther has entangled himself in so many lies, as will soon be apparent.

But first, dear reader, note what crafty manners Luther uses: he insinuates falsely that the most illustrious king brought forth no examples whereby Luther's inconsistency could be refuted.

Luther says, "He does not bring forth a single quotation, by way of example, with which to convict me of inconsistency. The glorious king merely spouts rhetoric such as this: 'Luther contradicts himself, who could believe him?' To have said so was sufficient for this new Defender of the Church."

Likewise, so that you, reader, may clearly perceive Luther's tricks and artifice, as well as his patent mendacity, I will copy below the illustrious king's own words by which he succinctly takes Luther to task, when speaking about indulgences, and shows him to be inconsistent and self-contradictory. Behold how he wrote: "Luther had previously admitted that indulgences were at least valid hitherto that one might be loosened — albeit not from fault — from any punishment whatsoever that the Church had established or that the person's priest had enjoined. Now, however, it is not by instruction — as he claims — but by ill-will that he has progressed as far as condemning indulgences in their entirety, in contradiction to himself."

Gentle reader, you now see one example that the king produced, wherewith Luther is shown to contradict himself. Have another: previously, Luther had denied that the papacy was of divine law and right, although he granted that it was of human right; now, being dissident against himself, he affirms that it is of neither one right nor of the other.

Here is a third example: he detested the schism of the Bohemians because they had separated themselves from obedience to the See of Rome, and he stated that they sinned mortally, whosoever would not submit to the papacy. Now he has fallen in with what he once detested.

Now a fourth besides these: will this be of a similar kind of inconsistency? In a sermon to the people, he taught that excommunication was medicinal and that it should be born patiently and obediently; somewhat later he himself was excommunicated, and that most deservedly, and yet he bore that sentence with such impotence that he went mad with rage, bursting forth into insults, affronts, and blasphemies to the point which the ear could hardly hear and bear. So now, kind reader, you have heard four examples given all at once, when Luther claimed mendaciously that the king had offered not a single example. Yet, the king did not refute Luther with nearly as few points as those to which Luther responds. Here you have his Royal Highness: "What does it benefit to fight against one who fights against himself? What should I try to prove by argumentation — if I should enter into such with him — when he now denies what he once affirmed, and affirms what he once denied?" So spoke the king. The reader therefore now sees that twice in one instance Luther lied: first when he claimed that the king had offered no example of his inconsistency, and then again when he falsely responded and fraudulently hid the force of the royal argument by asserting that the king had said nothing more than, "Luther contradicted himself and therefore who should believe him." Then he even added, "To have said so was sufficient for this new Defender of the Church."

What a shameless man it takes to feel no shame while so openly lying! From this the reader can also gather that that same book is entirely filled with lies when that author is revealed in his lies twice in one spot. Furthermore, it is clear that not only with one example but with several offered by that very king, Luther contradicted himself.

Here I should like for the devout readers to recall how

consistently Luther proclaimed — once upon a time — when he had begun to make his teachings public. "I protest that I wish to say nothing or hold nothing unless it is first and foremost in and from the Holy Scriptures, and then received and held hitherto by the Church Fathers and the Church of Rome, as is contained in the canons and decretals and can be contained."

Such is how he once protested — but now? "I want you all to be called upon as witnesses that I wish to be bound in no way at all by any authority of the Holy Father."

That is what he had for the Fathers but we will see clearly what he thinks about the cannons and decretal letters — because he would commit them to flames. He would not even admit holy writ, unless it were only those which he could wrongly twist from his own craftiness, since he did not even hold that the letter of James should be received — which letter he could not fashion to suit his own heresy. What intolerable madness! So, the Epistle of James, which the church has venerated for so many years as a truly Catholic [universal] letter, was not from heaven — but the pestilential teaching of Luther, filled with so many lies, did most certainly emanate from heaven? As you see here, my dearest reader, Luther sides neither with the Scriptures nor with himself. He is dissident with himself because what he protests to hold he hardly retains; dissenting from the Scriptures because he in no way admits the letter pinned by holy James, as it clearly combats his own heresies.

So the king vehemently takes Luther to task: "What does it benefit to fight against one who fights against himself? What should I try to prove by argumentation — if I should enter into such with him — when he now denies what he once affirmed, and affirms what he once denied?" Did he not hold indulgences at first to have been valid — for some time — before he later denied the same? And had he not extolled Pope Leo X with so much praise — before he would later call him an impostor and try to denigrate him with a thousand other wicked names? Previously, he had protested that he was going to admit all those Fathers that were received by the Roman Church, and now he completely rejects them. Once upon a time, he had promised to obey the cannons and decretal letters, and now he wholly refuses.

Are not all these things contrary and opposed one to the other? Therefore, the king is found to be most truthful when he argues that Luther contradicted his very own statements. But Luther is discovered to be a liar even twice in the same situation and citation: first because he taught and promised contraries, for which he could be no other than a liar, but also because he denied that he lied in any matter.

But this fox has many layers and hiding-places: see how he hides the subterfuge that he had prepared for himself. He was fearful lest the reader might catch him in lies or might think that from those lies he had contradicted himself and thus he distinguishes two genres in which he recalls himself to have written: the one is those matters contained in Sacred Scripture, such as faith, charity, hope, works, passions, heaven and hell, Penance, the Lord's Supper, sins, the law, death, Christ, God, freedom of the will, grace, Baptism, and such like; the other genre is on such things as are outside Scripture, such as the papacy, the doctors, purgatory, educational institutions, bishops, idols, devotion to the saints, decrees of the councils, indulgences, and things of that sort. Yet note what sort of trick he lays out here, how does it fit in this spot to have commemorated so many different titles, when he is only disputing what he will later claim? For if Luther is consistent with himself in all other things, how would he not be taken here, too, to dissent from himself? Would this not be enough to show that he is contrary to himself? In every way, yes. But this fox is thinking up tricks, since he hopes that from this universal stock of subjects he will overwhelm the reader's mind, lest the subject at hand be attentively kept in mind.

Regarding indulgences, as you have heard already, the king takes Luther to task because Luther was contradicting himself, and he does that precisely because Luther had previously — and for some time — admitted that they were licit and valid as far as it regarded the punishments which previous spiritual fathers or one's own priest had established, but now he asserts that they're completely invalid [of no effect]. Are these things not clearly contradictory? What, pray tell, could be more diametrically opposed than valid and invalid? It is certain that both dogmas could not have emanated from heaven together, and yet Luther shamelessly affirms that he has all his doctrines from heaven. Yet, he cannot back pedal that at various times he affirmed both the one and the other and that this happened before he had begun to be inspired by that evil spirit — that is, before he had set up his own heresy. For this reason, if his proper spirit had failed him in the prior instance, why could it not do likewise in the latter? Without a doubt it could have done so, because he received no greater certitude from heaven in the later instance rather than in the former.

In both cases he obviously followed a most fallacious conjecture of his own spirit, since whatever had seemed right to him could not be disproven either by argumentation or by the Scriptures, although it was most erroneous, and he nevertheless persuades himself that this came down from heaven. On this account, he is unable to agree with himself, nor can he refrain from lying so frequently, when his own human opinion is so frequently accustomed to change that what he judged true today, tomorrow he will sentence to be false. So that you can see that this is the manner in which Luther behaves, have this patent evidence on the matter: he admits, in the beginning of his work on The Babylonian Captivity — which he himself fabricated — that it was thanks to the help of Sylvester that he had conceived a new understanding about indulgences and here is how he puts it: "Whether I should be willing or not, as the days proceed I am forced to become more learned, as so many and so great teachers fight to urge me on and to train me; I had written about indulgences before, but in such a way that it now pains me greatly to recall that published booklet, because afterwards, with the help of Sylvester and the brethren — who had strenuously defended indulgences — I understood them to be nothing more than mere deceits of Roman sycophants." So spoke Luther. Is it not clear from his language that he changed his mind because Sylvester had so coolly defended them? Likewise, whatever Luther can convince humbler minds to believe by his criticisms, by an ingeniously depraved mode of thinking, or by a forcefully twisted sense of Scripture, he takes to have been confirmed from heaven.

Now whether or not such teaching actually proceeds from heaven, I'll leave to others to judge for themselves: I myself do not doubt that such teaching rather more proceeds from a human or diabolical spirit. They prophesy from their own heart — and not from heaven — to whom Ezekiel says in Chapter 13: "Woe to the foolish prophets that follow their own spirit, and see nothing. Thy prophets, O Israel, were like foxes in the deserts." Let others, therefore, judge whether or not we have correctly called him a fox, the one who follows his own or a hellish spirit, since this same Ezekiel calls that sort of prophet a fox.

It is enough for me that I have demonstrated how little these two teachings fit one with the other, that is, that indulgences once were beneficial for a while, and that these same indulgences are now worthless. Similarly, the one who taught thus is self-contradictory and plainly objects to what he held, and so he cannot have all his teachings from heaven.

Yet, this deceitful fox has still another trick: he contends that his teachings are not contradictory, unless he had stated them at the same time and had not first retracted the prior claim. We cannot let the fox hide in this sort of refuge because even if he took back his opinion which he had earlier put forward, would it not by that very fact be true that the revoked opinion is now false and that it is contrary to what he now holds? You see, even if he did not claim these things about indulgences at the same time, they are nonetheless contrary since — in the interim — nothing changed in regard to indulgences but only in that man's head, who was clearly wrong in one or the other case. It is necessary that in one of those cases he taught what is false and an error, but what is false and erroneous clearly did not come from heaven. Yet this fox still does not stop seeking new subterfuge: "Paul changed his mind when he called dung what before he had considered gain, wherefore we shall likewise damn all epistles of Paul." That was what Luther said and he thought that he had rendered himself safe with that defense, whereby he could likewise say contradictory things but without any contradiction or inconsistency. We can easily destroy this beast with this reasoning: if Paul at some spot in his epistles had approved that dung and then later disapproved of the same, then there would be no doubt in anyone's mind that he was contradicting himself and that he had thereby rendered suspect all the letters that he had written, lest anyone should hold them to be from heaven. But, there's no doubt that what, in his words, seemed dung to him was from before the time when he had been called by Christ, and that after such a time he did not consider them to be gain. Luther, on the other hand, committed both of these opinions to book form after he had begun his own heresy, that is he both taught that indulgences were valid, and then that those same things were invalid. For this reason, he is not only convicted of being self-contradictory but also that whatever else he wrote is not therefore from heaven. Yet Luther has yet another diversion: "We will also damn Augustine, who retracted many things in a single book, and taught very differently from what he had at first."

This also does not defend Luther's error: no one denies that Augustine could licitly retract what he had taught less than correctly before; likewise, Luther, too — if he should so will — can retract all the heresies which he has hitherto taught. However, the revoking that Augustine did does not make it so that what he had previously asserted would not clearly contradict that which he later affirmed, and so Luther's retraction will not make an excuse for the contradiction and inconsistency. Nor, too, was Augustine ever so shameless or arrogant as to assert that he had received all of his doctrines from heaven, nor such as to contend that the positions he had expressed at various times were not contradictory. So you see that this fox has done nothing with his twisting and turning; we have him completely, and there is nowhere he can flee. He cannot escape unless he first concedes that what he taught previously is clearly contradictory and at odds, and that therefore he does not have all of his doctrines from heaven, since necessarily one or the other is false — and nothing of that sort emanates from heaven.

Note where this cunning fox now tries to escape: he deceitfully attempts to transfer the argument to another sort of case because he denies that he contradicted himself in anything that belongs to Sacred Writ, that is, in any of those matters pertaining to the first genre, about which he had drawn up that long catalog. Yet, the king never made this an objection, because he did not mention anything about faith, hope, or charity as far as a contradiction, but he expressly mentioned indulgences because he had formerly approved of them and then completely disapproved of them. So it's not in question at this point whether or not Luther was self-contradictory regarding the matters of Sacred Scripture, but whether he had written contradictory things at various points, and the king convicts Luther of having written contradictory things.

For the present argument, that is enough. But this dogma about indulgences, too — even if Luther's false opinion does not pertain to Holy Scripture — in our opinion and in the opinion of the entire church this argument is completely reliant on the Scriptures, for we do not doubt that indulgences have their power from Christ's promise, since it is certain that Christ did not say to Peter in vain, "whatsoever you bind on earth will be bound in heaven" (Mt. 16). These words are so clear in the opinion of the entire Church that there can be no evading refusal: If Luther could show from other Scriptures that Christ did not say this or that if he did say it that he did not mean it taken in this way, then he would somewhat more justly claim that indulgences are worthless; but he will never do either of these things. So absolutely clear are the words of this promise, that there is not the least obscurity or ambiguity in even the shortest word of that phrase. We do not doubt that the same power which was granted to Peter was also fully preserved for the successor of Peter, since Christ's promise was not merely for those who lived then but also for all Christians who would succeed them. Yet, Luther contends that this promise was made to all the Apostles and to the entire Church without distinction — but this is Luther's teaching — not Christ's. I find this nowhere in the Gospels. I read in them that it was clearly said to Peter, "whatsoever thou dost bind on earth, it shall be bound in heaven, and whatsoever thou dost loose on earth shall be loosened in heaven." Now, if Luther denies that this was said to Peter, let him prove his denial — and from the Scriptures — just as he urges us to prove what we hold.

It will of course be reprehensible to so often object to us that we frequently assert many things without any proof if he labors under the same vice: he claims always that the Scriptures are abundantly clear and that they must be understood by mere grammar, since no grammarian could in any way interpret this Scripture in a twisted manner, except to say that Peter could loosen whatever seemed best to him according to his judgment and that whatever he had so loosened would also be loosened in heaven. I do not see why this should not also be truly believed by any and everyone, nor do we deny that similar words were said by Christ to the rest of the Apostles but that those words differed substantially and in their meaning, just as we have shown elsewhere.

Luther's Apology Hides His Vices

Luther, however, still contends that there is nothing at all left in the sinner which the Pontiff might wipe out after the absolution by any priest whosoever, but he still must prove this: we, for sure, believe that there is something left and which — unless it is expunged or purified previously in this life — will at last be expiated in purifying purgatorial fires. A man would be exceedingly foolish indeed if, overlooking the salutary remedy of indulgences he would—in a subject as serious as this—choose to believe in Luther's bare assertions. For if someone accepts indulgences according to the Church's faith, no danger awaits him for that fact; neither will anyone suffer loss because of that acceptance. Yet if one were to overlook them and yet there should remain something to be purged in such a man's soul, then he would at least sustain something unpleasant, which the excruciating pain of those flames would keep him for a time from the entrance into heaven, so long as that expiation was not yet fully consummated. It is for this reason that besides an obstinate hardness of heart, it is plain stupidity to completely despise indulgences, because even if indulgences were granted to be completely useless, nevertheless no one would mock them in the next life, no one of those who believed becomingly in Christ's words. If, on the other hand, they were to be found useful, would not then they be mocked who cast them out, and would they not simultaneously pay the price for such contempt? Luther cannot deny that something of sin remains after absolution, but he will say that all punishment due to sin is completely pardoned so that there is afterwards no need for any indulgences. Yet, he cannot prove this with any Scriptures nor did any one of the Fathers before Luther dare to assert such a thing — especially among those who affirmed purgatory — and that fact alone should warn all souls lest they trust Luther.

We, however, have cited many places in the Scriptures besides the sayings of the Fathers, and by these scriptural citations it is clear that those who are absolved from the guilt [of sin] are still liable to a certain punishment. Yet even if we were to grant as true what Luther holds forth — that through the absolution of any priest the punishment is also simultaneously and completely abolished — yet is it not safer for the sinner, due to the statements of the Fathers who deny that all punishment is taken away, to accept indulgences rather than so casually despising them with Luther? If Luther were to hold that something of the due punishment did remain after the priest's absolution, and yet that the same thing could not be done away with through indulgences, then certainly he could have more rightly asserted that the pontiff had thought up indulgences as a means of tricking the people. Yet now, when he grants to any single priest so much power that he could completely wipe away all punishment — which assertion he could never prove from the Scriptures — what does he still have whereby he might accuse the Pontiff, the one who not only from the statements of the Fathers of yore, but also from the Scriptures believes that after the guilt has been wiped away there still remains some punishment, and who promises the forgiveness of the one and the cancellation of the penalty due? You see, Luther promises all this solely from absolution alone, and he does so without the aid of the Scriptures or the testimony of the Fathers, whereas the Pontiff promises it from but two things — and not only from the testimony of the Fathers but also reliant upon the clearest of Scriptures. At this point, however, let us return to the point from where we departed.

Before he set out to establish his own heresy, Luther had taught for a time that indulgences were beneficial and then he later taught that they benefited nothing. So in the same doctrinal matter, he is convicted of being both self-contradictory and inconsistent and both cannot be believed to have come from heaven: the fox cannot escape that noose.

Because he so shamelessly denies that his teachings conflict in former matters, we will attempt to show that he is openly lying.

First as a summary: who does not perceive that in this matter he has gifted us broad ground for a dispute since he claims — as far as such matters pertain — that his teachings are nothing other than Christ's teachings, while we demonstrate that he is in disagreement with Christ's teaching, such that it immediately follows that he is self-contradictory in each of those points? Yet this happens in almost every one of the articles condemned by Leo X, and we do not doubt that this will be clear to him who reads this reputation at some later point, but let us now demonstrate this specifically in regard to some of his dogmatic claims. First of all, let us see if this is not clearly contradictory: "hardly any Christian man has the faith." And then again "all Christians have the Faith"? Yet these two clearly follow from Luther's dogmas about the faith, because he teaches us in his book on faith and works that "there can be no faith at all unless it is a lively and undoubted conviction whereby a man is certain beyond all certitude that he is pleasing to God." Yet what man is certain beyond all certainty that he pleases God — especially when Luther elsewhere affirms that no one can be certain that he is not sinning mortally due to that most hidden vice of pride. Whoever doubts whether or not he might sin mortally is not certain beyond all certitude that he pleases God, because whosoever sins mortally is lacking grace. Whosoever is lacking grace is not pleasing to God; therefore, no one who doubts whether or not he is sinning mortally can be most surely certain that he is pleasing to God. For this reason if — as Luther asserts — there can be no faith unless it is a living and an undoubted belief whereby man is certain beyond all certitude that he is pleasing to God, then no man has the faith unless it were to happen to be revealed to him that he had grace and was lacking any mortal sin and that he thereby was pleasing to God. Such an occurrence, I think, has only happened to very few people.

Similarly, in his book on Christian liberty he teaches that the one who has the faith is free by that faith from every law and that merely by such freedom whatsoever he does, he spontaneously does only what is pleasing to God — seeking no benefit or salvation — since he already has enough in being saved by God's grace from his own faith. That is what Luther claims.

How many will Luther give us from all of Christendom, who do all things voluntarily and — in whatsoever they propose to do — only what is pleasing to God, seeking nothing else besides it whether of benefit or spiritual health? For that reason if only such people were to have the faith then the one who actually possesses the faith would be a most rare person.

Again in that same little treatise he teaches that whoever has the faith is necessarily formed in all of his works by that conviction, so that the unique aim of such a one is that he might serve and benefit others in all that he does, having nothing else in sight other than his neighbor's needs and utility. Now, truly, if this is the case, there are very few who have the faith, because hardly anyone is found who aims in all that he does and in all his works only to serve and benefit others, having nothing else in view besides his neighbors' needs and advantages.

He likewise asserts in his resolutions against Eck:[2] "Given that faith is a right and good belief about God, that any belief whatsoever by its own force draws one to works, there can be no doubt that the one who has faith does all works; for if the belief and love of a woman does not allow one to be lazy, but rather causes one to do many things that are asked with no law or master, how would faith not grant even much more?"

From this the reader can see that hardly anyone would have the faith since barely anyone exists who from such great love does all and only such as please God, such as a man might do who is madly in love with a woman.

Besides this, in the twelfth of his articles, Luther says the following: "I said this by means of a hypothetical impossibility because it is clear from what has been said above that there can be no faith without contrition since grace is not infused except upon those who are greatly broken in soul."

The reader understands from this that grace is not infused without a spiritual brokenness of soul, nor is there any possibility of faith without contrition. For this reason, wherever there's not a great, true, spiritual contrition, there can be no grace or faith. But I should ask how many Christians experience this great brokenness in soul, or, if they once experienced it, did not then sin mortally and thereafter sense this brokenness again? On this account the one who has the faith would be the rarest of men and I think that from what we have said it is therefore clear that according to Luther's teaching there could hardly be one or two who have the faith.

For this reason, we will also show another of his dogmas: that there is hardly anyone who is called "Christian" and does not actually have the faith. Here is how he defines "faith" in his own works: "Faith is nothing else besides believing what God promises or says." There you have it, dear reader: if faith is nothing but belief in what God said or promised, then what Christian (who believes

---

2 Johann Maier von Eck (1486- 1543). The resolutions were made against the doctrines of indulgences, and delivered against Eck at the Leipzig debates.

whatever is contained in either Testament) ever did *not* have the faith, even if otherwise he was very evil and defiled?

Then, consider what he always says aloud: that works are in no way necessary to the faith or for justification. For this reason, if works are in no way required for justification, as Luther asserts, then what is easier than believing? All the difficulty is in doing, of course. The unfortunate people hear these things and easily believe Luther — that they have the faith — even if they do nothing at all.

Regarding this, in Article 14, he asserts that faith can most certainly be felt in the heart, if one actually has it. Who from among the people hears this and does not persuade himself that he has the faith, just as soon as he confirms that in his heart he assents to what must be believed? For, who makes this decision about having faith in his heart otherwise than by the mental assent which he experiences when he examines himself?

Add to this the fact that in Article 15 he says that the one who approaches the Sacrament of the Eucharist has no need of previous prayers or preparation, but that it is sufficient to believe that he will receive grace there, and as Luther says, faith alone makes such people worthy and pure. Who, hearing these things, does not gather that for him it would be sufficient for reception of the Eucharist that he only believe that he will obtain grace from it?

He gives another such example again in his Babylonian Captivity: "If the most abundant Lord were to depute to some poor — and even worthless and evil — slave a thousand gold pieces, he would certainly request and accept them and would mind nothing at all about his vileness and the huge sum attested. And if someone were contrary to him, mentioning his worthlessness and the grand sum, what do you think he would say? Of course, 'what's it to you? I'm not taking this because of my own merit or because it's my due. I know I'm unworthy and getting more than I deserve – nay more! even contrary to what I deserve — but I'm asking for it because it was appointed to me legally, thanks to someone else's goodness. If it wasn't unworthy for him to depute me, worthless as I am, why would I shy away from taking it because of my worthlessness?'" That's what Luther says.

Dear reader, you clearly see that Luther thinks that no man must abstain from the Eucharist: he believes that it was deputed for sinners. And what is easier to believe than that? As long as there is no want for a pseudo-apostle who will teach — against Paul — that the people only need faith, whereas Paul himself teaches that whoever comes forth for communion must first examine himself and that once he has examined, he might come, and that whosoever approaches unworthily will be punished. Luther rashly contends to the contrary that faith suffices and that whoever believes is thereby well suited to receive the Eucharist.

However, precisely as Luther either wishes or not, everyone believes or no one believes. This right here is his beyond the pale, vulpine fraud: he can never be retained in any assertion but can always flee to some hiding spot. As the reader can see, this is why Luther thought up a dual explanation for the faith. For the one explanation he can surreptitiously win over the people to himself, that is, by saying that the faith is nothing other than believing what God has promised and said, and there is hardly a Christian ever who hasn't thought that he has this sort of faith. The other definition whereby he protects himself from the Doctors, is that which claims that there can be no faith unless it is a living and an undoubted belief whereby a man is certain beyond all certainty that he is pleasing to God. Now according to this definition, of course it is true that it alone would suffice for the reception of the Eucharist with no need for other prior spiritual preparation, because if one is certain beyond on all certainty that he is pleasing to God, what could ever prohibit such a man from receiving the Eucharist as often as he wished? But now the people are sorely mistaken when they are so far from such a faith — unless perhaps someone or another was convinced that he was so certain that God's goodness was so great that no Christian, even mired in the worst sins, could ever displease God, which is a horribly impious thought. On the other hand such a conviction that one is certain beyond all certainty that he is pleasing to God by an undoubted, tenacious, life-long conviction is most rare and can hardly happen beyond some revelation. According to this other notion of faith, any Christian could easily believe that he has the true faith since he senses himself to believe all that God has promised and said, and in this way he will think himself sufficiently well-suited to go up for the most holy Body of Christ without any other preparation. So, I think that it is clear to all how unsteady, inconsistent, and finally even self-contradictory Luther is and his dogmatic statements about the faith, because if faith is nothing other than believing what God promises and says, then whoever believes thereby has the faith. In an identical way if someone is not supremely certain that he is pleasing to God then he does not have the faith, since according to Luther there is no faith that is not a completely convinced and perfectly sure conviction by which one is certain beyond all certainty that he is pleasing to God. Yet this notion of having the faith or not having the faith is manifestly self-contradictory.

Let us consider another matter that belongs to the same subject: Luther claims in several places that faith is a kind of emotion — not a quality that resides in the soul. He also claims that faith merits grace. Finally, he claims that whatever precedes grace in man — that is, every effort, every thoughtful preparation, every interior act by man that precedes grace — is sinful. Now these assertions hardly fit together, because if faith merits grace, then it must precede grace in the soul. And since, as Luther likes to say, it is also a kind of interior mental emotion, it is prior to grace, and since it is prior to grace, it is therefore a sin. Now it would lead us on endlessly to treat of hope, works, sin, free will, and other such matters wherein similar inconsistencies and contradictions could be brought forward, but what we have produced on the faith should suffice to show by what deceitful tricks this fox teaches his doctrines. So let us now go on to other matters.

In regard to his vice of snappy and biting severity, from which he tries to excuse himself, let us bring to the fore what the king first noted. After the king had criticized Luther's inconsistency and contradictions, since he had at first approved of indulgences but now calls them pure impostors, he then adds: "In this matter he is not only desecrating but he is also raving and raging, as is clear to all, because if indulgences are worthless but mere impostors, as Luther claims, then they were necessarily impostors before, and not only when Leo X and so many previous centuries-worth of popes mentioned them. Leo X, by the way, is even admitted by Luther, in a certain letter to that pontiff, to have been one of pure and innocent life and morals, and extremely holy from an earliest age, as well attested throughout the world." These are the king's words.

Luther, however, cannot and does not remove any of this, but only brings forth some examples of how he can, if he likes, attack anyone according to his good pleasure: "And why does Christ himself (Mt. 23) attack the Scribes and Pharisees so vehemently and accuse them of being hypocrites, blind, fools, full of uncleanness and hypocrisy as well as murderers? And Paul, how often does he speak vehemently against the circumcised — as he calls them — and the false prophets, who adulterate and corrupt the word of God? He calls them dogs, deceitful workers, apostles of Satan, children of the devil, full of guile and malice, deceivers, empty-talkers, busybodies and wandering philanders."

The reader can here note that Luther has gathered together whatever he could corral from the Gospels and from Paul that had any hint of blame or fault finding — whether it was what Christ said to the Pharisees or what Paul said to sinners and enemies of the cross of Christ. And yet the same man is not afraid of spewing out innumerable times against the one pontiff and prince of the entire Christian religion.

Furthermore, Luther did not take a very fitting example, since it was so dissimilar. He should have used the example of Korah,[3] who incited the people against Moses and Aaron, and became all conceited by saying, "The entire multitude consists of holy ones, and the Lord is among them: Why do you lift up yourselves above the people of the Lord?" In a similar manner now Luther is trying to put on an equal plane the Pontiff and the people, and with much worse accusations than Core had used towards Moses, but he is following in his predecessors' footsteps perfectly here, because almost all heretics have acted this way: attack the pope! It was for this reason that the Apostle Jude in his letter spoke of them who perished in Korah's rebellion, and just before that he had written, "These men despise dominion and blaspheme majesty," or, as Erasmus has translated it with a greater intuition: "they spurn their masters and hurl insults upon those who possess power." Luther is not afraid to do this now because he reveres the authority of no man, but rather has loosened the reins of his cursing tongue upon

---

3 Numbers 16:23.

all. So, he should have brought forth the example of Korah, which would have been much more fitting for him than that of Paul or Christ. He better plays the role of the barking Pharisees against Christ, or of the pseudo apostles who resisted Paul, and he actually instructed us well by those examples which he cited, so that we can compare the one who bitterly reprehends the Pharisees themselves or the pseudo apostles, as such action merits. Thus, Luther is not right to use the example of Paul or Christ for himself.

Also, who does not see another Arius, Novatian, Nestorius, Donatus and other similar men who pursued the popes of their day with cunning calumny and railing reproaches, who also dared to bring the same examples forward as Luther does as a pretext for their wickedness? And yet who would approve of those? Certainly no one — except whoever was a member of those sects — because everyone else would have hissed them away and completely driven them off.

Third, neither Christ nor Paul would have used those rebukes unless they had previously and plainly confirmed their authority by miracles. In fact, their miracles were clearly so great that of course anyone who dared to fight against their doctrines would have been rightly rebuked, since Paul writes in this way in Romans 15: "For I dare not to speak of any of those things which Christ worketh not by me, for the obedience of the Gentiles, by word and deed, by the virtue of signs and wonders, in the power of the Holy Spirit"; and in 2 Corinthians 12: "For I have no way come short of them that are above measure apostles, although I be nothing." Note here, dear reader, that he says, "in all patience" and "although I am nothing." This is the Paul who worked so many miracles, signs, and great deeds in all patients and reputed himself to be nothing; and this Luther who lacks all miracles nevertheless speaks impatiently, thinks of himself greatly, and spares no man insults.

We also know that Christ had proved himself by his deeds before he reproved the Pharisees. John 5: "The works which I do testify about me, that the Father has sent me" and in chapter 10: "The works that I do in my Father's name, these render testimony of me"…"If I do not the works of my Father, do not believe me," and later, "If you do not believe me, believe the works that I do]." In Chapter 15: "If I had not done among them the works that no other man has done, they would have no sin." So, here is your first point: Luther has no right to furnish himself with this abusive language on Christ's example unless he has first demonstrated by patent miracles his own authority. Likewise, not even Christ himself upbraided the Pharisees before he had shown miracles, for whom it was fitting so that they begin to have faith. On this point, unless Luther's malice has completely blinded him, he should see that we are completely free from sin and not believing his teaching to be true unless he should previously corroborate them with fresh miracles, because the things which we believe have been abundantly proved not only by Christ's words and deeds but also by the Apostles' and the Holy Fathers' openly visible miracles, so that if we are now wrong — I should dare say — it would be on God's effort that we were wrong.

But Luther will say, "My teachings are in no way different than what Christ and the Apostles taught." Yet this is completely false, because even Arius used this same ironic sophistry; that is, that he was saying nothing except the words of Christ — except that the words of Christ had been misused for his own party — just as Luther now does. Of course Christ's words — understood according to the mind of Christ — are to be received as Christ's own teaching. On the other hand, if they are conceived of according to the mind of a heretic, then they are not the teaching of Christ but merit rather to be called heresy. For example, the words which Arius leaned upon "the Father is greater than me," if they are taken according to how Christ meant them, are truly Christ's teaching, but not if they're according to how Arius took them, that is in the manner which Arius interpreted those words, because the sense that Arius had of those words was not Christ's teaching but rather completely expressed the Arian dogma. Since the Fathers had followed Christ's sense of these words, the Church therefore approved what those Fathers taught and not what Arius taught, just as she did when every other controversy between the Fathers and the heretics arose. You see, heretics have always insisted that the true notion of the Scriptures was to be found with them, but the Church has always been sufficiently taught by the Spirit of Christ, and so repelling the heretics' interpretations, while constantly adhering to what the Fathers thought and taught.

Luther's Apology Hides His Vices

Therefore, it is not as Luther boasts, "My teachings are nothing other than Christ's teachings," given that he is at odds with the Fathers; Luther's teachings, you see, are nothing other than scriptural interpretations that are twisted to be against the true sense of Christ, and since Luther's teachings have still not been corroborated by any miracles, Christians are not at all bound to give assent to his teachings, nor is there any danger that awaits the one who withholds his assent, especially since Christ himself said: "If I had not done among them the works that no other man has done, they would not have sin" (John 15:24). Yet, whoever does not believe those things that are taught by the Catholic Church will most certainly run a risk for his soul, since those teachings are clearly confirmed by the miracles of Christ, as well of those of the Apostles and Holy Fathers.

Let us come to the point now: it was perfectly licit for Christ to go after the Pharisees so harshly because his teaching proceeds from God and he proved it manifestly through the working of miracles. It was allowed to Paul to rebuke pseudo-apostles and bad Christians because he had verified the truth of his teachings by abundant signs, miracles, and wonders. Luther, however, is not allowed to do the same thing — he who is truly a pseudo-apostle, Satan's slave, and plainly a precursor of the Antichrist. By no miracles has he yet confirmed his heresies and his destructive inversions of Scripture — unless you call it a miracle that a man who is so swollen with rage and burning with fury is not immediately busted asunder. He has hitherto certainly not confirmed his pernicious teaching with any other miracle, which is why neither Christ nor Paul support Luther on this point; to the contrary, based on Paul's example which we find recounted in the Acts of the Apostles in Chapter 23, Luther is patently condemned by the same Paul who recognized the pontiff even of the ancient priesthood and gave him reverence, as well as recalling that ancient Scripture that "you must not curse the prince of your people." Luther, on the other hand, does not even recognize the prince of the new priesthood, but rather pursues him with cursing calumny. This Pauline example is what he should have imitated, as well as many others which the most illustrious king had put before him, since those examples could have easily brought him back from his mindlessness, except that he was simply the slave of Satan and Son of Perdition, because the king had shown in opposition to him many great popes who had granted remission from the sin and the penalty due to sin — some for a year, others for three years, some others for forty or another part of the full total penance — and some even granted a plenary indulgence. The king indicated that faith even in the worst bishops or pastors of old — in such great number, however — would be much more justly deserved than it would be for a single little brother, a sick sheep, but Luther did not respond to this. The king then demonstrated most clearly and by many explanations that Luther had not a lick of charity since he did not show any fear of accusing so many and so great supreme pontiffs of the worst, that is that they had been impostors: "If God said in Leviticus 19, 'Thou shalt not be a slanderer or bad-mouther among the peoples,' then what should we think of Luther, who is guilty of this crime not simply against one man but against many and even the most venerable bishops, and not only does he bad mouth in one town but he blasts it throughout the whole world." And Luther said nothing on this point.

The king then added, "If in Deuteronomy 27 a man is called 'accursed' if he furtively strikes his neighbor, then how stricken with a curse will be the one who openly insults those in authority with overwhelming reproaches?" Luther held his silence here too.

The king then closed with this, "If, as the evangelist says (in 1 Jn. 3), he is a murderer and does not have eternal life, whosoever hates his brother, then is this man not a patricidal killer worthy of eternal death, since he goes after his father in hatred?" Luther ignores all these rational questions with a deaf ear, and he makes light of his vice by calling it "severity," when he ought to have called it a dogged anger and beastly fury.

The audacity of this raving mother bear is remarkable since nothing is more often condemned in Paul's letters than arrogance, strife, and the violation of fraternal charity, nor is anything more frequently extolled then whatever is contrary to these vices; yet this man does not shame from taking Paul as the patron of his evilness and impiety. In Romans 12 we read, "bless and do not curse," but Luther teaches that we ought to not only curse but even fight, insult, and even rudely and stubbornly taunt whoever opposes us

— and he claims this upon the example of Paul and Christ.

Let others judge whether this dogma flowed down from heaven, but one thing I know: this is not at all Christ's doctrine, as Luther daringly asserts, "My teaching does not contradict itself in any part, nor could it, since it is Christ's." This shameless mouth does not shy from lying in such a manner, whereas his teaching is nothing like Christ's. I actually think that no other heretic has ever existed who was less consistent with Christ's teaching on so many points as Luther. But the teaching of Christ is not "whatever Christ said" unless you have also interpreted it according to the mind and Spirit of Christ, so whenever Luther so frequently interprets the words of Christ against the sense and understanding of Christ, his teaching is clearly not the teaching of Christ but rather opposes it greatly.

The reader should furthermore note what Luther has brought forward in his defense so far, since he says this about the king: "He knew perfectly well that I believe the papacy to be the kingdom of the antichrist, which even Job (3:6) commands to be cursed by those who were ready to raise up Leviathan. And the Spirit commands us in all places to convict the world of the sin of impiety, as well as it completely commends and requires this holy and just severity." Those are Luther's words, and we will respond to each point. He did know perfectly well: the king is truly a Catholic who knew that Luther was a heretic and had opined incorrectly about the authority of the sovereign pontiff. So what? Should he not have therefore chastened Luther's cursing tongue which goes on so insanely against the very powers that all orthodox believers take to be established by God?

Then Luther adds that Job commanded the papacy to be cursed by those who were about to raise up Leviathan. Luther continues to be just like himself, that is he perversely twists Scripture according to his own thoughts. Here you see Job's actual words when he curses his day: "Let them curse it who curse the day, who are ready to raise up a leviathan." Now who can gather from these words that Job commanded a curse of the papacy by those who were ready to raise up Leviathan? Unless it's one who argues in the same manner as Luther does: "Job commands that they curse their day namely, those who curse the day, who are ready to raise up Leviathan;

therefore, Job commands that they curse the papacy." This is the way the one who makes himself the teacher of the whole world interprets the Scriptures, with the result that he takes the word "day" for "the papacy." Who else can get such a sense from those words? Rather, who is more prepared to raise up Leviathan than Luther himself? Nobody doubts that the Church has been resting quietly for a long time, untroubled by heresies, and in this regard Leviathan had slept for quite a while. So, since Luther is of the number of those who attempt to raise up the sleeping Leviathan and whose number holy Job perhaps foresaw as most cursed, Luther therefore would have them curse his day, that is, those who hardly seem born for anything besides cursing. The Hebrews, on the other hand, interpret this verse differently, and here is how it could be understood literally: "Let them curse it, those who curse the day, those who take care to watch over their society." By "those who curse the day," the Jewish teachers understand "the mourners," whose duty it was to mourn and cry for the dead, and they take "Leviathan" to be their very own society, so that we understand this very holy man to have wished for the following: "Let them curse the day in which I was born, those whose duty it is to mourn and weep over the dead, those to whom it pertains to raise up others to mourn and weep." But let us assume as Luther does that Leviathan is the devil. Surely no one could be found more fitting for this office than Luther himself, because not even when Satan is loosened will he more easily raise up such a great disturbance in the Church, to the extent in which Luther has disturbed her. In any case, what is clearly the case is that this Scripture cannot be twisted to be made contrary to the papacy, as Luther would have it, and yet when he twists and corrupts the Scriptures like this, as he shamelessly and frequently boasts, these dogmas of his would have come down from heaven.

Now we move to the point in which he says that the spirit always commands that the world be convicted of the sin of iniquity and that this makes his bitter severity both laudable and completely holy! Now this Scripture does not support this teacher in any way, because never in Scripture do I recall bitterness to be required of anyone, but instead I find it to be prohibited. For so does Paul say to the Galatians in Chapter 5: "For all the law is fulfilled in one word:

'Thou shalt love thy neighbor as thyself,'" and then he promptly adds, "But if you bite and devour one another: take heed you be not consumed one by another." The Spirit in Paul does not command or praise this biting severity as something completely holy and just, but he rather fully condemns it as vicious and evil; therefore, it is false that the Spirit always demands and lauds this mordacity as holy and due.

Please, dear reader, see how this teacher of the entire world brags that he has his dogmas from heaven while he plainly lies about the Scripture; yet he does this so often and has become so completely accustomed to it that whenever he lies, he doesn't understand that he is lying. Instead, Luther will say that Christ foretold in the Spirit, in John's Gospel (ch.16), that he would convict the world of sin. Certainly Christ foretold that there would be a conviction, but not that there would be an attack of detraction or that Christ would make that happen, since — as far as I recall from the Scriptures — this phrase is always understood in a negative light. Furthermore, as Christ himself says in that same spot, as an interpretive key: "He will convict the world of sin — because they have not believed in me." Christ did not train his disciples to attack by detraction; he rather taught them to be meek and long-suffering, but let us hear Paul, too, speak of the same thing when he exhorted Timothy (2 Tim 4) to "reprove, entreat, rebuke in all patience." And then again, "But the servant of the Lord must not wrangle: but be mild toward all men, apt to teach, patient, admonishing with modesty them that resist the truth." So again, Paul commands him, among other things, to pursue patience and modesty. This teacher Luther of ours, on the other hand, finds no shame in admitting that he has lost patience, as he plainly professes, and that he has no care at all for patience. If he has not said these very things in his own accursed book, written against the king, then I am a liar. If, on the other hand, he did say so, then it is fitting that all of his teachings — of whatever sort — should be held to be not from heaven but rather from Satan. Christ's Spirit always and everywhere praises and pushes for modesty, meekness, mildness and things of that sort, which is why when the Apostles were stirred against the Samaritans Christ said to them: "You know not of what Spirit you are" (Luke 9:55).

So you, reader, must understand that Luther is teaching — clearly and not in some nebulous manner — and acting against Christ's teachings, nor is he ashamed of his shameful accusations against England's king, or being guilty of lèse-majesté by rebuking him in this way: "He lies against the divine majesty and against my king, who is the King of Glory, as he defiles him with his blasphemies." Those are Luther's words. Why else did he say these things besides the fact that the king had shown that when Luther had spoken of indulgences, he had contradicted himself. In this way it would be permitted to Luther to babble on, to lie, to contradict himself, to erroneously interpret the Scriptures — and whatever else he might wish to do — nor would anyone else object to these things, except such a one should be considered to have offended the Divine Majesty. Luther will be free to attack, bite, devour, and destroy anyone according to his good pleasure — but whosoever might, in turn, do any of these things to Luther, would be guilty of defiling Luther's king with blasphemies.

But who is this king of Luther? He is surely none other than the one of whom Job speaks when he says, in Chapter 41: "He is king over all the children of pride." But he cannot be called the same king of glory, except insofar as he once had a seat in heaven whence he attempted through ambition to usurp that glory.

At this point I don't think that I have left anything out in the necessary response to Luther, as far as these matters go, except the one place where he tries to demonstrate that the orthodox believers teach self-contradictory doctrines:

> "This is the Papists' insanity when (in Matt. 16) they make the rock both Christ and the pope, when Christ is holy but the pope impious, and when holiness has as much in common with impiety as light with darkness, or Christ with Belial. For the papacy only stands — or rather falls — by its inconsistent, contradictory, and lying dogmas, which teach, assert, and maintain both of these conflicting teachings at the same time. Let the reader then see from this one argument how asinine is the ignorance of the Thomists, or the impotence of their childish

minds, which does not allow them to understand their own words. Yet they dare to write a defense of the sacraments, and to boast of their bombastic elegance, which is the proof of their incredible lack of knowledge. For I think this book of the king's was written for this reason, that the world might never believe that I had falsely accused the Sophists of folly and ignorance, especially the piglets that are among them (I mean the Thomists), because my judgment was to receive both demonstration and confirmation by their own work and image."

At this point, you must weigh carefully the sort of insults that he levels at the Thomists, by which he seeks to denigrate the glory of this saint — whose name has always inspired great veneration among the most learned and experienced, since they variously called him the crowning flower of theology. Simultaneously you should examine by what sort of frivolous reasoning Luther does this, not to speak of his lies: I have not read where St. Thomas or the Thomists or some pope called someone other than Peter "the Rock," and besides, it was not merely Thomas, but Jerome and often even Augustine who openly spoke in this way. What would prohibit such a name when Christ himself predicted that he would be called "Rock" in John 1:42: "Thou shalt be called Cephas, which is interpreted Peter," or rock, or stone, as the evangelist notes. But please tell me what difference there is between a rock and a stone: what would keep Peter from being named "the Rock" when the same person is called a stone? The same Peter acknowledges that he is a sinner, when he said to Christ in Luke Chapter 5, "Depart from me, oh Lord, because I am a sinner." Therefore, there's nothing that would keep Peter, who is otherwise a sinner, from being styled "the Rock," simply because Christ, too, is called a rock. What is this? Can Christ not be a rock precisely because some other Christian is also called a rock, or is it rather that no other Christian can be called a rock since Christ himself is termed a rock? Did perhaps Peter say something contradictory when he wrote in his first epistle, "Unto whom coming, as to a living stone, rejected indeed by men but chosen and made honorable by God: Be you also as living stones built up, a spiritual house"? It would follow from Luther's reasoning that Peter here said something contradictory because he calls each and every Christian a rock, just as he calls Christ "rock" — although Christ himself is holy, and to the contrary so many Christians are sinners — well there is nothing less in accord with sanctity than sin, just as light in comparison to darkness, and Christ to Belial. For this reason, if a Christian is a sinner and can also be called a rock, just as even Christ is called a rock, what should keep Peter from being titled "the Rock," as the same title enjoyed by Christ? Does Christ not call himself "the Light" as well? "I am the light of the world" (John 8), while calling his Apostles the light of the world, too: "You are the light of the world" (Matthew 5)? Did Christ speak in a self-contradictory manner when he said these things?

Here, dear reader, you can clearly see how frivolous Luther's dialectic is, as well as how unjustly insulting he is against Thomas and the Thomists, when they have only said that Peter is called "the Rock." Whether Luther wills or no, Christ built his church upon this rock, and Peter is a rock. Did Paul not say to the Ephesians that Christians had been built upon the foundation of the Apostles and prophets, with the cornerstone being Jesus Christ? Who would miss that Christ Jesus is the great and capital cornerstone? Then, that the prophets and apostles are as stones set upon the foundation, and that, lastly, other Christians are living stones that are built on top of this foundation? For this reason St. Augustine called the prophets and the Apostles the church's foundations, according to what David had composed in Psalm 86: "Its foundations are on the holy mountains," although he does not deny that there is one principle foundation, to wit Jesus Christ, whom he calls the foundation of foundations, just as he calls the same the holy of holies and the pastor of pastors.[4] At this point it has become clear, I think, that Luther has not triumphed over Satan, nor did his dogma's come from heaven, but that he rather obtained diabolical discernment. Thereupon we demonstrated on many points how he had been self-contradictory — and not only on those points that do not concern Scripture, as he argued, but also upon the other matters on which the Scriptures do openly declare

---

[4] Or "great" pastor, as a Hebrew superlative — Editor.

something to be true. Third, it is clear that Luther's biting insults are inexcusable either as exaggerations, embellishments, or any other cause. Finally, there is no contradiction among the orthodox believers, as Luther has accused, in that the title of "Rock" should be common both to Peter and to Christ.

CHAPTER III
Regarding the Faithful's Communion, the Church's Custom
Should Be Observed

OW we will turn our pen to the principal matters about which there is the most serious controversy, and of course there are several points with which we shall deal singularly, so on this third point we will treat the matter of communion under both species; however, at the outset we must refute the points which Luther promised to dispute in general.

Specifically, Luther first objected to the king that the king represented his claims by no scriptural authority nor by any necessary reason, but that he rather brought forward and adduced only one, and that this was "custom," which Luther claimed to be an imitation of the Thomistic form of argument, that is, "it seems to me," "in my opinion," "I believe," and "it must therefore be this way," as if Saint Thomas rested upon no more solid argumentation than that — which is a complete lie, and clear to everyone, but Luther has become accustomed to lies so that it pains him not in the least to lie completely. Is this, too, not also a very patent lie, in that he accuses the king of bringing forward no other pressing reason? We will show that that is completely false in just a moment, but this sort of "opposition according to Luther" is of no consequence, because whenever the Scriptures fail to demonstrate some truth, for our predecessors "usage" and "custom" have always been very important, nor did the Apostles themselves always bring forward Scriptures to prove what they would, which is something that Luther falsely asserts elsewhere. It is clear from The Acts of the Apostles, Chapter 15, that they said just this: "For it hath seemed good to the Holy Spirit and to us," and they were persuaded that this proceeded from the Holy Spirit, whatsoever they had unanimously approved. Even when Paul had taught the Corinthians about how women should veil, he did not prove this from the Scriptures, but from reason and custom together: "We have no such custom, nor the Church of God." Yet, it is clear that many customs were introduced into the Church by the Holy Spirit besides those which the Scriptures delivered to us, or about which the Scriptures make no mention. So, too, through the Apostles and from the Scriptures themselves it is clear that many things had been handed on, but about which there is no explanation in the Scriptures, and for this reason it is manifest that wherever the Scriptures are wanting, at that same point it will suffice to adduce "reason" or "custom." Although Luther brings forward many reasons to the contrary, they are too weak to render powerless the force of custom, as we will promptly demonstrate, but we should consider this first: there is a great difference among customs. You see, some are good and holy, while some to the contrary are evil and demented, but amongst these it is not too difficult to discern the difference: if something is evil, then it is likely that it was introduced by an evil spirit; on the contrary, if the custom is holy and salutary, and generally approved of by all Christians, then I don't doubt that it was inspired by the Holy Spirit. Nor should anyone — unless he is an obstinate defender of his own position — dare to object that the custom is lawful and to be observed by all Christians. At this point however, it is likely clear that we are speaking of the Church's custom of communion for the laity under the species of bread alone. Surely this custom came forth from many approved conditions and is quite suitable to right reason, so that no one — unless he were wholly unholy — would dare think that this should be abrogated.

1. Now, this matter has ten such conditions: first, that its early introduction is free from any suspicion of corruption, either on the part of the clergy or on the part of the people, because no one could even suspect some sinister intention — either clerical or lay — for the sake of which the clergy would attempt to take away other part of the sacrament from the laity, or why the laity would not forthwith protest this fact, while it is certain that there was no

temporal gain or benefit to come from it for the one group or for the other.

2. The second condition is that there is a clear and great set of evils both for the clergy and for the lay people which gradually led to this custom. You see, there was the danger of spillage in the administration of the [Precious] Blood — and this happened too frequently — especially whenever there was a large multitude that needed to be communed. There was likewise risk in conservation, lest the species of wine should sour into vinegar, since parish pastors would have been obliged to have it ever ready for the sick. It was also perilous whenever it needed to be carried to the dying, whether one did the carrying on horseback or by foot; it was also a hazard that those who were to receive — especially those who are easily nauseated, as is the case for a significant number — that they would easily suffer nausea once they had the taste of wine. There's also a dangerous lack of wine in many parts of Christendom, where there is great poverty, so that one who lacked the species of wine might be led to believe that he had received less than the whole Christ. There was, finally, even the threat of a lack of faith, that is, that the whole Christ would not be believed to be wholly present under either species, were both species not always presented to all Christians. Now you can see what great fear there was previously of so many dangers which are now completely avoided by this custom.

3. The third condition for this custom is that it must not be against any precept in the entirety of the law, because Luther himself could not provide any precept from Scripture besides this one: "drink ye all from it." But this forbids nothing, because Christ then spoke only to the twelve, nor was he speaking to others when he had previously offered the cup said, "take it and divide it among you," and there were twelve present as Luke plainly writes (in ch. 22): "he sat down, and the twelve apostles with him." Now, if there had been more than twelve, the one cup would not have sufficed, which is why it is in accord with both reason and Scripture that this was said only to the Apostles, that is, "drink ye all of this." Luther, therefore, badly corrupts Scripture in this place when he contends that this was said to all Christians which was said to the Apostles alone, and he does not have another scriptural citation on

this point — although it is he who usually criticizes his adversaries for, "so it must be," "it has to be thus," and "it cannot be otherwise." You see, he renounced the sixth chapter of John's Gospel, which he plainly admitted to be completely unfavorable to the Bohemians.[5] Of course there can be a great delight for the orthodox believers in seeing this spectacle wherein there are mutual battles among these heretics, while one says the Scriptures have this sense, and another contends that it has the contrary sense. But we should follow upon our project: it is clear from these things, as it relates to our point, that holy communion under one or the other species is against no command from the Scriptures.

4. The fourth condition of this custom is that the examples from the new law greatly favor it, such as the account from the final chapter of St. Luke's Gospel wherein we find the two disciples with whom Jesus went to the town of Emmaus: "And it came to pass, while he was at table with them, he took bread and blessed and broke and gave to them. And their eyes were opened: and they knew him. And he vanished out of their sight." Here you have what pertains to the eating of that blessed bread, which according to the custom of the Scriptures is called bread, and that their eyes were opened immediately. Now it is by this precise indication that Chrysostom, Theophilus, and Augustine understand this to have been the true body of Christ. It is clear, too, from the very words, as we see in the consecratory formula that he used for his own body: "He took bread and blessed and broke and gave to them." Furthermore, from the fact that he immediately removed himself from their eyes, it is quite clear that they had received only this part of the Sacrament, which is under the species of bread and not under the species of wine too.

5. The fifth condition of this custom is that it must square well with the figures of the old law, because whatever liquid was offered under that law was also called a "drink offering" which was received only by the priest and not at all by the non-priestly people, since it had come to be the portion of the priests just as the liquid part of this sacrament is now solely reserved for the priest, and not likewise offered to the laity.

---

5 Namely, the Hussites. —Editor.

6. The sixth condition for this custom is that it should cause absolutely no man a loss. You see, whatever is contained under the species of bread is also wholly and completely contained under the species of wine, because the body and the blood, the soul and the divinity of Christ are fully contained under either species. For this reason, the one who receives under one species no less communes than the one who receives under both, as far as it means to receive Christ, since the species add nothing whatsoever to the sacramental power, but are only signs, and the signs themselves are not operative in the human soul.

7. The seventh condition is that the aforementioned custom came about not by any force of precept or command, but rather by a kind of tacit consensus that was sensed both from the people and from the clergy. Once all these dangers had been seen and had so often before happened throughout the churches of all Christendom, this manner was received by a sort of tacit support of all, before any sort of conciliar decree had ever confirmed it in writing. Because this is abundantly obvious from the many books written and published by various authors who lived long before the Council of Constance or the Council of Basel, it needs no other proof at all.

8. The eighth condition is also quite important: this custom arose among the people that is guided by the Holy Spirit, and no one doubts that the Church is ruled by the Holy Spirit, unless it is one who doesn't believe in the gospel of Christ, because in the gospel the Holy Spirit himself is promised — the Spirit of Truth — to remain in the Church in perpetuity, that he might teach her and lead her to all truth, and that he might proclaim what is Christ's, which he has heard from Christ, and that he might finally bring to mind all those things whatsoever Christ had long ago said to the Apostles. St. John the Evangelist clearly writes these things as from the very mouth of Christ in Chapters 14 and 16. And what else is it to bring to mind all things but to make known and offer to the mind whatever belongs to Christian truth? Thus, it is clear that the Holy Spirit himself — whom Christ calls the Spirit of Truth — should remain in the Church forever, instructing the Church and leading the Church into all truth, as well as proclaiming, ministering,

and administering to the mind whatsoever is of Christ, as well as simultaneously bringing to light all those things which Christ had once before said in an obscure manner.

9. The ninth condition is also of great importance, since this custom concerns something upon which the salvation of souls depends greatly. For the communion of the body and blood of Christ greatly pertains and belongs to the salvation of souls — which is something that Luther cannot deny, since he claims that upon the fate of this very thing one gains both the remission of sins as well as the heavenly inheritance.

10. The tenth condition is that all the chief leaders of the entire Church as well as two general councils wholly approved. You see, whenever any controversy over the Scriptures arises, as is known to happen very frequently by the force of heretics, there must be someone or some men here on Earth who can be held up as judges, and upon whose sentence the judgment will stand; otherwise, there would never be any hope of solving controversies. The heretic, you see, will strive to say that this Scripture has this meaning; the orthodox, on the other hand, will deny it. So, when will there ever be an end to this quarrel unless there are some judges appointed for this very matter? Likewise, their judgment — unless it is believed to be guided by the Holy Spirit — will be easily avoided and evaded by the heretic. It is for this very reason that we must believe that Christ was not going to desert his Church on such a dangerous point of agitation and vacillation, for which he did not refuse to shed his own blood. Who could be in doubt, therefore, when out of every corner of the entire Christian world the Fathers were gathered together to consult the spirit of Christ regarding what they should do upon this contentious point, that Christ himself and his spirit would be present? "Wheresoever two or three are gathered in my name there shall I be in their midst," (Mt.18) and again, "Behold I am with you all days, even unto the consummation of the world" (Mt. 28). Thus, whenever all Christians cannot agree together upon some point, and since the Fathers are always esteemed to be the greater portion of Christianity as a whole, then it is fitting that whatever they decree in the Holy Spirit whenever they are gathered together should be believed to be true by all Christians. There are many examples of this in the Acts of

the Apostles. For example, when there are councils mentioned in that book, not all Christians were asked to come, but only the Apostles and the elders, who were held to be mediators between God and the people, so that whatever they declared to be of the Holy Spirit once they had come together would no longer be seen as a mere human decree but rather something that the entire rest of the people should consider to be from God. It is clear that this was the manner in which they held the council that treated of the ceremonies of the ancient law, in the controversy of whether or not they should be done away with. What was established by the Apostles and elders there was sent to the rest of the Christians, as many as lived in Antioch of Syria and even in Cilicia. Nor did they assign any other rationale for the decision except that it had seemed well to them and to the Holy Spirit, once they had been gathered together as one. In this spot one can intuit the custom of the early Church — the same custom which later generations would retain, because although then there was hardly so large a number of Christians that they could have never all been called into one location, and yet nevertheless this was not done, but only the more senior defined what seemed right to them, and they passed on their definition as the law to be observed by everyone else. Nor did they reduce any other reference to Sacred Scripture, or any other reasoning: they simply held it to be clear that this had come from the Holy Spirit, since they had decreed it in unanimity.

Furthermore, one can also ascertain how sure this truth is from the proceedings of the Council of Constance as well as that of Basel: the aforementioned custom was approved clearly in each council by the Fathers who judged on the matter unanimously. It could therefore not be broken profanely by anyone, since that custom arose from no occasion of corruption but rather as a freedom from many dangers, and since it is not only against no command of the Gospels, but to the contrary it is most fitting with other examples from the new law, as well as befitting the figures of the old law. It harms no one. It was not brought in by force but was rather gradually introduced by the tacit support of all — in that society which is governed by the Holy Spirit — and it is in a matter that greatly concerns the salvation of souls. Finally, it should be noted that innumerable princes of the Church have twice approved it, so that one would have to have lost his mind to think that this had not proceeded from the Holy Spirit. This suffices for establishing the custom.

Now let us investigate how Luther's reckoning has no force to abrogate this custom: he first brings forward a quote from Matthew Chapter 15: "And in vain do they worship me, teaching doctrines and commandments of men." From this Scripture he tries to conclude that this custom, which had been introduced by men, was without force and authority. But Christ himself refutes this scriptural citation, since he said that it pertained to those who made void the precepts of God on account of the traditions of men. Nothing of the kind, however, is introduced through this custom, because it is not contrary to any divine command, as we have shown above. Christ cited this Scripture from the old law which would have the people obey the mandates of men, as is clear from Numbers 11 and Deuteronomy 17: you see, you had under that law the seventy elders, whose commands and institutions the people were bound to follow, under pain of death. Christ speaks of them in Matthew Chapter 23: "The Scribes and Pharisees sit upon the chair of Moses; All things therefore whatsoever they shall say to you, observe and do." Now if Christ had commanded that they should be obeyed in all things, whatsoever they might say, then he would have willed this obedience be shown much more so to his Apostles and to their successors, that is, that all should obey them, those about whom he had said, "whosoever rejects you, rejects me." Thus, Christ does not condemn the commands of men nor does he forbid anyone from obeying them, but he rather commands that in all things that are not contrary to God's precepts, they should completely obey. On this account, since the custom is not in any way contrary to God's commands, this reference aids Luther's case in no way, and it's rather quite surprising how Luther mockingly taunts as if by this one Scripture alone he had completely conquered.

Yet, what he then produces calls for mocking more than for any response. Who would not laugh at how he brings forward the long-standing nature of the Turks' belief, since that has nothing to do with our custom besides its long-standing nature alone? And yet, Luther is not ashamed to cite this in his defense: "So, how shall we prove that the Turks' faith is erroneous since it has been in vogue now for nearly a thousand years, and arose before Germany was converted to Christianity?" as if we had approved this custom of ours only because it had been in vogue for so long, which is clearly false. But we have instead shown that there are many other good and just conditions: it delivers from many evils, nor does it go against any commands of the divine law, it was introduced for good reasons into a people that is ruled by the Holy Spirit and by Heaven's own law, and finally that the princes and rulers of this people — by common appeal and acclaim — had approved of it.

Furthermore, the Turks' belief — no matter how old it may be — is clearly bereft of all these other conditions, because it is certain that it is both unholy, against the law of God, and that it is not the people ruled by the Holy Spirit, as is clearly the case from the patent promises of Christ to Christians. Likewise, there is no weight at all to what he produces, regarding the Jews, as a third reference: "In this way, who could not rightly justify the religion of the Jews, according to the method of this unconquerable Thomist, because it surpasses our own in length of time?"

To this we respond: the duration of the faith and law of the Jews does not support them in any way since it is clearly a fact that Christ had convicted them of infidelity, and that their faith had been rejected and that their law had long ago been superseded.

Then he objects in a like manner regarding the Gentiles: "According to Henry of England, why shouldn't the nations of the world be said to have rightly persecuted the new religion of Christ? Their idolatry, according to this excellent Thomist argument, ought to be regarded as the true faith because it has the support of so many thousands of years, of so many different countries, and of such long-continued usage!"

Here we respond that, no matter how long the custom of idolatry, it cannot save the nations, since it is not only impiously against God, but also most harmful in its laws. Yet, this custom about which we are now speaking is neither impiously against God nor contrary to his laws.

In the fifth place he tries to establish his error with reference to how common errors are among men: "Let us even state, with that same Henry as our teacher, that the errors of wicked men are the true faith, because from the beginning of the world they have surpassed in number, duration, and power the few and insignificant congregations of those who were godly."

We respond to this by saying that the errors of the men that have been since the beginning of the world can be helped in no way by their long duration, since they have no other author but Satan — that same author of Luther's teachings.

You see from our responses here, dear reader, what sort of rock-hard arguments this new teacher of the entire world has produced, he who boasts with certainty that he has received his doctrines from heaven and who glories that he has overcome Satan. You see what sort of spoils he has brought back from such a glorious victory!

We should not, however, overlook what a Herculean and invincible reason he produces at the end: "The sum of the whole matter is that if the sayings of men are able to be made into articles of faith, why should not my sayings be made articles of faith? Am I not a man?"

In response, I say that I certainly think you are anything but a man: did you yourself not call yourself a she-bear and a lioness? Since no man would ever call a she-bear or a lioness a man, but rather a beast, then you clearly don't seem to me a man, but a beast. Four, if you were a man, there would be some other indication of humanity in you. Your books would not be littered with so many lies. You would not abound in abuse. You would not be furiously raving with such rage and futility. With this settled, let us go on to other matters.

He then jeers, "If we claim that these customs come from the Holy Spirit, the Turk will laugh at this, and furthermore, insofar as we maintain this without Scripture, we barely differ from the Turkish custom." First of all, we do not assert this without the Scriptures, rather we showed how this was actually created on account of the Scriptures; then, the Turks have no faith in our Scriptures, which we would otherwise produce in potent abundance. Third, the Turk would not believe Luther, although he claims with certainty to have received his teachings from heaven, even if he would try to confirm them with the Scriptures — which he never does.

Besides this, he goes on at great length and grumbles in so many words that we have put down a foundation other than Christ, we who obey men. Now this, too, is wholly false, because the supreme foundation of our faith is Christ, and thereupon the Apostles whom Paul himself — although they were men — also calls "foundation," which is established upon Christ who is the chief cornerstone. Upon these men, too, other apostolic men are used in the edifice as living stones, and upon all of these, as a support, the rest of Christianity leans.

After this, he asserts that Paul "[s]anctions with his great authority that our faith should rest upon the words of God when he says, 'My speech and my preaching were not with the persuasive words of man's wisdom, but in demonstration of the Spirit and in power, that your faith should not stand in the wisdom of men but in the power of God'" (1 Cor. 2).

But this Scripture goes much more against Luther than it does against us, because Paul taught what was his by a demonstration of the spirit and of power, that is by the openly clear working of miracles. The Fathers who succeeded Paul, too, taught what was theirs in a similar manner, that is with the testimony from heaven, in marvelous works. For this reason, what is ours has been confirmed abundantly by the testimony of the Spirit and of power. You see, just as Paul taught what he did in his day and confirmed all of it by patent miracles, so, too, did the other Fathers enlighten us with their teaching in the following ages by a great holiness of life, which was also confirmed by the great light of miracles.

This is why, if Luther wishes to introduce other things than that which the Church has hitherto believed and which are clearly different from what she has believed up to this point, then he must do so by a demonstration of the Spirit and of power; that is, he must prove it with signs and miracles, rather than by a twisted misinterpretation of Scripture that goes against the meaning that Christ and so many and so very learned and holy Fathers gave as their unanimous decisions, those who have preceded us by many centuries. I would rather have Luther's words of human wisdom than his many diabolical lies, as well as the cursing and contentious censures that he gives in abundance whenever he writes anything. I mean that the reader will always find those writings to be full of lies and cursing rather than any efficacious arguing.

After another heap of reproaches, he closes by saying that Christ "built his Church not on the length of time, nor on the multitude of men, nor on "It must be so," nor on the usage and sayings of the saints, nor even on John the Baptist, nor on Elijah, nor on Jeremiah, nor on any of the prophets, but upon that one and solid rock, upon Christ, the Son of God."

We, too, claim this same principle and primary foundation of our Church, upon which foundation, though, we have the Apostles as well as the prophets closely laid, and of course it is clear that they were men. Then we, too, are built upon them, just as Paul says in Eph. 2: "Built upon the foundation of the Apostles and prophets, Jesus Christ himself being the chief cornerstone: In whom all the building, being framed together, grows up into an holy temple in the Lord." But, Luther will contend that nothing else is meant to be understood of this foundation here than Christ. I, on the other hand, would refute this, and for this reason we need some judge who can settle this dispute between us.

So Augustine, in his explanation of Psalm 86, calls the Apostles and the prophets the foundations of this city, that is of Christ's Church; and he calls Christ the foundation of foundations, just as he is sometimes called the shepherd of shepherds and holy of holies. Thus, the reader sees that the Apostles and prophets are called the Church's foundations and that there is nothing to be feared from such a truth, although they, too, were men, since they have been established upon that chief cornerstone that is Christ Jesus. It follows again from that same point that Peter must be understood to be the rock in Christ's prior words, because why else would Christ call him elsewhere a stone, such as when he said in John Chapter 1, "Thou shalt be named Cephas," which is interpreted as "stone" or "rock," as even John says. What else is a stone or a boulder, but a rock? If Luther wishes to contest that this is not how that passage should be understood, then we will need to have judges — and we have provided a fair number of them against him in article 25 of his refuted assertions.

Now let the reader note in what way he tries to prove that the Church of Christ is founded only upon Christ and not upon those foundations.

"He cannot lie or deceive; but every man is a liar." I do not know what he means here except that he is perhaps attempting to cover his lies with this citation, that is, that there is no reason for Luther to blush, since Scripture says that every man is a liar. But I do not think that he means that Paul was a liar, or Peter, or some other of the Apostles, in those things which they bestowed to the Church, because in that case then whatsoever they wrote would also be brought under suspicion. Now, if you do not want this to be said of them, then what would keep them from being called "foundations," upon which the Church — after Christ — rests firmly?

He then brings forward another two scriptural citations which serve his purpose in no way, but actually combat against it. The passage from 1 Pet. 4:11, "If any man speak, let him speak, as the words of God," clearly condemns Luther since he so frequently speaks nothing but curses, criticisms, and reproaches, which are rather the words of Satan than of God. Yet, lest Luther should say that we have produced no example of such a thing, it will not weigh upon us, too, much to place one or two before the reader: did he not already attack with a diabolical reproach the supporters of St. Thomas? "These are the arms by which heretics are conquered today: fire and fury of the dumbest asses and Thomist swine. Yet let those swine proceed and if they dare, let them burn me — here I am; I am waiting for them. Even if my ashes should be thrown into a thousand seas after death, I should come back to tirelessly pursue the vulgar abomination, the Summa. While I live, I will be the enemy of the papacy; if I am burned, I will be twice the enemy. You Thomist swine, do what you can! You will have Luther for a she-bear along the way and as a lioness in your path. He will attack you on all sides, and will give you no rest until he has broken into pieces your iron necks and bronze foreheads, either for your salvation or for your destruction. Until now it has been enough to have lost patience; from now on, since you continue to be hardened and blinded to raise your horns and willingly become incorrigible and unreformed, let no one expect me to say anything against you — you deplorable monsters — that is either sweet or mild, because I want you to be irritated more and more until all your strength and fury are exhausted and you fall down, one on top of another. He that first silences the other, let him be the victor.

As you wish, so let it be done to you."

These, dear reader, are the words of Luther. Do they seem to you the words of God, or rather the devil's? Then again, he speaks of the servants of the supreme pontiff in this way: "I will silently despise them. If I have to deal with them, I will do it with all the violence that I can in order to irritate and anger them sufficiently; rather, I will provoke the stupid blocks, the ignorant asses, the fatted swine, since they deserve nothing else other than to be led to their punishment. I will do this for the glory of Henry's Church and of Henry himself, its renowned Thomist defender, lest he be able to complain that he had condemned my bitterness of speech with his most holy curse, all in vain."

So, are these the words of God, the sort which Luther so frequently speaks? Who would not rather characterize them immediately as diabolical?

So that we may now return to our intention, Peter teaches in those words above that whatsoever Christians might say, they should say with modesty and sobriety, as if they were speaking the words of God. For that reason, this Scripture provides no benefit to Luther. Less than no benefit, however, is provided by the following citation — which, however, he makes up from his own brain — since it was never written in any place: "Let every prophecy be in analogy with the faith." Since Paul did not say this, but rather, "Let prophecy be used according to the rule of faith," that is, that the gift of prophecy among men is greater or lesser according to the greatness of faith. What does this have to do with the subject at hand, since we could say nothing that is not from the Scriptures? Furthermore, although these Scriptures adduced by Luther do not prove this point, no one would deny that for those who should prophesy, it should be in accord with the Scriptures, and that they should pronounce nothing at all that is in any way contrary to the Scriptures.

Although Luther has not proved these things either from the Scriptures or from reason, let the reader hear how he then boasts: "These are our towers of strength, against which the Henrys, Thomists, and papists — and whoever is like them and their impure, foul, filthy, wicked and sacrilegious sort — are forced to be silent, and since they have nothing to reply, they lie confused and prostrate before the words of that thunder. Still, we wait for whatever the king, together with all his sophists, will dare to mutter back against this."

Does the reader not see how this beast is clearly insane, since he furiously blathers and spews forth only jests and trifles, all while he calls others the jesters and triflers? And who thinks that the stinking pestilence of his mouth is so formidable that it would cause everyone else to be quiet?

Luther then adds, "For the sentence remains fixed, that faith is not due to anything except to the certain word of God, as it is said in Romans 10: 'Faith comes by hearing, but hearing [comes] by the word of Christ'."

This, of course, supports our position very much, because those things which we believe, we have accepted from the orthodox believers, and they in turn heard these things from other orthodox, and this happens in a continuous line all the way until we arrive at those very first hearers of the Apostles. But, if you were to seek from Luther once he had received his faith by hearing, he could indicate no one else besides a follower of Wycliffe or some Hussite. Luther, you see, knows how to gather whatever he might like from any Scripture; of course, it hardly follows logically that since faith should be given to the word of God, that it should therefore be given *only and solely* to the word of God.

For the time being, let us grant this to Luther: let faith be given only to the words of God and to those things that follow from God's words. Now, we do not doubt that the matter with which we are dealing should be just like that: "And I will ask the Father, and he will send you another advocate, that he may abide with you forever, the spirit of truth." Again: "when he shall come, who is the Spirit of Truth, he will lead you into all truth." And once again, speaking of the same Spirit: "He will receive from mine and he will announce it to you."

On top of this: "But the Paraclete, the Holy Spirit, whom the Father will send in my name, he will teach you all things and bring all things to your mind, whatsoever I shall have said to you." Now, who could examine these Scriptures carefully and doubt within himself about the consolation of this Spirit? Especially when apostolic men and elders from throughout the Christian world came together into one place for the sake of consultation, that is what they should do for the cause of the faith — which is certainly a cause which concerns the salvation of souls to the greatest extent possible. If this Spirit is "of truth" and may abide with us forever, it cannot be a waste of time to demonstrate the veracity of this matter. If he will lead into all truth, why would he not indicate it if he had been so devoutly employed? And if he will teach you all things and bring all things to your mind, whatsoever Christ had said, why would the Holy Spirit not explain this solicitous spot among Christ's words, if only he is asked? Here, for sure, we could throw this back at that beast and heap all of his criticism back upon his own head, most especially since we have the example of Christ's deeds, beyond those same Scriptures, that is that he made use of the single species of bread when he gave this sacrament to the two disciples [on the road to Emmaus]. Not only Christ, but even his Apostles are recorded to have done this more than once. But we have handled this matter at greater length in our refutation of his articles.

Yet, Luther does not reign in his foolish talk: he tries to show from the above words that "therefore whatever is brought forward that is beyond the word of God, this will be at our disposal, as though we were lords of it, to believe or not to believe, to condemn or to approve, as it is written: All things are yours, whether Apollo, or Cephas, or Paul, and you are Christ's." Yet not even this proves what Luther would have it prove, because Paul has not understood Christians to be Christ's in such a manner that they should not obey their superiors, because he writes in the final chapter to the Hebrews: "Obey your prelates and be subject to them." Then he gives the rationale: "For they watch as those who will render an account of your souls." See here that Paul wants Christians to obey and be subject to those who preside over them, since those same will render an account to God for the people's souls, and Christ likewise commanded in Matt. 23: "Whatsoever they say to you, do."

Finally, he teaches that "it is for us to judge the pontiff — not for us to be judged by the pontiff — because the spiritual man is judged by no man, and he himself judges all."

This logic is clearly silly — unless Luther first teaches that all the people are spiritual — because Paul had said this of those who preside, and not about the people, as is abundantly clear from that citation, because he would soon add, "but we have the mind of Christ," as he spoke of the leaders, and then what did he say about the people?: "for you are still carnal." He then shows who he called carnal: "For whereas there is among you envying and contention, are you not carnal?" See here, dear reader, how the authority of Luther's judgment vanishes before us, since he is openly contentious, envious, and thus carnal. If the works of the flesh which Paul enumerated in his letter to the Galatians make any man carnal, then Luther is completely carnal because he is completely kindled by enmities, contentions, jealousies, anger and fighting, dissensions, sects, and envies. For these reasons, neither he nor his followers can be suitable judges.

What he then produces from Augustine is in no way opposed to us: "to the canonical books alone should the honor be given of firmly believing that there is no error whatsoever in them, and for other books, no matter how much authority and holiness they may enjoy, are not worthy of equal honor." Augustine did not mean this so that nothing at all should be believed unless it is found in the Scriptures, since he himself teaches against Donatus that there are many things that should be believed which are not contained in Holy Writ, just as we mentioned in our refutation of Luther's articles on the same matter. Rather, Augustine judged that we should show such a deference to the decrees of general synods just as if they had proceeded from the Holy Spirit.

Up to this point we have omitted nothing, dear reader, that was worthy of any response, although we have passed by many taunting insults lest we should wear you down with a boredom from our loquaciousness; but, after many more words, Luther tries to sneak something in, lest he should seem to be praising and protesting Pope Leo on the same point and thus seem self-contradictory, but there is nothing going for him here. If Leo X was an impostor, as Luther calls him, then he was hardly a good man; and yet, the same man was called by Luther "a good man" — unless he wishes to admit that he said that for a fawning flattery or that he had written a lie.

Luther then snarls about the papacy, and insinuates that the most illustrious king had been more silent than a fish in regard to the scriptural references, when Luther himself, however, did not produce in the entire book of the Babylonian Captivity a single citation that would overthrow the papacy. Furthermore, since we have abundantly responded to Luther's contentions against the papacy in our refutation of his articles, we will here deal with the matter in fewer words. I don't think that there is anyone who expresses doubts on this matter, and who could yet sufficiently compare Christ's words with what happened in reality, because who is so blind that he doesn't see that what we call "the Church" has come down to us from Peter? I will not make a contentious point about whether or not other Apostles set up other churches, that is, Paul, John, James, Matthew, Barnabas, and the rest of those whom, at various points and throughout the world, Christ had sent to convert the world. Yet, as these others passed on, there were either complete extinctions, or the churches were so upended by schisms and heresies that they could hardly be believed to belong to the Church. Now, since the Church is not called a segregation but a congregation, then those who are not united with the other members are justly considered not to belong to the Church. Therefore, solely that succession of Christians which flowed from Peter retained the right name of the Church. It is on this account that when Christ said, "Thou art Peter and upon this rock I shall build my church," and also promised elsewhere that the same man would be called "Rock" or "Stone," who does not easily see that Peter is the one being called "Rock" by those words? Here is why: nowhere else, in all the Gospels, can you find anyone other than Peter being called "Rock," and it is clear that Christ's words cannot deceive or be of no effect, such as when he said, "Thou shalt be called 'stone'." So it follows that Peter is rightly called a rock in this place, upon which Christ would build the entire succession of his Church — against which succession the gates of hell have not prevailed and will not prevail. It is true that the Church remains up to this day in an uninterrupted succession, and so shall she remain, doubtless, as long as the world shall last. What does it matter to us if the Bohemians and the Indians do not want to recognize this rock as the foundation of the Catholic Church, but wish henceforth to be separated from her? She nevertheless remains the one dove of Christ, as in the Song of Solomon, and that others make themselves outside of her when they willingly leave her. Whether or not you say that Jerome called the Roman Church — his own — also the mother Church of the world makes no difference in the matter, since it would be a mere denial, but that Jerome was not then in the Diocese of Rome, but instead living in Jerusalem, and would not therefore call the Roman Church his mother, and less indeed that she were the mother of the entire world. Nevertheless, let us hear what Jerome thinks of the Roman Church, when he wrote to Damascus, the Pope of Rome: "because the East is torn apart by ancient anger among their peoples, it has ripped at that unbroken tunic of the Lord and bit by bit tugged at the cloth; therefore, I thought it fitting to consult the chair and the faith that is praised by the Apostles." And further on: "With your beatitude, that is, with the See of Peter, I am connected in communion. I know that that Church has been built upon the rock." There you have what Jerome thinks about Peter: "I know that that church has been built upon the rock." He added: "If anyone is joined with the chair of Peter, he is mine." This is why he candidly said that he did not know Vitalis, that he rejected Miletus, that he did not accept Paulinus — those who were adversaries of this See.

He even said in the end that they all scattered — that is that they were schismatics and outside the Church — whosoever did not gather with the successor of Peter. From all these things, who would not gather how much deference Jerome thought was owed to the Roman Church? Thus, there is no reason why Luther should prattle on that the King of England is some ignorant and unlearned layman: if only we priests ourselves were not so inferior to the king, both in erudition as well as in eloquence!

But let us now come to the point at hand, which Luther had forestalled up to this point through his great verbosity. You see, we had to respond to each and every point, and the order which he followed we, too, had to observe, so that readers might promptly find all the points. First of all, we will solve all the citations and rationales which Luther calls his "robust strength" and which, he falsely claimed, had been omitted by the king, whereas Luther himself actually skips over many things which press him to some extent, and to which he offers no response, but this is one — and far from the only — vulpine fraudulence whereby Luther gravely reprehends his adversary in a matter of which he is much more delinquent himself. Still, we will now go over and examine the seven things which he calls his great strength.

1. "First, I advanced the authority of the evangelists, who tell in one unvarying narrative that Christ instituted both species to be received by those who were to observe his memorial; and that he significantly added to the giving of the cup the words: 'Drink ye all of this'." To this we respond: it is true that Christ instituted this sacrament under both species, but we deny that he commanded it to be given under both species to everyone, whosoever should keep this memorial, nor does the citation "drink ye all of this" prove that it was given to all Christians and not to the Twelve Apostles alone, as we previously demonstrated.

2. "The second argument is that if, at the Supper, Christ had given the sacrament to priests alone, it would hardly be right to give any part to the laity since it is not lawful to change the institution and example of Christ." We respond here that to two of his disciples who had not been made priests, Christ himself administered this sacrament under the species of bread alone, and thus Christ's institution is not changed on this account, when the very same sacrament is given to the laity — albeit only under the species of bread — since Christ himself first did this very thing when he communicated the laymen on the way to Emmaus, just as we have said earlier, and which is clear from the final chapter of Luke's gospel.

Furthermore, we say that a general council can licitly change some things of Christ's institution due to urgent causes, just as those first leaders of the Church changed the form of Baptism to a form quite different from what Christ had instituted.

Third, we say that the mode of administering this sacrament was left to the Apostles' judgment, which Augustine teaches Januarius when he says, "The Savior, in order to commend the depth of that mystery more effectively to his disciples, was pleased to impress it on their hearts and memories by making its institution his last act before going from them to his Passion. And therefore he did not prescribe the order in which it was to be observed, reserving this to be done by the Apostles, through whom he intended to arrange all things pertaining to the Churches" (Letter 54).

Paul taught the same thing in 1 Corinthians 11, namely that some things regarding the sacrament needed to be ordered differently, which is why he added, while speaking on the matter, "I will arrange the rest when I come."

3. "The third argument I brought forward was that if one part of this sacrament can be taken from the laity, then a part of Baptism and Penance can be taken away by the same authority and whatever else Christ ever instituted can be partially taken away. If this cannot be done, then neither can the other part [of communion] be taken away."

In response we say that it is not at all similar when treating Baptism and Penance, since neither of these has two parts in either of which the entire sacrament would be contained; yet, whoever receives the sacrament of the Eucharist under the species of bread or under the species of wine, receives the whole Christ in either, because whoever receives one species receives just as much benefit as would be contained under both species, and there is nothing greater under the both species than what would be received under one alone. You see, the species are just the signs and not the reality [res], and they do not add anything of power or virtue since Christ is not contained by a mere sign. To this you can add that the words of Baptism, differently from what Christ patently said, were changed by the Apostles for some time in the primitive Church, just as they oversaw in some other matters, wherein they noticed just causes for the change. For this reason it is doubtlessly licit for the Fathers and the Holy Spirit to do the same thing.

4. "Fourth, that Christ says his blood is shed for the remission of our sins, and therefore to those to whom that remission of sins is given, it is not possible to deny the sign of that forgiveness which Christ has given them."

We grant that in this sacrament the blood is contained which was poured out for the remission of sins, but we deny that this is the sacrament of the remission of sins, but rather the sacrament of the union of the faithful with Christ and with God the Father through Christ; it is not a logical consequence that "this is my blood which will be shed for many, unto the remission of sins," and therefore the Eucharist is the sacrament of the remission of sins.

5. As a fifth point: "If the wine can be taken away, the bread can be taken away, too, and consequently the whole sacrament can be taken away, and the institution of Christ is done away with. If the whole cannot be taken away, then neither can a part be taken away."

Here we respond that in the administration of this sacrament under the species of bread, there do not arise the sort of dangers which are hardly avoided should it be administered also under the species of wine, and that on this account it does not follow that because it seemed necessary to the Council and for just causes to remove this portion from the laity, that therefore the other portion could be removed beyond all reason and any cause. Yet sometimes, with reason, both parts are withdrawn, for example from the dying, when there is risk of vomit, and from infants who do not always digest what they ingest, or who often expel or spit out what they have ingested.

The sixth strength fled him, nor dared to make itself known: it feared lest the same thing would happen to it as what happened to its fellows.

7. Seventh, "Paul shuts the mouths of all disputants, when (1 Cor. 11) not alone to priests but to the Church and to all the faithful he gives the whole sacrament."

We respond here that Paul is only going over with the Corinthians what he himself had already received from Christ regarding the sacrament, and that was so that he might increase in them their reverence towards this nourishment, while simultaneously removing abuses which had by that point crept in among them. Nor do we dispute that at times this sacrament has been administered under both species to all the faithful — and especially during the times of the worst persecutions — by which one might note that the faithful themselves, from their frequent consumption of Christ's blood, which had been poured out for them by Christ himself and which they would behold under the species of wine, would thus much more willingly be enlivened and disposed to suffer martyrdom for Christ's name. On the other hand, when that persecution had ceased and many difficulties arose more and more day by day, such as we have recounted above and on account of which the faithful souls began to tremble, the other species was taken away by a silent consent that steadily arose throughout all the churches. In this way, the people avoided an ever-growing number of dangers by this tacit unanimous vote, as we noted earlier, so that it was agreed that this sacrament would be offered to the laity henceforth only under the one species.

You can add to this that Paul completely omitted that inclusive "drink ye of it — all [of you]" in his epistle, and it is upon that precise wording that Luther leans so much, so that there would be not the least occasion for later Christians to believe that it would be necessary for them to drink the blood from the chalice, just as the priests now do. Perhaps Paul foresaw that this manner of communion would finally lose force, as we ourselves now see.

I think that it is now clear to all how Luther's strengths are bereft of all force, upon which his gigantic arrogance has for so long lifted its brow, so that we can very rightly throw back into his face whatsoever he had previously and wrongly spit out at the most illustrious king. We only change the insulting words by which the king is mentioned.

The reader understands Luther's evil from these points. Now see whether or not there is a drop of Christian blood in that entire body or whether in his soul there is any spark of a good man: who, I ask, is not incensed at the incredibly sophistic ill-will, as well as the shamelessness, whereby he willingly and purposefully goes mad against the known truth, that he should wish not only for his hearers but also for the whole world to lose and see buried this reasonable and salutary custom? Clearly he is a chosen vessel of Satan and most fitting as the chief-enemy of the Catholic Church. His attempts and other areas upon which he writes have the same tendency, but the devout reader can learn to be wary of him and to circumspectly view him in all his extremes by this note, that is, to beware the bilge of death. He's worthy of no concession and there is no error here, but pure evil and an obdurate malice that is intent upon lying and blaspheming. But that is enough of his own words that we have heaped back upon the head of Luther, and which words fit no one so well as they do Luther himself.

Let us know that the king has done more than enough in response to all of Luther's scriptural citations and reasoning, but that Luther on the other hand has bypassed many things which the king had objected to him. First, and as we noted above, as regards the Scriptures, Luther has provided none that would command the sacrament to be received by all under both species, besides the one, "drink ye all of it." Yet, Luther himself denies that this forces the laity to receive under both species, which is why the king also accused Luther of inconsistency. Here are the king's word to that effect: "But please see how Luther waivers and contradicts himself: at one point he says that Christ says this in command to all of the faithful at the Supper, and not merely as a permission, 'drink ye all of it,' but afterwards he seems to fear the laity — whom he prepared with adulation to hate the priesthood, and so Luther adds these words: 'It is not as if they sin against Christ when they only receive under one species, since Christ had not commanded that they receive both, but had only left it up to each one's judgment when he said, "however so often you do this, do it in memory of me".'" Those were the king's words. Does the reader not see how Luther affirmed both, that is both that Christ had commanded it and that he had not commanded it, and that these are manifestly at odds with one another?

For this reason, the king added: "Therefore, what need is there for us to contradict him, he who so often contradicts himself? It is therefore clear from Luther's words that this was not a command to all: 'drink ye all of it'." Given that Luther could provide no other command from the Scriptures, his Royal Highness sufficiently overturned Luther's first strength, and he is rather completely silent about his conviction of inconsistency.

Luther's second strength, too, is easily demolished by the king: Luther teaches that it is not permissible to change Christ's institutions, but an institution of Christ could be changed because of just causes, just as is clear in several cases historically, such as how Christ instituted this after the Supper itself, whereas the Church has commanded that it be taken by those who are fasting, or how the Church has commanded that water and wine be mixed together, which we find expressed neither in Paul nor in the evangelists. The king even showed from Augustine's words and ample testimony wherein Augustine did not shy from asserting that this change proceeded from the Holy Spirit! But even

Augustine himself would attest later on in that same spot to how Christ had left it to the Apostles to determine the disposition and order of that entire sacrament, an opinion that he gathers from Paul's words, such as when he said, "For the rest, I shall order them when I come" in 1 Cor. So when it is clear, therefore, that Christ did not command that both portions should be given to all Christians, but that this set-up was left to the Church's judgment, who could doubt whether the Church — which is ruled by the Holy Spirit — did not also ordain by the instinct of that same spirit that this sacrament should be conferred to the laity under a single species?

Likewise the third strength is rendered infirm, since the teaching is clear that Baptism was commanded in a different manner than was the Eucharist, since Baptism was distinctly commanded when Christ said to the Apostles, "Going therefore, teach ye all nations; baptizing them in the name of the Father, and of the Son, and of the Holy Spirit." In no place of Scripture do we see such a clear command about the sacrament of the Eucharist, which the king even draws from Luther's own words, because Luther had said that there was no precept for the laity that they should drink from the chalice. So this isn't a like matter, in regard to Baptism and the Eucharist.

The fourth strength is dissolved as well, because the Eucharist is not the sign of the remission of sins, nor does the logic follow: "Christ said that his blood was shed for the remission of sins therefore this sacrament is a sign of the remission of sins." If this followed logically, it would benefit the Bohemian heretics greatly, and it would rightly incite the hatred of the laity against the priests, and the king strongly strikes Luther on this point when he says, "Yet, in the meantime he takes pleasure in throwing dust in eyes by a fraudulent adulation of the laity, as he tries to incite hatred against priests, because when he had decided to render suspect the fate of the Church, lest its authority should have any weight, thereby was the path first paved for the eventual aversion of all the most important points of the Christian religion. And he strongly hoped to obtain the people's applause for that attempt, since he had opened an old wound which Bohemia had long ago suffered, that the laity could not receive the Eucharist under both species. When he had previously treated this matter — at least as he phrases it — he said that the pope would do well if he took care to establish something by a common council so that the lady might receive under both species. Afterwards, I don't know who or how this was denied him, but he wasn't content to remain with what he had said, but made it worse so that he condemned the entire clergy of impiety because they had done this and not waited on a council." So spoke the king.

The fifth point of strength falls apart because the Church had taken away both species from infants, although they had at some times received communion. He does not even deny that this was justly taken away from them, since in his *Babylonian Captivity* he recounts from Augustine how they commune in the body and blood of Christ beyond the sacrament. Yet let us hear the king once more: "But I marvel that Luther is so angry over the removal of one species from the laity, because it does not disturb him at all that neither species is given to infants, although — as he cannot deny — long ago they did receive communion. If this custom was rightly omitted — although Christ does say "drink ye all of it" — and no one doubts that serious causes for the omission came up, even if no one is currently recalling them, why don't we also then think of the good and just reasons that are now so much ignored, and for which reasons the custom of the laity receiving under both species (long-standing though it may have been) was abolished?"

This is what the king said. Here, the reader notes that although Christ had said, "drink ye all of it," both species were nevertheless taken from infants, and thus whenever suitable causes are present, one or even both species may be taken away by the Church.

The sixth strength never appeared, so the king was not able to refute it.

The king takes the seventh strength, too, right out of Luther's hands — although Luther proudly glories that this argument said to the asserter of the sacraments,[6] "touch me not" (a reference to Our Lord's words to Mary Magdalene). He touched it and he completely crushed it — which was not difficult, since it was bereft of all force. You see, he accomplishes nothing more than

---

6 There is a wordplay here in the Latin which is lost; it is a reference to the title of the king's work, the *Assertio VII Sacramentorum.*

establishing that the custom of Paul's time was that the faithful received under both species — which no one denies. Thus, the king declared that the custom had given way due to just causes: "Furthermore, even if I did not see the reasons why the Church had decided that both species should not be administered to the laity, I could still not doubt that the causes were suitable, due to which they, once upon a time, made it so that this should be omitted and now to make it so that it should not be reintroduced." He then teaches with the strongest logic that the clergy did not do this without a very justified reasoning: "Nor do I at all agree that the entire clergy, throughout so many centuries, was so stupid that they bound themselves to an eternal punishment for something which would bring them no temporal benefit." At the end, he adds a powerful reason: "What is more, there is not even the least such risk [of temporal gain from a damnable error], because God himself not only welcomed into heaven, but also willed to be honored by men as venerable upon the earth not simply those who did such but even those who wrote that this should be done; among such men, so as not to mention so many others, was that most learned and likewise most holy Saint Thomas Aquinas, of whom I gladly make mention here since this man's sanctity is something which the impiety of Luther cannot bear, although all Christians venerate him while Luther everywhere execrates him with his own defiled lips. Although there are a huge number of those who — although not publicly recognized as saints — are nevertheless noteworthy either for their learning or for their piety, this number of men who hold the opposite position on this matter is so great that Luther cannot be compared to them; among them you have the master of the sentences, Nicholas of Lyra, and so many others whom all Christians should much more profitably believe than Luther."

Behold, dear reader, how ably the most illustrious king brings to complete naught the strength of Luther, and how plainly he teaches that all of Luther's strengths are therefore just like the arrows of little children, which can do no harm.

Luther, on the other hand, declined to engage the king's strong arms, since he does not respond to the contradiction which the king brought up to him, that is that Christ would have both commanded and not commanded all to drink of his blood; and lest

Luther should wiggle free of this contradiction, we will note here the specific places wherein he wrote this. He speaks this way in his first "Captivity": "I admit that I am overcome by this invincible reasoning: I have not read, nor heard, nor found anything to say against it, given that Christ's word and example here stands most firmly when he says not as a permission but as a precept, 'drink ye all of it'." Again, at the beginning of his second "Captivity," he says: "It is not that they sin against Christ when they receive under one species, since Christ did not command this usage, but he rather left it to each one's judgment when he said, 'As often as you do this, do it in memory of me'." See how he says in the first work that Christ commanded it and in the second that Christ did not command it. But when the king said that there was no fault among the priests, whom Luther — on the other hand — had accused as guilty, Luther offers no response, just as he cannot justly fabricate any guilt for the priest at all on this matter, since there is no precept anywhere that commands the giving of both species.

If there is such a command, let Luther bring it forth. If he cannot do so, then why is he asserting this without the Scriptures, since he would allow nothing to be admitted besides the Scriptures? Now, when the king clearly teaches that this custom came about while the laity were in no way against it, Luther remains completely silent, so let us hear the king on the subject: "Therefore if anyone should ask him how he knows that this custom came about against the people's will, I don't think he can show us. So, why does he condemn the entire clergy for having taken something that was rightfully theirs from an unwilling laity, when he can in no wise prove from documentation that this happened against their will? How right was it to pronounce upon the consensus of the people for a custom that endured so many centuries, if it could not have been rightly instituted in the first place unless the people were willing? I surely cannot easily believe that the people would have allowed this, since I see what things the clergy can never obtain from the people, unless they were even to go so far as to allow their bodies to be buried under the altar itself! That they should have been unwilling and yet — by contempt — pushed away from something that was rightfully theirs, and in such a great thing as this? I rather believe that it was instituted for numerous suitable reasons and with the laity's accord too."

You do not hear a peep in response from Luther.

When Luther asserts that the Romans are the greater heretics, unholy ones and even schismatics, than the Bohemians or the Greeks because — as Luther says — they have presumed against God's clear Scriptures by their own fabrications, the king did then oppose him in this manner: "If Luther admits nothing else besides the clear Scriptures of God, then as I have said, why does he not command that the Eucharist be received by those who are eating Supper? For so was it done by Christ, as Scripture commemorates. How much better would it be for Luther to believe that it is not by human fabrication but by God as its very author that in the Church, the laity would not receive the Eucharist under both species — and yet at whose instigation should it be received by those who are fasting? Because it pleased the Holy Spirit, as Saint Augustine says, that the body of the Lord was received by the Apostles after other foods and at dinner, and that in the Church it is received by those fasting and before other foods. It therefore seems likely that the Holy Spirit, who rules Christ's Church, led the laity from the reception of both species to the reception of one, just as he changed the sacrament of the Eucharist from something to be received by those at Supper to its reception by those who fasted, because whoever could change the one, could also change the other, no?"

Now let us listen to Luther's complete silence.

Yet, so as not to seem indolent to his followers, he furiously goes after two small sections and he tries to stomp all over them, although he is not successful, because he does not even justly represent the king's argument, but rather uses his foxy manner to hide the best part of the argument: "The Church, he says, gives the sacrament in the morning, which Christ gave in the evening. Also, we mix water with wine, concerning which the Scripture relates nothing. Therefore, if the Church can do or institute that, it can also take away part of the Sacrament." Luther here surveys the king's work and yet mutilates two of the arguments by his "great strengths." Hear instead, dear reader, the king's actual words in that argument, because after the king had brought forward the point about the removal of both species from infants, and that this was done for good and just reasons, he says that doubtlessly "it follows that this could be done justly and equitably, with the result that one species might be removed from adults for just causes." Then he adds to this point: "Furthermore, if Luther recalls precisely the passage from Luke's Gospel, there is nothing therein which offers a permission to the Church. Why is there no command to receive at Supper — or rather after Supper?" Here the reader can note what the king is attempting to do; that is, if the Church (which he takes to be "guided by the Holy Spirit," as it comes most persuasively from the Scriptures) could change anything in the setup which the Gospels narrate, then she could also change more or less, as the suitability of causes necessitated.

Nothing is more precisely narrated at that point than the time itself, since just as Christ gave his body and blood under the species of bread and wine, so, too, did he give it in the evening after Supper. For this reason, if the Church was able to change the circumstance of the timing, for good and just reasons, and is believed to have done this not otherwise than at the Holy Spirit's instigation, then why could she not also similarly change something of the other circumstances, wherever just causes are equally present?

Yet, the king added to the argument along these lines: "In the end, there is no less damage, in regard to this sacrament, in doing what you ought not, than in not doing what you ought. Therefore, if the custom of the entire Church is not doing what is right in the removal of the species of wine from the laity, then by what reasoning does Luther dare to pour water into the wine? Because I do not think that he is so audacious as to consecrate without water, but in the mixing thereof, he does not have an example from the Lord's Supper, or from apostolic tradition, rather he only learned it from the Church's custom. If he thinks that the Church should be obeyed in this part, then why does he arrogantly oppose the Church in the other?"

The reader can see here that the king's other argument is different in length from what Luther goes over, since any argument is quite easily explained away if one is allowed to mutilate the opposing argument in this way, according to one's good pleasure. The king has no other intention here than showing that the arrangement of this sacrament has been left to the judgment of the Church's leaders — and he clearly teaches this by the many arguments that he has gathered together: "Because men of such great sanctity and knowledge — as well as being notable for their miracles — would have never dared in any way to change such an august thing in any circumstance whatsoever; they certainly would have never forbidden that the Eucharist be received after dinner and after other foods, and they would have never commanded the mixing of water and wine, unless they had taken it as distinctly settled that it was wholly licit for them to do such; nor, otherwise, would the laity have ever so unanimously consented to have one species removed from them or both species taken from their infants."

Luther, on the other hand, approaches these matters in a completely different manner and as if he were in charge, and once he removed the force of any argument, then when it had been sufficiently mutilated, he set out to destroy it; but he attempts to destroy his own arguments — not the king's — because no argument from the king mentioned the phrases "outside Scripture" or "against Scripture," and yet Luther shows no shame in asserting that this was the manner of the king's argument: "Something happens outside Scripture, therefore it is believed to be against Scripture." Nowhere in his entire book did the king argue thus, much less in the manner which Luther would then add: "Wine is mixed with water outside the testimony of Scripture; therefore the Scripture which establishes a second part must be condemned." In this manner, the shameless monster never ceases lying. It is not only false to say that the king used these arguments, but even Luther's attempt — both in the preceding as well as in that argument which followed — was completely against the truth, because Luther tries to establish that in the Scriptures, when the Lord's Supper is described, both species were given as necessarily to be received by all, and from that very argument depends all that he will later say with such wordiness.

Yet the reader must note how fraudulently this fox words the matter: "Scripture establishes the second part." Yes, of course, it is true that the Scripture established the other part, but it is not true that it established that both parts had to be received by all, which is what Luther wanted to be understood by these words; in fact, to the contrary, Scripture did not establish either part for all. Now, if

Scripture did not establish that either part should be received by all, how will it then be against Scripture that one or each part be taken away? Or, how do those who are moved by good and just causes condemn the Scriptures when they remove one or the other part?

Once again in the preceding argument, when Luther tries to show that it is outside the testimony of Scripture that water and wine should be mixed, this is not universally true, because although, granted, it is not in the scriptural account of the Lord's Supper, it can still be gathered from other Scriptures; and not only from the Scriptures, but also from revelation, as well as from apostolic tradition, just as we will show hereafter from the expressions of the ancients. It is then abundantly clear that Luther opposes his sense in vain to evidence that is so abundant and so solid; it will be clear that this is no figment of the human mind, nor does it have some terrible significance, as Luther impiously contends. Let us now close up the king's argumentation, as he himself ends it: "Whatever Luther growls and about whatsoever he is snarling, I believe that it is much safer to believe that laity should commune under one species than to believe that the entire clergy — throughout so many centuries — should be condemned on this account, because it is towards this accusation that he is compelling all the impious and other such folks, to be guilty of offending the Gospel's majesty."

It is of course much safer to believe that laity rightly commune under one species alone, rather than that the entire clergy should be condemned over this one issue, since it is certainly clear that the Church is guided by the Holy Spirit, as we have so often said.

We now, therefore, return to what we had promised, to show that it is right for the water and wine to be mixed.

First, Cyprian says that he received this very thing from the Scriptures and from the Lord's revelation: let us first see about the revelation, because in an epistle to Caecilius, wherein he wrote about the mixing of water in the Chalice, he confesses that he was told by the Lord to do it this way, that is to mix water with the wine. "Nor must you think, dearest brother, that I am writing my own or human thoughts; or that I am audaciously taking this for myself of my own will, since I always consider my mediocrity with lowly and modest moderation. But when anything is prescribed by the inspiration and command of God, a faithful servant must obey the Lord, and he is acquitted by all of assuming anything arrogantly to himself, seeing that he is constrained by the fear of offending the Lord unless he does what he is commanded. Know then that I have been admonished that, in offering the chalice, the tradition of the Lord must be observed, and that nothing must be done by us but what the Lord first did on our behalf, so that the chalice which is offered in remembrance of him should be offered mingled with wine."

Those are Cyprian's words. Note here, reader, that this most holy and learned martyr states that this had been commanded by an inspiration and mandate from God to himself, that the chalice should not be offered with water alone nor with wine alone, but with the wine and water mingled. Then, he asserts that Christ did the very same thing at the Supper, which he then confirms from the Scriptures, and especially from Solomon: "Moreover, the Holy Spirit by Solomon foreshadows the type of the Lord's sacrifice, making mention of the immolated victim, and of the bread and wine, and even of the altar and of the apostles: 'Wisdom has built her house, she has laid her seven pillars underneath; she has killed her victims; she has mingled her wine in the chalice; she has also provided her table; and she has sent forth her servants, calling them together for her cup with a lofty announcement: whoever is simple, let him turn to me; and to those that want understanding she said: Come, eat of my bread, and drink of the wine which I have mingled for you'," to which Cyprian then adds, "He declares the wine to be mixed; that is, he foretells with a prophetic voice that the chalice of the Lord had mingled water and wine, so that it is shown that what was done at our Lord's passion had been predicted."

You can add to this that the blood of calves and goats, with which Moses confirmed the Old Testament, also had water mingled with it, just as Paul says in his letter to the Hebrews: "When every commandment of the law had been read by Moses to all the people, he took the blood of calves and goats, with water...and sprinkled both the book itself and all the people," but that blood was a figure of this blood, because by that blood the old was confirmed, but by this blood is confirmed the new covenant. So, dear reader, you understand that Cyprian confirmed this necessary mingling of water and wine both from revelation as well as from Scripture. Luther, however, stands without shame as a violator of the Scriptures and of the mysteries, as he follows his spirit and understanding, and grants that it would be better and safer not to mix the water in the wine, since he calls it a mere human creation, and that it has a twisted or even horrible meaning. But woe to the prophets who follow their own spirit, as Ezekiel says, and the greatest woe to him who does not hesitate to lean upon his own spirit rather than upon the statements of so many orthodox Fathers. It is not Cyprian alone who states this, but Jerome even openly adds: "That the wine of Our Lord's blood should be mixed with water is shown not only by tradition but also by Our Lord's sort of death and passion, out of whose sacred side flowed blood and water, when struck by the lance" (Jn. 19).

So you see here how Jerome brings another Scripture to the fore, besides apostolic tradition, that is that water and blood flowed forth when the spear pierced Christ's side.

We can consult Chrysostom here, too: "A deep mystery is consummated at this point, because blood and water came out — not by chance did these fonts simply spring forth, rather because the Church is made up of both; the initiated know this, for they are regenerated by water, and nourished by the body and blood. It is from this place that these mysteries have their beginning, so that as often as you approach to behold the chalice, so may you approach as one taking drink from his very side."

John Damascene also supports these when he affirms that Christ had wine mixed with water in the cup at Supper: "likewise, as he took the cup of water and wine, he gave it to them and said: drink ye all of it."

Ambrose also gives assent to this when he says: "Before the words of Christ, the chalice was full of water and wine; when Christ's words had done their work, there was the blood made which redeemed the people."

Augustine, too, is added to this number when he explains that Gospel passage: "And thenceforth blood and water came forth: that blood was shed for the remission of sins; that water regulates the salvific cup," and again when he says, "In the Eucharist it is not pure water that is to be offered, as some have been fooled to think under the pretext of sobriety, but wine mixed with water."

The reader understands from these citations that water had to be mixed with wine, since both from the revelation to which Cyprian makes appeal, as well as from the Scriptures and testimony of the Fathers, we have a complete confirmation on the matter. We will now show from these same things that the mixture does not have some very bad significance, as Luther recklessly claims.

Let us first hear Cyprian's own opinion: "The divine Scripture in the Apocalypse declares that the waters signify the people: 'The waters which thou didst see, upon which the whore sits, are peoples and multitudes, and nations of the Gentiles, and tongues,' which we evidently see to be contained in the sacrament of the chalice too. For, because Christ bore us all, in that he also bore our sins, we see that in the water is understood "the people," but in the wine the blood of Christ is shown. But, when the water is mingled with wine in the cup, Christ is made one with the people, and the assembly of believers is associated and conjoined with him in whom it believes; this association and conjunction of water and wine is so mingled in the Lord's chalice, that that mixture can no longer be separated. Whence, too, nothing can separate the Church — that is, the people established in the Church, faithfully and firmly persevering in that which they have believed — from Christ, in such a way as to prevent their undivided love from always abiding and adhering. So, therefore, in consecrating the cup of the Lord, water alone cannot be offered, even as wine alone cannot be offered. For, if any one offers wine alone, the blood of Christ is disassociated from us; but if the water is alone, the people are separated from Christ; but when both are mingled and joined with one another by a close union, a spiritual and heavenly sacrament is then completed."

That was Cyprian, but Jerome's testimony is in complete accord with that: "We note in the waters the prefigurement of the Gentiles, as John says in Chapter 17 of the Apocalypse: the waters which thou hast seen are many peoples; but in the wine the blood of our Lord's passion is displayed, as if whenever water and wine are mixed in the oblation of this sacrament, then by that very fact we see signified that together with Christ the faithful people are incorporated, conjoined, and united, by that connection of perfect charity." That is Jerome on the matter.

Yet, others understand a mystical significance in this mixture, by means of the redemption of the people which happened through the mediation of that blood which was shed for them; Ambrose seems to have been of this opinion when he said that, at first, wine was together with water in the chalice, but thereafter the blood which redeemed the people.

Augustine thinks that the water was mingled with the wine to signify that water, too, had flowed from the side of Christ; later, Paschasius also seems to have sensed this when he said: "The reason why water is mingled in that chalice is primarily because from the side of Christ, when the passion was fulfilled, blood and water both flowed."

Bede hands down a double significance of the occurrence: one, that which Jerome and Cyprian note, "but, because we, too, are in Christ and Christ must remain in us, in the chalice of the Lord water and wine are mixed, because as John says, 'the waters are peoples'." Yet, he later adds another meaning of it: "And because Christ could not suffer without a love for our redemption, nor could we be saved and offered to the Father without his passion. It was as if he had said, 'water is mixed with wine so that the water might signify the people and the wine his blood that was poured out, so that we might understand that we could not be redeemed in the least without Christ's passion'."

Yet still, Luther's audacity is such that he fears not to oppose his own sense to those of so many Fathers: "And in my opinion it would be better and safer not to mix water with the wine, since it is merely a human and sinister figment, or rather, it has a very bad signification. For it does not signify our incorporation into Christ, since the Scripture has no similar sign." These things are said by Luther, who is certain that he has his dogmas from heaven, although he is plainly lying in this spot as well, because in the sacrifices wherein wine was offered, water was mingled with them, too, which even Jerome thought worthy of mention in his *Hebrew Questions:* "It is noteworthy that wine, which was to be offered to God and sacrifice, was mixed with water." Now if wine was mixed with water in the sacrifices that were offered to God, then this mixture could not lack some mystical significance, which would also not be "very bad," as Luther claims. Nevertheless, because once in the Scriptures this mixture is understood in a bad sense, that is enough for Luther to take it that it should always and everywhere be so, as if there were not many such things, that for one reason are taken in a bad sense, but for another reason are accustomed to be taken in a good sense.

From this, therefore, it is clear that water must be mixed with the wine in the chalice, as it comes both from Scriptures and from revelation, as well as from the testimony of the Fathers; nor does this mixture need to have a very bad meaning. One may perhaps say to me at this point that I have undermined the king's reasoning, which gathered that it was listed to change some things in this sacrament to something other than what Christ himself handed on, because in our mixing of water and wine in the chalice, we are doing other than what Christ did. My response is that the king's reasoning in his point against Luther is completely valid, that is that Luther denies that water should be mingled because, he says, in those Scriptures which treat of the Lord's Supper, there is no mention of the water at all, and so that for Luther, "not to be present" is the same as "not to be done"; and the king completely overturned that claim, as we, too, have shown more than once, since there were many things that were handed on to the Church by the Apostles which are not found anywhere in Scripture.

This will suffice against the first part of Luther's Captivity.

CHAPTER IV
The Substance of the Bread Does Not Remain with the Most Holy Body of Christ

IN the fourth place, Luther maintains that, after the consecration of the Eucharist, bread still remains and that the same [bread] is the body of Christ. Here he first attacks the king as if — besides Ambrose's statement "and it must be thus" – he had brought forward nothing else that might refute Luther's opinion. Now, were it true, then Luther is not lying; if, on the other hand, it is completely false, as the reader will promptly and plainly see, then who will protect him from the lie? Understand from this, too, how great the man's shamelessness is, since he spreads lies all about, and nevertheless dares to assert that he is sure that his teaching comes from heaven.

You, dear reader, will understand that Luther has brought nothing new here, except insults, of which he offers himself a masterful artisan, and in which he trusts much more than in any solid argumentation. He hopes to enchant and fill the ears of the reader so much with them that there is no time left to note his errors. The sincere reader will keep another ear reserved for the most illustrious king, and he will gather that Luther's attempt is not solidified by these words, rather they are all completely squandered. He brings forward this first argument against the transubstantiation of the bread in his Babylonian Captivity: "The main rationale for my opinion is, first of all, that there should be no violence done to the divine words, neither by man, nor by angel, but insofar as is possible, they should be preserved in a most simple meaning, and unless a manifest circumstance demands, they are not to be taken beyond what the grammar and proper meaning give, lest occasion should be given to our adversaries of cheating all Scripture. Since the evangelist is clearly right, therefore, that Christ took bread and blessed it, and the Acts and Paul the Apostle use the word 'bread' thereafter, there must be understood here true bread and true wine, just as there is a true chalice, because even they do not say that the chalice is transubstantiated." At this point the illustrious king focuses all his force on the matter, and lays Luther so completely flat, more potently even than someone who was perfectly trained in the schools, both in his genius and in the logical power; but let us hear from the king himself:

> As Luther tells us, this is his great and primary rationale, which I hope I am going to treat in such a way that everyone will absolutely understand it holds nothing of importance. For, when he first relays what the evangelists clearly say — and although they do speak clearly — this nevertheless proves nothing for Luther; instead, what would prove anything for Luther, they nowhere say. He says, "Do they not say right that he took bread and blessed?" So what? We, too, say that it is written that 'He took and blessed'; but that he gave to his disciples bread after he had consecrated his body, we incessantly deny, and the evangelists do not say that. And so that this matter may be even clearer, and that there be less room for evasion, let us hear the evangelists themselves in Mt. 26: "And whilst they were at Supper, Jesus took bread and blessed and broke and gave to his disciples and said: Take ye and eat. This is my body. And taking the chalice, he gave thanks and gave to them, saying: Drink ye all of this. For this is my blood of the New Testament, which shall be shed for many unto remission of sins." And these are Mark's words: "And whilst they were eating, Jesus took bread; and blessing, broke and gave to them and said: Take ye. This is my body. And having taken the chalice, giving thanks, he gave it to them. And they all drank of it. And he said to them: This is my blood of the New

Testament, which shall be shed for many." Whereas Luke narrates it in this manner: "And taking bread, he gave thanks and broke and gave to them, saying: This is my body, which is given for you. Do this for a commemoration of me. In like manner, the chalice also, after he had supped, saying: This is the chalice, the New Testament in my blood, which shall be shed for you."

From all these words of the evangelists, I see no spot wherein, after the consecration, the sacrament is called bread or wine, but only body and blood. They say that Christ took bread into his hands, which we all confess as well, but when the Apostles received it, it is not called bread, but the body. Yet, Luther fashions the evangelist's words to his side with this interpretation: "Take ye, eat ye — that is, this bread which he took and broke, is my body." This, however, is Luther's interpretation — not the words of Christ, nor the sense of the words. If it were the case that the bread which he received — and just as he received it — he then and in that way handed over to the Apostles, and had not previously changed it into his flesh and offered it with the words, 'take ye, eat ye,' then it would be right to say that he offered what he had taken into his hands, because there would have been nothing else there for him to offer to them. Since, however, he had first changed the bread into his flesh before he gave it to the Apostles to eat, they no longer receive the bread which he had taken, but rather his body into which he had changed that bread.

That is how the King wrote.

Kind reader, whoever you may be, you who have taken this book into your own hands, I pray by your very learning that you pay close and full attention here, and that you diligently weigh how accurately the king has hit the point and what an unavoidable death blow he has struck against Luther. First note how effectively he solves the difficulty that had to be argument, that is that Christ's body was rightly called "bread" — that is, "wheat bread" by the evangelists; he tried to show this both from the evangelists, as well as from the Acts of the Apostles as well as from Paul; therefore, the king reviews the three evangelists, Matthew, Mark, and Luke and he teaches clearly that by none of these was Christ's body called bread, nor that the bread was simultaneously the body of Christ. Rather, it was bread when Christ took it into his hands, but when he gave it to the Apostles it was not bread but truly the body of Christ, just as he said, "This is my body" — not "this bread" — as Luther interprets it. This is because, after he had taken the bread and before he had given it to the Apostles to eat, he changed it into his body, with the result that the Apostles did not receive bread but Christ's body into which the bread had been changed. If this bread had remained bread, it would not have been changed into Christ's body, and Christ would have said, "*this* is my body," so that the pronoun would have been in the same masculine gender as the word "bread," which had just been mentioned, because "bread" is in the masculine gender in Greek just as it is in Latin. But so that what he did say should be clear to all, the king gave an example: "Just as if someone had taken a seed, and then once it had become a flower, had given it to another, and the other had received what had then been given, so Christ took bread but did not give bread, but rather his own body, into which the bread had been changed. Therefore, that Christ might make this change clear, he deigned not to say, 'this bread is my body,' but 'this is my body,' which demonstrates his very own body, into which the bread had changed. So, since not one of the evangelists says that Christ gave bread to his Apostles, but only that he took it and then gave his own body, then the Gospel testimony is worthless for Luther's side, as the reader now understands."

Thus, Luther's reasoning — which he bragged to be so great — is nothing now, as it pertains to the evangelists' testimony, but it rather openly fights against Luther, because if we ought to follow the grammar, then who does not perceive that the article and the neuter gender is pointing to something in the neuter gender – "body" — rather than what would be referred to by the masculine gender – "bread." Yet, Luther does not even deny that Christ's body was truly present in that which Christ gave to his Apostles — even before he gave it to them; what, then, would keep Christ from having shown his body when he gave the same to the Apostles, saying, "this is my body?" What violence is then inflicted on Christ's words? None at all, whereas you most certainly do violence to the words when you change the "this" to refer to "this bread." We will show this very thing from Luther's own words, because he affirms that it is open to anyone, as he pleases, to believe his words, whether this be or not be bread. Yet, if the "this" truly refers to "bread," then there is no longer any freedom! Therefore, whoever interprets it in this manner, is definitely doing violence to Christ's words. I think that this is so clear that no one — except the most pertinacious defender of Lutheran opinion — does not clearly see this, and nevertheless Luther tries so hard to escape from this that he accuses the king of begging the question, *petitio principii*, since the king responded to his reasoning and plainly demonstrated that the reasoning was not approved as credible.

Let the fair reader observe, too, how loosely the king proves what he said by an example that is "begged" from Scripture.[7] For, just as Aaron's rod was changed into a snake in Exodus 4, and then likewise from a snake back into a rod, it was never simultaneously a snake and a rod; neither likewise is the bread that was changed into the body of Christ simultaneously bread and the body of Christ, because if a snake could not remain a rod, so that the two were one, how much less so could the incomparable substance of Christ's flesh remain bread, thus having it said to be both bread and the body of Christ? And yet someone will say on Luther's side: "It could hardly have been otherwise than that he gave true bread to the Apostles, since Matthew clearly wrote the following: 'But while they were eating, Jesus took bread and when he had given thanks, he broke and gave to his disciples'. This word *bread* is governed by three verbs: *took, broke,* and *gave,* so that the bread was *taken, broken,* and *given.*" Luther, you see, has already injected this objection. He says, "The text says the following: 'He took bread, blessed, broke, and said this is...etc.'." You see here that all those verbs – *took, blessed,* and *broke* — are said of the bread; and it

---

7 Pun on "begging the question". —Editor.

is proven by that same pronoun that is in the neuter that he took blessed and broke *this* — in the neuter. *This* was taken, blessed, and broken — as it is said, "this is my body," which is not the predicate but the subject. He did not, you see, take his body, bless it, and break it, but rather, he took bread." This argument implies nothing, because we read it written similarly in Luke's Gospel, regarding the Chalice: "Taking the cup, he gave thanks and said, 'take you and divide among you'." Now, although it is written that he took the chalice, gave thanks and said, "divide among you," it is clear that he did not intend for the chalice to be divided. But, we will try to resolve this Lutheran objection with a still clearer example: history tells us that Julia, the daughter of Caesar Octavian, warmed an egg in her lap for so long that the entire substance which had been contained within the shell was turned into a chick. At this point, if you say that Julia took the egg and thereafter fostered it for a long while, broke it and gave it to the one who would nourish it, you would be telling the truth; yet, it is still not true that what she gave was an egg, but rather the chick which had once been within the shell of an egg. So, too, was it that here, when Matthew refers to Christ and says that he took bread and, having given thanks, broke it and gave to his disciples, I do not doubt in the least that in the meanwhile Christ had so handled the bread, that before the disciples would receive it, it would be changed into the true flesh of Christ. For this reason, Christ did not also show bread when he said, "this is my body," but he was indicating his very own body, under the species of bread, which bread had been changed into his flesh.

Similarly, too, when Christ made wine out of water at the wedding, it is true that the ministers filled the six jars with water, and that they then again took from them, and finally that they offered to the head-steward, but it is plainly false that they took and offered water, although they had poured water in, since the water had — in the meantime — been turned into wine. Christ also said that this was water that was poured into the jars, just as, when it was poured out and offered to the head-steward, he called it wine and not water (which did not remain), and thereby indicated that it was completely wine. So, it is clear from these two examples, I think, that Christ pointed out that this was no longer bread but rather his body into which the bread had been changed; because there is no doubt that if he had designated this as bread, he would not have used the neuter article, but the masculine article, just as the Royal Intelligence noted above. Scripture's manner of speaking does much for us, since the demonstrative article so frequently matches with the thing demonstrated, and this is abundantly clear from all Gospel passages. In John's Gospel, for example, Christ spoke of John the Baptist: "He was a burning and a shining light."[8] The article was in agreement with the thing demonstrated. Again he says in Matthew, "The stone which the builders rejected, *the same* is become the head of the corner." The conversation had been about the stone, the pronoun is in the same gender as that of the word "stone", just as when, in this place, when there is a clear change of the gender, such as when he speaks of the body, versus when he speaks of the blood; it is clear that he wanted this change to be understood in both places, and there was also a demonstration of that into which the thing was changed — that is — not into bread, but into the body; not into wine, but into blood. The grammar perfectly fits in these cases, when he spoke of the blood, "this is my blood," and of the body, "this is my body." Thus, both Scripture's manner of speech as well as the grammar support the king's response.

Moreover, Luther was mistaken and thinking that he had drunk of Scholastic theology, when he glories of having read something from Cardinal Pierre d'Ailly of Compiègne, specifically, that it is much more probable and to be considered much less of a superfluous miracle, if true bread and true wine were to be believed to be upon the altar, and not only the accidents. You see, Luther has fallen into this intellectual darkness from having not understood this opinion well enough, such that Luther opines that d'Ailly and company consider that the same bread remains after this change, and that is clearly false. Although they teach it as a possibility, how a substance of the bread may remain, they do not however intend it to be possible that this is the very same bread that remains, that is, what was here before is the same "subject" [*suppositum*] of bread, as those men put it; for, in this case, there would be no change at

---

[8] "That man," literally, the masculine demonstrative pronoun —Editor.

all, and nor would Christ be there sacramentally, but only locally. Nor would it be true to say that this bread which Jesus took is this body of Christ. All of these things are clear to the experts and to the well-exercised debaters, because, if Christ's body were not otherwise in the bread then as the same body had been in the door or in the wall when he came in to the disciples while the doors were closed — which occurred outside of any transmutation of the door or the wall — then it would be no truer to say that "this bread is the body of Christ," than to say, "this wall is the body of Christ." Yet, I don't think that anyone is so silly as to believe that, given Christ's mere presence in the wall, that the wall itself was the body of Christ, because no conjoining — no matter how intimate it may be — makes it so that one thing can truly be said to be another. You see, although the form may be most connected with its matter, so that it is truly one composite that is constituted by the two, yet no one will assert that this matter is this form, or conversely, that this form is this matter; rather, from these two one composite is made up. What, however, could be imagined more intimate to our souls than God? And yet, God forbid that we should affirm that the soul is God, when not even the soul of Christ — which is in the same subject that is God — can be called God. Therefore, it is not true that this very same bread which Christ took and broke, did so remain with the body that it could ever truly be said that this bread is this body, because if that very same bread remained, then there would have been no change in the bread.

So that this might become clearer, as regards the present issue, let us consider three things about the bread: first, the very substance of bread, upon which there is unanimity among all bread. Then, that by which it may be said that *this* bread subsists, and as they say, that the subject is not only different from any other bread, but also from any other thing which is not this very bread. Third, the accidents which follow from this bread. Now, if all these things which were previously in the bread remain, then I pray you: what change has taken place in regard to the bread so that it could be said to be the body of Christ, any more than a wall into which Christ entered on his way to the disciples, or a rock through which he exited from his sealed sepulcher, or finally, the Virgin's womb through which he was born into the world? Luther himself brings forward the same examples, so that it's remarkable that he could be so blind as to not see that he slit his own throat with his own sword: "What will they do? Christ is believed to have been born of his mother's intact womb. Let them even say here that the flesh of the Virgin had been annihilated, or that it might be said more properly, to have been transubstantiated, so that Christ would come forth from those accidents, fully wrapped in those accidents. The same thing will need to be said about the closed door and the closed opening of the tomb, through both of which his flesh entered and exited." That is Luther's take.

We, however, do not say that the Virgin's flesh was annihilated or transubstantiated, Luther; nor do we affirm that this flesh of her womb is exactly the same as the flesh of Christ, but as different as there is a different body of each person. So, too, do we not say that the Virgin's womb is Christ, although Christ had been in it; nor do we dare to say that the door of that house through which Christ entered to the Apostles — nor even the door of the tomb, through which the resurrected Christ exited — were Christ himself. God forbid we would have such rashness. Yet, if Christ were not in the sacrament in another way than how he had been in that wall or in the door, then the sacrament would not be truly Christ, any more than that door in the house or the tomb were. Therefore, you see how patently your very own examples sink you.

Why should I recount what you said about iron and fire in trying to show that the glorious body could simultaneously be present with the bread, since no one is disputing it? Neither do we protest the possibility that the body of Christ could be there simultaneously with the bread — minus any mutation of that bread — but we do deny that the body of Christ stems *from* the change of this bread for the following reason: unless the bread be changed with respect to one of the three descriptions mentioned above, this bread will never become the body of Christ; however, the change of the accidents does not suffice, such as it is in the mixing of fire and iron, the example of which Luther makes mention. He says, "So, it is this same way in burning iron, that the fire and iron are mixed together so that any part whatsoever is simultaneously fire and iron." This is plainly false, because even if there were no portion of the iron — no matter how small — in which there was not found, simultaneously, fire too, still this mixture would not yet be truly a union, such that this fire became that iron. That is because these two natures remain different in their substances, even when such changes as described above do occur. Thus, by an even stronger argument, there's no place in this sacrament where the body of Christ would also be bread, if — as Luther argues — there is no change of the bread. Therefore, as we can see, while the accidents of the bread remain, it necessarily follows that unless the very substance of the bread has completely disintegrated, or at least that means by which the bread was said to subsist — or both of these — then it would never rightly be said that this is the body of Christ. So Luther is clearly in error when he so interprets Christ's words that "this is my body" becomes "this bread... which he took and broke."

On this, although the most blessed soul of Christ is so united to his most holy body in one and the same infinite subject[9] that the whole is in every part of the body; nevertheless, these facts do not suffice to make it so that this soul is truly this body, or on the other hand, that this body is truly this soul. For this reason, as long as the bread remains the same as it had been previously, with nothing changed whatsoever, it can never be said — simply due to Christ's true presence alone — that this bread which Christ took and broke was also the same body. Therefore, dear reader, you see that Luther has not proven from the Gospels that it was bread that was given to the Apostles, unless it was bread that was thereafter changed into the body of Christ, and that in the meanwhile Christ said, "this is my body," not, "this bread," as Luther falsely interprets.

Luther takes for himself such license in the Scriptures that he can twist, add, take away, invert, and do whatever he pleases with them, according to the mere madness of his own brain; but, whatever he thus does, he also desires to have ratified without any reasoning, but only, "it must be understood thus," by which sort of reasoning he frequently presumed to condemn in the king's book.

Now, if by some recherché subterfuge, Luther is saying that

---

[9] The Latin word here is *suppositum*, which can mean a substance, i.e. what underlies all of the accidents of a thing; in other words, the subject of the very existence of a thing. —Editor.

the bread was changed by Christ's words in such a way that it was assumed into the unity of Christ's *suppositum*, or personal subject, as those who agree with Peter d'Ailly would have it, still these latter do not affirm and could not defend Luther's daring interpretation, whereby the bread which Christ took is the body of Christ; but, the Scriptures cry against their opinion, if — as Luther would have it — the Scriptures should be taken according to their simple signification and grammar. Four, since they say "the bread is the body of Christ," they would not have this to be understood of the body, that it is one part of a composite, but about the body as a genus. Yet, it is clear that as the three evangelists, Matthew, Mark, and Luke are covering Christ's words "this is my body," they understood this to be the body as one part of a composite person, and not of the body as a genus, because if they understood this of the body as a genus, they would have written rather that Christ said, "This is the body which I am," and not, "This is my body." So, not even this evasion can safeguard Luther's error. To this you can add what David says in Psalm 15: "Thou shalt not give thy Holy One to see corruption," which citation all expositors understand of Christ's body; but even Peter in the Acts, Chapter 2, and Paul in Chapter 13, use this scriptural witness in regard to Christ's body. Peter says, "For David said in the spirit: I saw the Lord before me always, because He is at my right hand, lest I should be moved. Therefore was my heart glad and my tongue rejoiced, and my flesh will rest in hope, for Thou shalt not leave my soul in hell, nor wilt thou give thy Holy One to see corruption." So Paul, too: "And to shew that he raised him up from the dead, not to return now any more to corruption, he said thus: I will give you the holy things of David, faithful. And therefore, in another place also, he says: Thou shalt not suffer thy holy one to see corruption. For David, when he had served in his generation, according to the will of God, slept: and was laid unto his fathers and saw corruption. But he whom God hath raised from the dead saw no corruption." See here, dear reader, that Christ's flesh could not see corruption, therefore how is it possible that this bread — which, if it were to remain, would be subject to corruption — should be this flesh of Christ, since, as you have just heard, the flesh of Christ could not see corruption? For it has more than once come about that from the remains of the bread in this sacrament, and through the priests' careless omission, worms and putrefaction have come about. For this reason it is safer for any sensible observer to believe with the Church, that the flesh of Christ is not this wheat bread, which is clearly subject to decay, although the priest had previously blessed it; nor can it be rightly said, "this bread is this body."

There follows upon this what we said above about the Holy Spirit, to wit, that he is the Church's perpetual guardian, according to Christ's promise, to suggest and offer to the minds of the faithful — and especially to the Fathers who gathered together for this very reason — the truth of Christ's words, if ever some obscurity should arise from them.

So that is why, at the Lateran Council, 1,315 Fathers came together from the entire Christian world for a declaration of this truth, and these very same men considered that Christ's words should be explained in such a manner that we would believe that no bread remained with the body; nor is there the least suspicion that the same Fathers had their focus turned anywhere else than to the pursuit of this truth. For my part, since the matter stands thus, unless Christ in vain promised the help of the divine spirit for the clarification of such doubts, or unless the very Spirit of Truth fooled so many orthodox Fathers — although he was so devoutly beseeched by them — there's no doubt whether this decree which the same synod of so many saintly Fathers at the Lateran did pronounce is much more surely trustworthy for any Christian, than any of Martin Luther's creations, no matter how artfully crafted they may have been. Furthermore, if anyone should perhaps seek out the words of that same council, here is how it handed over what was to be believed by the faithful on this matter: "There is one Universal Church of the faithful, outside of which there is absolutely no salvation. In which Jesus Christ is the very priest and sacrifice, whose body and blood are truly contained in the sacrament of the altar under the species [appearance] of bread and wine; with the transubstantiated change of bread into the body and wine into the blood, by the divine power." That is what the council said, so Luther is not right when he relates Christ's words, saying: "When he says, 'this,' He means, 'this bread...is my body',"" given that a synod of so many Fathers affirms that the bread and wine are transubstantiated by the divine power into the body and blood of Christ.

Now, someone may say that Luther holds this Council to be of no account. Fine: we hold Luther's exposition to be of like value. Likewise, no sane person disbelieves Christ's promises in regard to the promised Holy Spirit — which we have recalled time and again. Christ cannot possibly fool us, for which reason his promise is most true, that is, that the Spirit of Truth will give to us to know all things, whatsoever Christ long ago said to the Apostles.

On top of this, since Luther contends that everyone has the free will to believe what he wishes, why would we not rather apply our belief to so many fathers rather than to one Luther? Because, there is no danger in disbelieving Luther, while no one can escape a manifest judgment of his own soul for having ignored the same Fathers.

Yet still, let us see with what ingenious operation the most illustrious king confounds Luther's other shrewd argument: "Luther argues thusly: 'Does not Christ seem to have wonderfully met this curiosity when he does not say of the wine "this [thing] is my blood," but, "this is my blood?" [now Henry]: See what Luther contends — or rather pretends — to do for the simplicity of his faith, when he says that Christ did not say of the wine "this [thing] is my blood," but rather "this is my blood"; I am amazed at what comes into the mind of that man when he is writing such things, because who does not see how little Christ's words do for his argument — rather, on the contrary, how much it would have done for Luther's argument, had Christ said "this [thing] is my blood?" For at least Luther would have had an excuse for his supposition about the definite article referring to the wine, since that would have been in the neuter; whereas Christ did not say that, but used the masculine; such as, on the contrary would have been the case, or gender, in a reference to the bread of "this is my body." Yet we have neither instance in either case." That was the king's response.

One can truly see here the king's lively intelligence, when he so acutely perceives Luther's hallucinations, and how he notes that what Luther argued in his own defense was actually an argument that refuted his own case, and did the exact opposite of what he had intended, because it would have doubtless done much more for Luther's intention had Christ said, "this [thing] is my blood," rather than saying, "this is my blood." You see, since wine is neuter in Latin, the neuter pronoun would have referred to it, nor would it have easily fit the word "blood." Yet Christ did not use those pronouns, but instead used the masculine [in Greek, too] to refer to the blood, as is clear. So he clearly teaches us that this is not bread, which would have been in the masculine gender [in Greek and Latin], but his body [as in the neuter, in Greek and Latin]. So all of this goes completely against Luther's proposal, but let us hear the other argument, as Luther continues the ridiculous: "However, that there is a neuter pronoun in Greek and Latin, has to do with the agreement in gender; yet, in Hebrew, where there is no neuter, it refers to the bread, so that one could say: 'this [bread] is my body,' which the manner of speech and common sense prove, since the subject is demonstrative of the bread and not of the body, whenever he says, '*this* is my body'."

To these words of Luther, the king thus responded: "Now, because Luther wants the pronoun 'this' to refer to the 'body' not because of Christ's intent but rather due to the fortuitousness of the Latin and Greek languages, and that he would thus send us back to the Hebrew, is ridiculous, isn't it? Since the Hebrew language does not have the neuter gender, then he cannot so clearly tell us to which of the two Christ wanted this part of speech to refer, as the Latin and Greek actually have it. You see, in Hebrew, if the article were masculine, then the 'this' would remain ambiguous in its reference, since it would not necessarily refer to something of that gender; yet in Latin the words 'bread' and 'body' have different genders and thus different articles, as in the original Greek from which it was translated, because it was discovered to have been phrased thus, with this reference to the body, by the evangelists themselves." And that was how the king put it.

At this point the reader plainly sees how thoroughly the king has explained Luther's tricks. First, that Luther would send us to the Hebrew, which does not have the neuter, demonstrates only an uncertainty about which of the two would have been signified.

You might add to this that it doesn't matter, since we do not have anything written in that language, and so he is asking us to seek for something that cannot be found.

The Substance of Bread Does Not Remain

Furthermore, since it is taken for granted by all that Mark is more succinct than Matthew, it would be necessary to show the same thing in both places, such that the pronoun would agree with "body" and not with "bread" in Mark, and thus would it be for Matthew, writing in Hebrew.

What is more, in the words that pertain to the blood, it is clear that the article must refer to the blood, since Christ recalled both — that is the chalice and the blood — and made no mention of the wine, that it would be one of these two, that is, either the chalice or the blood to which the pronoun would necessarily refer. Yet no one is so insane as to claim that the chalice is here designated, since the chalice is not the blood of Christ; therefore, the blood was truly signified, just as it's impossible to believe otherwise about the body, that is that the pronoun referred to the body and not the bread.

Finally, since both "chalice" and "blood" are in the neuter, and wine is masculine in Greek, then the evangelists would have necessarily referred to the wine with the appropriate masculine pronoun. Therefore, since none of them did so, as is clear, it is also clear that they did not intend to refer to the wine, just as they could not have been referring to the chalice either, as we have shown; so it could only follow that Christ could have only been referring to the blood, and doubtless that this would have followed for the body as well. Then, the most illustrious king uses still one more line of reasoning to refute Luther's prior play: "Now that Luther has admitted that there is the same difference in gender among the Greeks [as in Latin], it could easily be known that the evangelists, who wrote in Greek, knew what article to put that would refer to the bread, as they would have been mindful of the Lord's mind on this matter, so they must have willed to make it known to Christians that by this reference to the body, Christ did not give bread in communion to his disciples, but his own body. Likewise, that Luther interprets these words of Christ 'take and eat: this is my body' for his own position, that is 'this bread which he took,' I shall not combat — but Christ himself teaches that his words meant otherwise, that is, in what he offered to them that it was not the bread that it seemed, but his very own body, that is, if the evangelists rightly recall Christ's words; because otherwise he could have said not *Hoc* (which could be explained for *Hic*) but rather more clearly, 'this bread is my body,' (*Hic panis est corpus meum*) by which manner of speech his disciples would have been taught that which Luther now teaches the church, to wit, that in the Eucharist are likewise present both Christ's body and bread; but he speaks in that moment such that he manifestly shows that to be only the body and not bread."

Here, too, his Royal Highness has clearly laid Luther out, because all who know anything about Latin and Greek understand that there is the same difference in these words, that is "bread" and "body," in Greek as in Latin. Therefore, when the evangelists who wrote in Greek put an article that did not agree with "bread," but with "body," it is clear that they did this with full consciousness of Our Lord's intentions, so that they willed to teach everyone with this demonstrative pronoun that this was not bread but that the body was communicated to the Apostles, and so they signified "body" and not "bread." Even Christ, had he willed that bread be understood, could have said so with equal facility: "This bread is my body." Thus with the addition of one word, he would have completely handled the dispute. Therefore, since he did not say anything like that, and yet Luther would have us believe that the bread remains, and that it is the same as his body, it seems to follow that either he did not foresee this controversy to be coming in his Church, or that if he did foresee it, he nevertheless willed that his Church should err: both of which are patently false. And so that you can understand this more clearly, dear reader, I beg you to consider the following few points:

First, with what great charity Christ has loved the Church, for whom he did not refuse to undergo a horrific death.

Next, how great was his attention to our harmony and union, for which he left us his own peace.

Third, how lovingly he promised that not only he himself would remain with us to the end of the age, but also that he would send another comforter, whom he called the Spirit of Truth.

Fourth, that the Spirit would lead us into all truth, and would open up for us those things which he had said more succinctly.

Fifth, that if anything should seem obscure, he promised that it would be clear to those who asked, sought, and knocked.

The Substance of Bread Does Not Remain

Sixth, how often the Church has suffered to see these very burdensome disputes and contentions arise over this matter, due to heretics, as all know.

Seventh, that the Church herself gathered 1,315 fathers at the Lateran, so as to consult the Divine Spirit, that she might discern what was to be believed on this subject.

Eighth, how it is likewise sure and certain that no corruption overtook those Fathers, by which they would have been moved to treat this affair in an insincere manner.

Ninth, if the substance of bread is converted into the body of Christ, as they defined, then Christ could not have spoken otherwise than he actually spoke.

Tenth, if the substance of bread were to remain, then Christ ought to have spoken otherwise, not least with the addition of one word that could have handled this entire dispute; because if he had said, "this bread is my body," "this wine is my blood," any and all controversy would have been completely removed.

Who, therefore, would consider these things precisely and not be persuaded that Christ, had he wished the substance of bread to remain, had then willed to speak so obscurely, such that many dangers would await souls; then that he would have, later on, not even deigned to clarify the truth of the matter to the 1,300 Fathers gathered together because of what he had promised, to seek, ask, and knock, that they might receive, find, and have it open to them? To whom would this seem believable, that Christ would have not willed to teach his Apostles the same thing more openly, given that he would have foreseen this future tragedy, that is, if he actually thought that the bread remained? He could have taught this very thing more clearly to the Apostles, doubtless, or he could have at least indicated the truth through the Spirit of Truth, to those Fathers who then begged it of him so resolutely. Nothing seems more unlikely, or further from the truth, than that Christ would have left this matter to Luther, who would now take up for himself this magisterial office to teach the Church, having followed his own spirit, while twisting Christ's words for his own heresy, after he ignored the Fathers and showed contempt for the presence of that spirit which would reside within the Church. So, since Christ spoke so clearly, by using a part of speech that obviously matches "blood" and not "wine," and indicated "body" and not "bread," Luther's interpretation is convincingly shown to be false and a patent error, when he says that "this" is "this bread...which Christ took," and the other "this...wine," which word was not added but could have been, had Christ wished.

The king, however, does not leave anything untouched that could have the least importance, so we now return to tackle Luther's other cunning crafts in regard to the wine. Here is what Luther had said: "It is even much clearer when he adds the noun 'chalice,' saying: 'this chalice of the new covenant in my blood': does he not seem to wish to hold us all in a simple faith, yet only that we might believe his blood alone to be in the chalice?" Then Luther closes his first argument: "It must be understood to be true bread and true wine, just as there is a true chalice, because even they do not say that the chalice is transubstantiated."

His Royal Intelligence likewise strikes down these two pitiful arguments with one blow: "That Luther would now boast so grandly that Christ is also speaking of a chalice, which no one says to have been transubstantiated, makes me marvel that this man is not ashamed of such intemperate silliness. When Christ says, 'This is the chalice of the New Testament in my blood,' what does this do for Luther? What else could it mean, other than what he offered to his disciples in the chalice was his blood? Or, will Luther show us from Christ's words that the substance of the wine remains, because Christ is speaking of his blood? Or, that the wine could not have been changed into blood, because there is still a chalice?"

Dear reader, you see how Luther has gained nothing here at all, since there is no need — simply because the chalice remains unchanged — that we must understand this same thing to be the case of the bread or of the wine, because the chalice would be much more fairly compared with the pyx upon which the body of Christ rests, rather than a comparison to the bread: three correspond to another three, that is, the chalice, wine, and blood to the pyx, bread, and body. Among those things, of course the chalice remains unchanged, but the wine is changed into the blood; and likewise in the latter, the pyx remains as it was, but the bread is changed into the body. Now, because his Royal Highness so convincingly refutes Luther at this point, and demonstrates that he has both impiously and pertinaciously erred, he then adds: "I wish that Luther had picked a game for himself from some other field, in which there was less danger in the play, given that he excuses the Bohemians and Greeks from any guilt of heresy, so as to proclaim all Romans heretics, by which Luther all the more shows himself to be the heretic: one who not only denies the faith which the whole Church believes, but also counsels that worse things should be believed than what the Greeks believe, or than even the Bohemians have ever believed."

The king handled this very prudently, because the Bohemians have hitherto not dared to assert that the bread is Christ's body, from which assertion Luther's daring has shown no fear. Since the king has copiously shown up to this point that it cannot be gathered from a single one of the evangelists that bread remains with Christ's body in the Eucharist, he now does likewise with Paul's words, since Luther had previously objected: "Paul says, 'is not the bread which we break a participation of Christ's body?' He does not say 'in the bread,' but the bread itself is the taking-part of Christ's body."

His Royal Highness responds: "The Apostle sometimes uses the word 'bread' according to Scripture's custom of speech, by which he might call something not that what it is but that which it had been, such as when Aaron's rod devoured the magicians' rods, which were then no longer rods but serpents; or perhaps he was content to call it that which its appearances gave forth, since he surely considered it sufficient for the people still new to the faith, who were fed milk, and that he was not so demanding on the people that, in whatever way they should believe that Christ's body was there in the sacrament, that they might, little by little, grow and grow up upon more solid food in the Lord."

The reader clearly notes here how Luther has been overcome with a double-edged sword: first with citations from the Old, and then by references to the New Testament. First, from Exodus in the Old Testament, when the serpent into which the rod had been changed was still called the rod, although it had been a rod and was now a serpent, as the king recounts above. So, too, in this sacrament, Christ's body — because bread had been changed into it — is likewise called bread by Paul, but it is not so because bread did remain there, anymore than the rod remained with the serpent. Surely it is a much greater stretch to call a serpent a rod, compared to the body of Christ into which the bread had been changed, than it should be called bread, since the serpent did not retain any indicator of its prior state as a rod, except perhaps its length. In the sacrament of the Eucharist, however, absolutely all of the accidents of the bread remain. Therefore, when Scripture calls a serpent a rod, according to its previous name, but which was no longer a rod, why should we marvel if the body of Christ is now called bread, since bread had been changed into it? Luther has not yet sunk his teeth into this example, at least not by way of any response, although he does play around with the matter in this way: "Sure, it's true that the serpent — which had been a rod — is called a rod: so by following logic of this sort, since bread is what it is called here, not because it is bread but because it was, then what? Should we — against the Scripture — simply fit every Scripture to what might be found in one place?" To Luther's games, we respond thus: the king is not attempting to say that what happens in one place of Scripture must be indiscriminately foisted upon all others, but that, rather, as a serpent was there into which the rod had been changed, and yet retained the name of "rod," although it was no longer a rod but truly a serpent; so in like manner here, the body into which the bread had been changed does retain the name of "bread," while the substance of bread is completely gone: who does not see the logical similarity here?

Furthermore, the king produces another offensive from the New Law: "Paul speaks to the Corinthians thus: 'brethren, even I could not speak to you as if to the spiritual, but had to speak to you as carnal; as babes in Christ I gave you milk and not solid food upon which to be nourished, for you were not yet able, nor are you able now.' And again to the Hebrews: 'and you are become such as have need of milk, and not of strong meat. For every one that is a partaker of milk, is unskillful in the word of justice.' From what Paul said, it is clear that Paul did not say all things as openly as he might — not because they should not have been said, but because the people were too young in their faith to be able to understand such mysteries."

It is for this reason, too, that the king teaches how Paul could be moved to call the sacrament by this name of bread, since it retained the species or appearances of bread. Paul considered it enough that a people still raw and unformed in the faith should be fed milk, and that at the beginning he did not seek to require more of them than that they should in any way believe that in this sacrament the body of Christ is contained. Whether or not the substance of bread remained, he did not yet openly teach, but he only used the word "bread" because of its likeness, since it had to be denoted by some name, nor was there a more fitting name: this is both because it contains the true Heavenly Bread within, as well as because it had been bread before, and still retained the exterior appearance of it. But even the Scriptures called Christ's body bread, although not of course of wheat, but spiritual, just as Jeremiah says when he takes on the persona of the Jews: "Come, let us give him wood for his bread." We understand by "wood" the cross, and by "bread" Christ's body. So likewise did Tertullian and Lactantius, as well as many others who interpreted this phrase. Lactantius said, "The wood signifies the cross and the bread, his body: because he himself is the food and life of men who believe in the flesh which he bore, and in the cross upon which he hung."

You can add to this that, whenever in Scripture something edible is denoted, the word "bread" is used frequently. For example, in 1 Kings [1 Sam] 14, when, upon Saul's oath, who ate "bread" before the eve of that day should be cursed, and that Jonathan incurred this curse, as is there noted, although he did not eat any common bread, but had only tasted of some honey. Likewise, in 4 Kings [2 Kings], when Eliseus only said that bread should be put before him, and yet a great variety of food was prepared for him. And in Matthew 5, when the Pharisees were accusing Christ's disciples because they had not washed their hands before they were to eat bread, and yet it is clear that bread was said in that place for any sort of food, generically. Therefore, it is clear that under the name of bread, any sort of food is understood, but even the common manner of speech shows that the Eucharist is thus called bread, because the egg of which we spoke earlier, even when it is turned into the substance of a chick and its flesh, it's still sometimes called an egg in common speech, and nevertheless is in no way an egg, but truly a chick. And on that account it retains its former name, due to its appearance, just as it is in the sacrament, which can be called bread by common speech and sometimes retains the name "bread" in the Scriptures, although there is no substance of bread there present.

Luther, however, is still not content with even this twofold solution to his problem, and he pertinaciously insists on his assertion that bread is still truly present: "Paul says, 'Is not the bread which we break a communication of the body of Christ?' nor does he say 'is in the bread,' but that 'this very bread is a partaking of the body of Christ'." He here tries to arm himself with Paul's words as if by some impenetrable shield, but which shield he will soon after try to throw back as an arrow. Furthermore, if we examine Paul's words more judiciously, they will no longer seem to be effective in the least for Luther's portion, as Luther himself thinks. You see, it is clear that Paul had just before that said similar things about the chalice: "Is not the chalice of blessing, which we bless, a communication of the blood of Christ?" and immediately following: "And the bread which we break, is it not a participation of the body of Christ?" Luther can surely not gather anything from the latter portion, as it pertains to the bread, which we might not likewise apply to the previous part, as regards the chalice; whereas, it is clear to all that the chalice is not the blood, for which reason neither is the body of Christ shown to be bread from these words. Therefore, dear reader, you see how Luther has only one Scripture upon which he leans, and that it is now falling apart completely, since the same words of Paul do not make the body of Christ the bread any more than they make the blood of Christ a chalice. For this reason, since it is now completely clear to all that the chalice can in no wise be said to be the blood, so neither is it to be believed that the body of Christ is bread.

Moreover, because Luther mentioned the Acts of the Apostles, too, that is that the sacrament is called bread therein, the king likewise handles this objection as he did the previous, and it melts away before him. For the king had added this: "The same thing could happen in the Acts of the Apostles, when blessed Peter spoke to the people and did not thrust upon them the faith of Christ with those very same words; but he did not dare to make plain to them everything about his divinity. In this manner the Apostles did not carelessly cast about the hidden and recondite mysteries to the people."

See how many different ways he demonstrates that, in the early Church, not all were indiscriminately admitted to the more solid food, and to the very depths of the mysteries; but they were first nourished for a while on milk, so that not even Peter, when he was addressing the people about Jesus our Savior, dared to speak of his divinity, but called him the "man approved by God in all virtue, signs, and wonders, who was raised from death to life by God." So, too, as it pertains to this sacrament: when he was speaking to the people, he was not accustomed to use a word other than bread, due to the exterior similarities of bread, as we have said. Furthermore, when Christ spoke to his Apostles, to whom it belongs to know the mysteries — as well as to be fed with more solid food — to them he explained it by point and clearly, that the substance of bread and wine no longer remained, but that each had retained its appearances, while being completely changed — the bread into flesh, and the wine wholly into blood. Wherefore, Christ indicated that the bread which was once there no longer was when he said, "this is my body," and he showed that about the wine when he said, "this is my blood," because the wine had been changed into blood, just as we have so frequently declared to you.

In the end, the most illustrious king confirms what he said also by the word of Christ, who called himself bread, and yet could not have wished it to be understood that he himself was wheat bread. And just as he was called bread, so, too, could he allow in reference to this sacrament, on account of the appearances of bread, that it be called bread, although it is in no way made of wheat; but let us hear the king himself: "The context of this Scripture makes clear that the word 'bread,' when the bread itself was changed into flesh, is nevertheless used without any violence done to God's word, since it signified the appearance of bread and not its substance. Would Luther so adhere to the propriety of language that he would believe Christ to both be in heaven and to be wheat or barley bread, since he did say, 'I am the bread which came down from heaven'?" That was the king's response.

Yet, Luther still tries to resolve this by distinguishing between spiritual and wheaten bread, that Christ spoke of the first and that

Paul was treating of the latter: "What follows from the words, the very absurdity of the matter, the irreconcilable understandings, then one's own interpretation forces the matter, so that Christ was speaking of spiritual bread, as when he said, 'my words are spirit and life,' and we find nothing of that in Paul's speech about bread: rather all of his language urges us to believe that Paul was speaking about wheat bread." Those are Luther's words.

Now let us see how much truth there is in all that: first, when he says that Christ was speaking only of the spiritual bread, that benefits our interpretation, because he also speaks in that place about this sacrament, which the ancients abundantly reference — but Christ's words themselves clearly teach this too. He says, "The bread which I shall give is my flesh — which I shall give for the life of the world." The reader is here begged to note that Christ said twice, "I shall give," once for the bread which he was going to give in the sacrament — and which he affirmed to be his flesh — and then again for the flesh which he would give for the life of the world. Both are shortly given to them by the Father, to whom he was then speaking: Jesus gave his very self to them as both teacher and servant, in whom they could believe. There were still two ways in which he would give himself: the first is how he gave himself in the sacrament, and the other is as he gave his flesh to be crucified, for both of which he said: "The bread which I shall give — that is, in this sacrament — is my flesh which — in death — I shall give for the life of the world." Here as well, I sincerely hope that the reader will consider what follows from those words, whether any absurdity or contradiction of some meanings, to see what else did they suggest other than that Christ was here speaking of the sacrament. Yet neither would Christ's words, "my words are spirit and life," actually be for them spirit and life should they make Christ wheat bread, that is, what would enter into the stomach only to then be expelled into the privy. But for us who believe that Christ is such a bread that makes us into him rather than converting him into our flesh, Christ is truly the spiritual bread, and his words are truly spiritual. If Christ were wheat bread, he would thus be digested into our flesh, and changed in our stomach, which is completely absurd, and those who speak thus are in no way taking Christ's words spiritually, but are rather understanding them in a carnal manner. Therefore, we do not dispute that Christ spoke there of the spiritual bread, rather, we readily affirm that he thereby mentions the sacrament.

It is likewise false that Paul was speaking only of wheat bread: "We who are many are one bread and one body, for we all partake of the one bread" (1 Cor. 10). If Paul were here speaking of wheat bread, I'm dying to know what sort of wheat bread could hold such a large company, and of which all Christians might partake. For that reason, Paul, too, is speaking here of Christ, the spiritual bread, and not of wheat bread. Dear reader, you decide which should be considered more set in stone: when the king interprets Paul's and Christ's words spiritually; or how Luther rather crassly and carnally interprets those same words, so that he makes Christ the bread that is cast into the privy. Who would ever believe that such bread could grant eternal life, rather than him alone who — once consumed by us — takes us, changes us, and transforms us into himself, and who could never be deformed inside us.

Luther, nevertheless still insists obstinately on his opinion, moaning in this manner: "Thus, my Paul stands unconquered against these futile transubstantiators and says, 'the bread which we break, etc.' and he wounds them with a two-edged point. First, because they cannot assert their claims with any reason nor with any authority; second, they do nothing else with their cold logic than to so unsyllogistically beg the question, and the greatest they might accomplish is only to show that it could be as they imagine, while they should have shown that it was done and that it was right that it had been thus done." There is Luther, and we will respond to him, point by point.

First, regarding the citation of Paul, "The bread which we break, is it not a participation of the Lord's body?", does not prove that the body of the Lord is bread, just as what is said close by — "The chalice of blessing, which we bless, is it not a participation of Christ's blood?" — does not prove that the blood of Christ is a chalice. But I will be even bolder: Luther cannot prove from any words of Scripture that Christ's body is wheat bread.

Next, we contest that it is a most false lie to say that we can make no claim either by reason or authority, because it completely goes against all reason to say that Christ is the bread that is digested and becomes feces, or that Christ's flesh is bread that will "see corruption." You see, besides the witness of the evangelists, we also have the many Fathers' statements that support our claim; we have, too, the decrees of a general council, which depend on the authority of the Holy Spirit. All of this shows clearly that Luther is not only a liar on this matter, when he says that we can make no claim with either reason or authority, but it is the greatest of lies to interpret Christ's word such that his neuter "this" is twisted into the masculine "this bread."

To his third point, about us as the worst beggars of the question by our frigid syllogisms, we respond coolly that this violation of logic, *petitio principii*, comes from an initial argument — not from the one who responds to the argument.

Finally, when he mentions the most that we might accomplish, is to show that it can be done just as we actually assert, should seem quite impressive to any Christian, that is to teach the possibility of what is to be believed. This is because our Creed is full of things that are difficult to believe, so much so that it is easier to impugn than to establish them.

Luther opposes still more: "And I wonder at this most wise Thomist, why he does not transubstantiate the accidents, too, since those words of transubstantiation, according to his brain, denote only the body of Christ: 'this is my body.' Therefore, there will be nothing there unless it is the body of Christ, according to his Ambrose, and therefore no whiteness will be there with the other accidents. Or, why does he not argue: 'What prevents the bread from being there, in the same way that the accidents are present?' I beg you, where is the necessity for doing away with the substance, and keeping the accidents?"

Note first of all, dear reader, that from all the authorities which the most illustrious king cited, Luther follows up on Ambrose alone, and see what sort of sophistry he engages in: you see, the king quoted Ambrose as follows: "Although the appearance of bread and wine are seen, yet nothing else should be believed to be present besides the flesh and blood of Christ." Then, this is how Luther argues: if "nothing else," then there is no whiteness with the other accidents. As if even children would not see this sophistry for what it is, since Ambrose's words have to do only with an exclusion of "what it is," that is, any other substance, and not its qualities or other accidents. And yet, Luther would shamelessly place the blame of this error on Ambrose: "We can almost touch what Ambrose has here so patently gotten wrong." With this, there is nothing more mendacious than Luther, nor should you find anything more shameless than he. Ambrose is clearly confessing that the accidents remain when he says, "Although the appearance of bread and wine are seen," and he is denying another substance with, "yet nothing else...is present besides the flesh and blood of Christ." That is, no other substance remains at all. It surely seemed this way to Ambrose — who was an ancient author — and to those other Fathers who lived more than a thousand years ago, so that when the body of Christ came, the substance of bread immediately departed. That is how they all taught the Church in their own times, and we have — more recently — followed their footsteps, and we call this arrival and departure "transubstantiation." But now Luther, rising up to rumble all things, is asking why not even the accidents are transubstantiated, as if it were reasonable for the accidents to be changed into another substance as well.

But Luther still presses forward: "What need is there of destroying the substance but keeping the accidents?" The fathers will say to him that they feared lest someone of this sort might arise, who would deny that the body of Christ was substantially present, since something of the bread remains there; well, Luther is such a one who would say that this presence of bread is there — and that it is the flesh of Christ, which to the Fathers was both false and completely absurd. Therefore, the Fathers were moved by the Holy Spirit who is the Church's moderator, so that they might foresee either error proscribe it for posterity: the substance of the bread does not remain, because no one has any doubts about the accidents and whether they were the body of Christ, so the Father has had no fear that such an imbecile of a heretic would that the accidents were the flesh of Christ.

Luther then adds: "I here pass over that rhetorically dressed up contempt, and meanwhile I adjoin two most cogent comparisons: iron heated by fire and the Incarnate God. And in neither case must iron give way to fire, nor the divinity to humanity; you see, although it is not necessary for me to assert my own opinions, I will nevertheless take on enough of this work for the assertor, if I might possibly show that his imagination could have it otherwise. Thus, I can say that the body of Christ is in the sacrament while bread remains, just as the fire can be in iron while the substance of iron remains; and God is in man while human nature remains, whereas in either case the substances are so mixed so that each has its own operation and nature still, and yet they constitute a one. So I can speak thus, I say, even while the papists take away the comparison not by any Thomistic contempt, but with a claim about their faith. It is their business to prove their affirmative, which in one particular at least I am able to disprove. For it is not a defense of the sacraments, when you pass by and despise the arguments of one's opponent, as this senseless Thomist does; rather it is to demonstrate that they are null and void — otherwise the defender forces men to think his opponent's arguments are invulnerable when he engages in silly dissimulation, and, like a coward, dodges the issue."

I said it once and it is so clearly true: it is much easier to combat our assertions than to establish them with proof, since they come from faith rather than from human reason. It is sufficient for us to follow what was left for us by the Fathers, who were most excellent in learning and in sanctity. If some heretic will not believe them, then that same person must render a sufficient reason why he would not be forced to believe in this way, otherwise he should not be given an ear. You see, it isn't enough that he can just reject our beliefs if he says that they are not sufficiently proven; but he must bring forward a reasoning that is clearer than any light for why these things must not be believed. Luther has brought nothing forward like this, and now — after so many uproars and disturbances — he is trying to escape, as if it weren't incumbent upon him to prove his own opinions. He says: "Although at this point I am not required to defend my assertions, yet I shall give my opponent enough to think about if I prove that what he has alleged can be taken otherwise," and thereafter, "It is their business to prove their affirmative, which in one particular at least I am able to disprove."

Well, at least I agree with Luther on this point, that it is an easier duty to be able to walk away from an opponent's assertions, and to oppose what someone establishes — in some sense — by his sophistry, because, as they say, it is easier to tear down than to build up. But I completely disagree that the one who attacks another's arguments should not have to assert his own, or that he can walk away from the matter at hand. Otherwise, I don't know what he means by an "affirmative," because, as far as the present matter goes, our claim is a "negative": that is, the body of Christ is not bread, and the substance of bread does not remain, from which facts it can be gathered that a transubstantiation of the bread has taken place.

But now let us confront his comparisons: I'm not amazed that Luther is lying, given that he almost never tells the truth: he here says that the king has a Thomistic contempt for his comparisons, that is that he bypasses anything about iron and fire, and the Incarnate God, but you will see that this is false, if you open up the king's book, because he wrote in the following manner about the first example, not long before Luther finished this "Captivity": "I certainly do not think that any of the holy Fathers of old would have approved of Luther's brief comparison of iron conjoined with fire, because none of them ever said that iron was changed into fire, such that the appearance of iron was left but the substance of iron had been changed into the substance of fire — which is what all the ancients believed about the bread and Christ's flesh." That is how the king addressed the subject and by those words he roundly refuted Luther's opinion, by which he sustains that the body of Christ is bread. Now, if Luther says that, by this example at least, it is proven that it is possible for the bread to remain with the body of Christ, then the king responds to him that he here disputes about reality itself, and not about the possibility of reality, since the king spoke of what actually happened and not what was possible.

To this you may add the point from logic: that from *posse*, or something's possibility, to [*ad*]*esse*, or its present reality, there is no valid conclusion, but just above we have given the reasons why it seemed to those Fathers who were full of the Holy Spirit that the substance of bread did not remain, and the king reviewed the many statements of those numerous Fathers. What kind of consistency of dogmas is there when Luther claims that bread is the body of Christ, but at another time that bread is not the body, but only remains with the body?

Neither claim comes from a man who surely has all of his dogmas from heaven. Therefore, as regards the example of the fiery iron, it is clear enough that the iron is not fire, and that the fire is not iron; for this reason, nothing is proved with this example such that the bread could be truly called the flesh of Christ, which error Luther nevertheless continues to push. Nor is the substance of iron changed into the substance of fire, as the Fathers teach that the bread becomes the flesh of Christ. That should suffice for the king's response to Luther in regard to the example of the fiery iron.

Furthermore, because Luther contends by this example that the substance of bread could remain together with the body of Christ, the king adds something from his own faithful fervor which he has for the most holy Body of Christ: "Whoever considers the most blessed Body of Christ as he ought, will more easily allow that any two other substances could simultaneously remain conjoined, rather than that any other body might remain together with the venerable Body of Christ, because no other substance is worthy that it should be mixed with that substance which created all other substances." Here, the king did not intend the flesh of Christ to be considered the creative substance, as Luther would blather about in so many words later on, but that Christ himself created all things. The king, you see, did not deny the possibility of such a union — if only it had seemed fitting to God — but he admitted how unworthy it would be for perishable bread to be so mingled with the imperishable Christ, and who does not understand that even human nature itself is not worthy to be mingled with the Word? Although his human nature was preserved from corruption, lest that which the Word had assumed should suffer corruption, yet if the bread should remain, de facto it would often suffer corruption, and often actually cast out. For this reason the king judged it something unworthy to be mingled with the incorruptible Christ. Nor is it true, as Luther banters about, that the accidents are mixed with Christ's body, as the accidents of fire are mixed with iron, because in this way Christ would — by "whiteness" — be white bread, just as iron would be fire by its very heat. So, that is enough in regard to the first example; now let us go on to the other example which the king does indeed mention: "Beyond this, I think that Luther's comparison would have not been agreeable at all to those Fathers of old, whereby Luther would have the bread remain simultaneously with the flesh, just as God remained with man in the one person of Christ; you see, just as each and every most learned and most holy ancient Father confessed that the bread was changed into flesh, so, too, was no one so impious or ignorant as to express that his humanity had been changed into the divinity, unless Luther could perhaps create for us some such new person, who would have God assume man, and thus God and man assume bread and wine. If he does believe that, then I think that he will be considered a heretic by all those who are not heretics."

The reader here sees that the king did not overlook any comparison, as Luther lyingly states, nor did he deny that the bread could be taken as a subject (*suppositum*) by Christ, if only Christ had willed it; but, because the Fathers unanimously profess the contrary, the king does not hesitate to hold him as a heretic (and proclaimed such by all who are not heretics), who would disagree with so many holy and erudite Fathers on such a profound matter.

Furthermore, this second example is very different from the first, because there the two natures — that is, human and divine — are united in the one subject of the Word, but because the same "subject-making" or person-making is beyond the powers of nature, just as is the change of the substance of bread into the flesh of Christ, it would also bring with it many absurdities as well, and specially that Christ would have separated from himself what he had once so often admitted into the unity of his person. For this reason, the king does not think that it can be allowed, and especially because not one of the Fathers is seen to teach that.

At this point, if Luther could have proved that this subjectification of the bread in Christ actually happened, de facto and not just as some possibility, then we should agree with him against the Fathers, and cede his point, but I know that he will never be able to do that. In the meanwhile, it is well for us to follow the fathers' footsteps, as well as what seemed good to the Holy Spirit to hand on to us through them; it is better to embrace that than Luther's tortuous meanderings, all the while he just seeks more entangled and entangling knots for the weaker souls — always under the pretext of "liberty" — so that, in the end, he leads them to the ultimate perdition. The king brings forward for his part many Fathers who were famous for their learning and holiness, to wit, Eusebius, Emisenus, Augustine, Gregory of Nyssa, Theophylact, Cyril, and Ambrose, as well as others who professed the same thing, that the bread's substance was changed and did not remain after the consecration. The king introduced them to this extent because Luther contended that the Church had believed for 1,200 years that the bread remained, and that nowhere before 300 years ago did the Fathers mention any change of the bread — which is patently false, as the king showed from so many citations. He even added that, were this to have been decided for the first time only now and yet the Ancients did not believe the contrary, then even if no one had ever thought of the thing before, why would one not rather obey the present decree of the entire Church being persuaded that what was revealed to the Church had laid hidden before? For the Spirit blows where it wills, and it so blows when it wills. That was the king's point.

Yet Luther turns a deaf ear to these things, just as he boldly passes over most of the rest of these matters. He took Ambrose alone out of all, and handled him with such futile sophistry, as we showed above.

I bypass many other things, lest I never finish, and especially if I aimed to respond to all of Luther's insults, which are limitless; nevertheless, I don't remember omitting anything that was worthy of a response, such that I have no doubt that the judicious reader will judge the king to have rested on solid reason and solid Scripture, whereas Luther on the contrary rests on the most frivolous. Although this is truly how the matter stands, and yet I hear Luther boasting of his victory at the end of this fourth part: "And so not to be ungrateful to my teacher, the Lord Henry, I only now wish to transubstantiate my opinion and say: before this I had laid it down that it was of no consequence whether a man thought in one way or another concerning transubstantiation; but now, having seen the reasons and lovely arguments of the Defender of the Sacraments, I decree that it is impious and blasphemous if any say that the bread is transubstantiated, and that it is Catholic and pious if anyone says with Paul: 'the bread, which we break, is the body of Christ.' Let him be anathema who says otherwise and

136

changes one jot or tittle of the Scripture, although he should be our new Lord Henry, and a master Thomist." That is how Luther speaks.

Note first of all, dear reader, how inconsistent this man is, he who glories of having his dogmas all from heaven. If that first dogma had come from heaven, how could it happen that this thing that is contrary to it would have also come from heaven? You know for sure that contrary teachings cannot both come from heaven, but these two manifestly contradict one another: "one may" and "one may not," for he first taught that it was "of no consequence" whether one thought one way or another, and now he decrees it to be impious to think one way.

Consider this, then, too: he says that it is Catholic and pious if one should say with Paul, "The bread which we break is the body of Christ," but Paul never said this. This teacher given to us by heaven does not sense shame and lying about Paul: Paul did say, "The bread which we break, is it not a participation of the body of the Lord?" yet, from that it does not follow that the bread which we break is the Lord's body, because the same Paul had said above: "The chalice that we bless, is it not a partaking of Christ's blood?" From this, however, it does not follow that the chalice is Christ's blood. So, neither from the other citation does it follow that the bread is the body of Christ. You will see later, if you observe Luther, how openly he strikes his own self with an anathema: "Let him be anathema who says otherwise and changes one jot or tittle of the Scripture." For this reason, since Luther cites Paul quite otherwise than Paul himself spoke, then should we not gather from Luther's own words that he has bound himself by an anathema? And so we conclude our fourth point.

CHAPTER V
The Mass Is Not a Testament

BUT now we must examine in the fifth place whether the Mass should rightly be called the New Testament. Luther attempts to add that the Mass is a testament (or "covenant"), and that this is a sort of immovable foundation upon which he might set up his diabolical concoction, and he tries in all manner possible to establish it. We, however, do not hesitate to demonstrate not only that this is no immovable foundation but also that those things which he strove to set up upon it are founded upon absolutely nothing firm. You see, he also infers from the same foundation that the Mass is no sacrifice, and that is something which is averse not only to all both modern and ancient authors but also to the Scriptures themselves, as we shall make clear in its place later on.

Furthermore, the cause of the entire error is that Luther thinks that the Eucharist is the sacrament of the remission of sins when it's actually not for remission but rather the sacrament of a certain union, because it signifies our union with Christ and it grants that same union with God the Father no less efficaciously. We will demonstrate this not only by the Fathers' witness, but also by the Scriptures themselves.

First Dionysus in Chapter 5 of the *Ecclesiastical Hierarchy* calls the same sacrament a synaxis and communion which perfects our Union with God.

St. John Damascene likewise calls it communion because through it we commune with Christ and take part in his flesh and divinity and we commune and are united to one another through the same.

St John Chrysostom, too, in his commentary on First Corinthians, while speaking of this sacrament says: "Why did Paul not say 'participation'? Because he wanted to signify something more and to show the great congruence among these things, for we commune not only by participation and reception but by unity. Thus, as that body is united to Christ, so, too, are we joined together in union through this bread.

Hilary is numbered among these same as he states in the 8th book of his *On the Trinity*: if Christ truly assumed the flesh of our body and that man who was truly born of Mary is Christ, and we truly receive the flesh of his body in the mystery, we will also be one through it because the Father is in him and he is in us: how is the unity of the will asserted since the natural property through the sacrament is perfectly the sacrament of unity?

Augustine signs on in this way: just as when the species of visible bread is present many grains are strewn into one, so that it might be present which Sacred Scripture says about the faithful: "There was among them one soul and one heart for God," that's, too, regarding the wine. Brethren, recall how it became one: many granules hung on the grape but the granules' liquid was mingled into one, thus the Lord Jesus Christ signified us — that he willed for us to belong to him. He did consecrate the mystery of our peace and unity on his table. Elsewhere he says: "As you see that it has become one so you, too, be one by loving one another by clinging to one faith, one hope, undivided charity; when heretics receive this they receive a testimony against themselves because they seek division, whereas this bread indicates unity."

From these things therefore it is clear that this mystery of unity and communion is a sacrament and mark. What need have we of more authors when Paul testifies to this abundantly? He says, "The cup of blessing which we bless — is it not the communication of the blood of Christ? The bread which we break — is it not the communication of the body of Christ?" What else does Paul mean by these words other than that these are the sacraments of communion and union? For this reason, in the following chapter, after he recalls the divisions among the Corinthians, he adds, "It is no longer licit to eat the Lord's Supper," just as if he had said,

"The Lord's Supper is the mark of harmony and does not admit of dissident souls, yet you dissent one from the other and set to eat not a meal in common but each one his own private fare." Add to this the fact that Paul makes no mention at all of the remission of sins, while he yet goes over the entire order of this mystery just as he had been previously taught by Christ.

Who does not clearly understand now from the sayings, the authors, and the Scriptures that the Eucharist is the sacrament of union and not of the remission of sins? Because sins — as far as guilt is concerned — must first be wiped away through the sacrament of Absolution, because the absolved one — as Luther claims — is bound to believe this. Now if the sins are truly forgiven, what need is there to receive another sacrament for the remission of guilt, since they were already remitted through the sacrament of Absolution? Furthermore, Luther contends for this reason that the Mass is the sacrament of the remission of sins because there is made mention of the remission of sins in the consecration of the blood. Now the fact that this conduces in no way to his proposal we shall show forthwith. Yet on this basis he seeks to build — and most pertinaciously — so that we might believe that the remission of sins is promised to us through this sacrament and, as it almost happens, once one error of any sort is admitted, we will fall straightforward into many others. Thus does Luther throw himself into many other most obscene and absurd errors once this error has been posited. Among these, this one is the most poisonous of all: that the most criminal and wicked men may safely approach this sacrament. Up to this point, the entire Church, full of all the right-believing, has considered this opinion to be, as it were, the most detestable, as Paul himself cries back out since he says that whoever approaches unworthily eats and drinks judgment upon himself, by not discerning the body of the Lord. For this reason, it is necessary first of all to be revived and recover from sins and simultaneously to receive Absolution from some priest before one would presume to approach this sacrament. But after one should have worthily done such thing I don't deny that the Eucharist confers much for wiping away smaller bits of sins, and most of all in so far as it is offered to God as a sacrifice for sins. You see in so far as it is a sacrifice, it represents the great sacrifice of Christ by which he offered himself to the Father upon the cross, and where he poured forth his blood for the remission of sins, because he promised that beforehand at Supper when he said: "This is my blood of the New Covenant, which will be poured out for you and for many, unto the remission of sins." Behold the remission of sins is promised for the spilling of blood, not for drinking from the chalice. Nor did he say, "This is the blood which will be drunk by many unto the remission of sins." Therefore, it was not for the drinking of the cup at Supper but for the spilling of blood on the cross that remission of sins was promised.

For this reason, neither is the Eucharist the sacrament of the remission of sins since it ought only to be offered to those who sins had previously been forgiven, for such are suitable to be united through the Eucharist to God, but not to those who are yet to be cleansed, nor for those who have not yet fully renounced their sins. Furthermore, it is certain that the pouring out of blood on the cross is able to forgive all sins and thus, since the sacrifice of the body and blood offered in the Mass does represent the very sacrifice of the cross, it happens that each time in the Mass when we offer under the species of bread and wine the body and blood of Christ, each time, too, something of the rust of our sins is taken away and the very remnants of sins certainly wind up more remitted for whosoever this sacrifice is offered. But it does not follow on this account that those dirty and sinful ones who have not yet expiated themselves may have these holy things conferred upon them since once upon a time Christ had forbidden this very thing when he said, "Do not give what is holy to dogs, nor cast your pearls before swine." This most holy sacrament, therefore, is not to be granted to just anyone who might be conscious of some mortal sin and had not previously and diligently purged himself of it, but only to those who had previously prepared themselves and as much as was possible had diligently cleansed themselves of deadly stain infecting them. To these, I say, this sacred food may be administered, but not to the swine and dogs, because these latter have in no way proven themselves, nor have they discerned the body of the Lord; rather, with unwashed feet they are rushing headlong into this most sacred repast.

Therefore, there are two things that we shall refute in order.

First, that the Mass is a testament; second, that it is not a work and sacrifice — because Luther attempts to affirm both positions to a great number of people. We will speak first of the testament since this is like an unshakable foundation which Luther has laid for his whole project. For he wrote thus in his *On the Babylonian Captivity*: "Let therefore this stand first of all and infallibly that the Mass or sacrament of the altar is the testament of Christ which when he died he left behind him to be distributed to his faithful ones, for here are his words: this chalice is the New Testament in my blood." Let this truth, I say, stand as the immovable foundation upon which we shall lay all else that is to be said, since you shall see this so that we might overturn all the impieties of men which have been brought upon this most sweet sacrament. Christ therefore is truthful and truly says that this is the New Testament in his blood which was poured out for us." That is Luther for you.

Response: here first of all note, dear reader, how cunningly he professes his dogma by including all things together — the Mass and the sacrament of the altar and the testament of Christ — and thereby, from these three things he makes one. He says, "Let it stand first and infallibly that the Mass or the sacrament of the altar is the testament of Christ." But you will find later on more than once that he calls the Mass a promise, and the sacrament of the altar to be something connected to the promise. It is quite clear that the Mass or the sacrament of the altar is not a promise, even if through its reception many good things are promised, but we will speak about this more shortly.

Then what he adds when he says that "dying, he left it behind to be distributed to his faithful ones." Who has ever heard of a testament that is made up of the things which must be distributed? But this is the man's cleverness: to confuse all things, mixing all together, and involving it all together. In other words, whenever he finds himself pressed in a corner, he immediately slips out of one's hands by some sort of cover. But even the words of Christ which he produces benefit this not one wit, because Christ did not command by his words that anything should be distributed besides his body and blood, so if something else is attached here it must be either the body or the blood of Christ, because we read nothing here of the forgiveness of sins. Nor is the remission of sins promised for the drinking of the blood, as we have said, but for the pouring out of the same on the cross.

Now Christ has already mentioned the testament, as it happens, so that he might show how he confirmed this by the spilling of his blood on the cross not that he might make the blood or the chalice a testament as Luther fallaciously suggests, but rather so he might teach that the New Testament — that is, the new law laid down by him — as well as all the things which are promised in it, are corroborated in full strength by his blood.

Furthermore, we will see shortly hereafter how Lutheran is this immovable foundation, and just how firm of a structure it raises thereupon. That he says at the end however, that Christ is true is of course true; nay, Christ is most truthful, but there is none more mendacious than Luther, he who fears not to ascribe to Christ what Christ truly never spoke. For, it is most false that Christ, in Luther's sense, ever asserted that the chalice was the New Testament, which we will show here below. In the meanwhile, let us see with which words the most illustrious king censures this error: "I will not contend with him about the testament and the promise, and regarding the entire definition and application of the testament to the sacrament. I will not be so bothersome to him as he might find with others, who might subvert a good part of his foundation here, and who also call the New Testament the promise of the gospel-law, just as the Old [Testament] was for that of Moses, and they would deny that Luther had treated this testament with sufficient intelligence, since it is not for the "testator" to name or call by name the inheritor whom he set up as sole heir. Nor regarding the remission of sins which Luther names as the inheritance which would be the same as the kingdom of heaven, but is rather the path to heaven. All these things and many others might be urged on and pressed so that the foundation of Luther's structure would in several places come crashing down on the scaffolding. But I will leave this to those who want it. Thus far the words of the most illustrious king.

With what frank and few words his Royal Majesty hinted at how this error might be overturned, and although we have shown this more fully in the refutation of Luther's articles, we would now however like to add a little something. Let whoever wishes peruse all of Sacred Scripture, no more than what is called the New Testaments, and he will find but one. There is one sole New Testament for Paul just as is clear in the eighth and ninth chapters of the letter to the Hebrews, as we shall show below. Nor do I think that Luther can wiggle out of this, lest he should speak of the New Testament (singular), because his proofs make this clear: for he proves from it that the Mass is the testament which Christ pronounced: "This chalice is the New Testament in my blood." After this he adds, "Christ is truly truthful therefore in calling this the New Testament in his blood." For which reason neither can Luther speak here of anything but the New Testament. Furthermore, as he is of a rather crafty and clever character, he introduces a certain definition of "testament" which he tries to accommodate to the Mass. Now of what sort this is, let us first listen: "A testament is without a doubt the promise of one who is about to die, by which he names his inheritance and establishes his heirs." Now we do not dispute this definition of a testament, rather we will teach that it belongs to the new law and that it fits most appropriately with what is called the New Testament by Paul, because in it Christ, who was about to die for sinners and was about to shed his blood to confirm the testament, promised his inheritance, that is, the kingdom of heaven. But he instituted as his heirs the poor in spirit, the meek, those who mourn, the justice-seekers, the merciful, the pure of heart, the peaceful, and finally those who would suffer persecution for the sake of righteousness. He says, "Blessed are the poor in spirit, for theirs is the kingdom of heaven, etc." Now this definition here of the saying meshes quite well with the new law since each one of its members fits. Now, that Luther would attempt to fit this to the Mass is so unbecoming as one who would drag the unwilling by the hair. The good reader will easily perceive this if you consider all Luther's words by which he tries to adapt his definition to the Mass.

He speaks thus, "He therefore wraps up as a testament first the death of the testament-maker, then the promise of the inheritance and the naming of the inheritance."

Note, dear reader, in what a wrapped up way he delivers his own words. He says that the testament wraps up into itself first the death of the testament-maker. Of course a testament requires the death of the maker for it to be fully established, and Paul stipulates as much when he says, "A testament is confirmed in the dead" (Heb. 9). Further, whatever is confirmed by death must necessarily be something other than the death itself, and death itself must precede that thing. For this reason, the testament does not so involve the death of the testament-maker as a thing clearly connected, but as the confirmation of those connected things. Luther, however, contends that Christ's death was not thus involved as the thing connected because he adds, "In these words we clearly see that Christ is making his death the testament when he says 'this is my body which will be given up...this is my blood which shall be shed'."

Here, dear reader, this Luther is having Christ make a testament of his death, not however to be confirming the testament by his death, which is clearly against Paul, who proclaims that Christ corroborated his testament by his death, and neither do the chapters which he cites from Paul provide any sort of help, since Paul clearly says in Chapter 9 of Hebrews that he is differentiating the Old Testament from the New when he says that Christ is the mediator of the New Testament: that by means of his death for the redemption of those transgressions which were under the former testament, they that are called may receive the promise of eternal inheritance. Now, dear reader, Paul is explaining most clearly by these words that a certain prior testament had gone before, that is to say the old law, which was the occasion of many transgressions, after which there followed another and new one, of course the new law, whose mediator was Christ, who by his death so established it that it would fully abolish all those transgressions. By this New Testament, the kingdom of heaven was promised as an eternal inheritance, but the heirs were set up to be those who were called.

So you now see, dear reader, the difference between the Old and New Testament. You see, too, that the death of Christ is not the testament itself, but rather the ratification of the testament. You see likewise who the heirs are, that is those who are called, and you see finally what the inheritance is: not of course the remission of sins which were dissolved through Christ's death, but rather eternal beatitude in heaven, to which none will rise except those who sins have been forgiven. Furthermore, there's none who misses that the death is different from the testament, and Paul teaches this most clearly in the same spot where he says that for there to be a testament, the death of the testament-maker must precede because the testament is ratified once such a one has died, since it is not valid as long as the maker lives. Who misses here that the testament goes before the death of the one who makes it, although without his death it would be in nowise valid, because he explicitly says that it is not yet valid while the testament-maker lives. By those same words there is the clear conviction that the sacraments of the body and blood of Christ were not the New Testament since they would have been invalid as long as the testament-maker was not yet dead. Therefore, it is very clear from these things that Luther associated these things in an inappropriate way when he afterward added, "You see therefore that the Mass, as we call it, is the promise of the remission of sins, which promise was made by God and is confirmed through the death of God's son."

At this point, unless Luther thinks that everyone who reads these things is completely blind, I'm surprised that he was not ashamed at some point to blab such a gathering of things, since nothing was first proven, from which he might proffer such a collected mass. He is completely insane if he thinks that he can stuff men full of such ridiculous things. This fits right along with what we find in the Gospels, wherein we are promised the remission of sins and the heavenly kingdom — but not for the Mass — because the promised remission of sins was not on its account but on account of the shedding of blood, as we have already said and as we will say again more clearly.

Therefore, if anyone should wish to define — properly and according to the Scriptures — this New Testament, he would rightly say that it is the new law from Christ and signed in his blood, and those who profess it are set up as the inheritors of the kingdom of heaven. Here you have a definition that is fully integrated with all its causes: the material, when we say "law"; the formal, when we add "new"; the efficient, when we subjoin, "from Christ"; the instrumental, when we add "signed in his blood"; and finally the final cause, when we write, "those who profess it are set up as the inheritors of the Kingdom of Heaven." Furthermore, we will confirm each part of this definition abundantly with scriptural citations.

THE MASS IS NOT A TESTAMENT

First of all that the New Testament is the new law, Paul demonstrates not only by those things which we have brought forth above from the letter to the Hebrews, Chapter 9, but even more clearly from Chapter 8, where he teaches that Christ received a more excellent priesthood than the priests of the Old Testament, and that he was there for the mediator of a better testament, that is to say the one which — as he cites — Jeremiah had predicted: "Behold the days are coming, says the Lord, and I will consummate a New Testament upon the house of Israel and upon the house of Judah, not according to the testament that I made with their fathers and that day when I took them by the hand and led them out of Egypt, because they did not remain in my testament, and I forsook them, says the Lord" (ch. 31). Paul cites that prophecy there and then continues to teach what the New Testament is from that same prophet: "For this is the testament that I shall make with the house of Israel after those days, says the Lord God, as I give my laws into their mind and inscribe them in their heart."

Now here you already have, dear reader, what the New Testament is, that is to say, the new laws written in human hearts. Christ himself laid and promulgated these laws, not writing them by pen and paper, but in the hearts of the hearers. In addition, he ratified them by his own blood, as Paul clearly asserts just a little after in the 9th chapter, where he also teaches that this new covenant is ratified by the precious blood of Christ, just as that old testament was confirmed beforehand by the blood of cattle: "When Moses had explained every precept to the people according to the law, he took the blood of cattle and goats, together with water, crimson wool, and hyssop, as well as the book itself and he sprinkled the entire people, saying: this is the blood of the covenant which God has mandated for you." That is what Paul says.

Note here, dear reader, how Moses used similar words to confirm the Old Testament, to those which the evangelists refer to as Christ's, in the confirmation of the New. Moses speaks thus: "This is the blood of the covenant which God has mandated for you." That is what Moses said for the Old Testament. Matthew and Mark, however, have Christ saying similar words when he offered the cup of his blood to his disciples at Supper. Mark writes in this way: "This is my blood of the New Testament, which will be shed for many for the remission of sins." First, the blood of cows and goats was shed for sin in the old law, before the confirmation of the Old Testament, but that blood was quite impotent not only for wiping away sin, but also for establishing the perfection of that covenant. You see, it was powerless to cancel sin, just as even Paul attests when he says, "The blood of cows and goats could not take away sins." The blood of Christ, however, (by which the new covenant was ratified) was shed unto the remission of sins, just as truly it granted that remission. Who doesn't notice here how each corresponds to every other completely — I mean to say Moses to Christ, the cup to the chalice, blood for blood, testament to testament. For just as Moses, once he had taken the cup in which there was the blood of cattle, set forth to establish the old covenant with it, so, too, Christ, having taken the chalice in which his very own blood was contained, completely confirmed by that same chalice the new covenant.

Therefore the blood is not the new covenant since the new covenant is confirmed by the blood, because who doesn't perceive that these must be two distinct things, to wit, that which is confirmed and that instrument by which something is confirmed? It's for that reason that the chalice of Christ's blood is that by which the New testament is confirmed, just as Paul gave us manner to show here, because as that old covenant had been confirmed by the blood of cattle, so likewise was the new by the blood of Christ, and since this is the way things are, Luther is clearly betraying his own ignorance, he who would call either Christ's blood or the chalice of his blood the new covenant. Therefore, the blood is not the new covenant, although the new covenant is most firmly confirmed by that blood. All the Fathers agree with that opinion, whosoever are considered to be orthodox.

This, too, should be noted that as Moses spoke, that is, "This is the blood of the covenant," we must supply some word that signifies its ratification, so that we might say, "This is the confirming blood for the blood that establishes this covenant which God has mandated to you." So, too, must Christ's speech be supplied; that is, we understand Christ to have said, "This is my blood [confirmation] of the New Testament." So it is extremely clear that neither Christ's blood can be called the New Testament just as the blood of bulls and goats was not said to be the old testament.

Add to this as well that it's quite clear from Luke's words, wherein Christ did not say: "This my blood is the New Testament," but rather, "this cup is the New Testament in my blood," in other words, "through my blood" as Matthew rendered it. The blood then, is not the New Testament and the chalice or cup can much less be said to merit such a title. Who would be so crazy as to think that the cup or wine-bowl which Moses held in his hand, full of blood, was itself the old covenant? Now, if neither the cup nor the blood in the cup is the New Testament, then it is clear that this phrase suffers from an ellipsis and is missing a word that would express its full sense — the sense which hitherto all Fathers have attributed to the words of Paul and Luke. Nor can one find before Luther anyone who dared interpret the blood or the chalice to be the testament. Christ in this place therefore makes mention of the New Testament insofar as that is what would be ratified by Christ's blood, and not because the Mass was a testament, such as Luther noxiously invented. You see, Luther arrogated to himself the freedom — nay the license — of interpreting Scriptures of any sort according to his own brain's dreams, and with insane reasoning. Just as above with Christ's words, when Luther said, "this is my body," the "this" is to be interpreted as "this bread." But now he says that the chalice, that is the Mass, is the New Testament. But neither is the chalice the Mass nor is either one of these the New Testament, which is abundantly clear to all who are far from ignorant of what the new covenant is.

In this regard, when Christ had spoken of his body, he made no mention at all of the testament — be it New or Old — but who doubts that the body as well as the blood nevertheless is part of the Mass? It is abundantly clear that he did this because the outpouring of blood is an indication of death. And since Paul says, therefore, that the testament is ratified in death, and the full pouring out of blood is no poor symbol of death, then it was fitting that the testament be established by blood. Because if Christ had willed by his words here to have the Mass understood as the New Testament, then he would have made mention not just of the testament when he spoke of his body, rather than just of his blood, since the Mass proper is equally a sacrament of his body and blood. So it is patent from these things that the New Testament is the new law given by Christ and that it was sealed by his blood.

Now, as regards that final part, to wit, that those who profess this are established as the heirs of the Heavenly Kingdom, it is so clear from the Scriptures that it was for this end that the other holy things were given, that is that men would observe this law, so that they might obtain the heavenly kingdom as an inheritance; such that it's completely unnecessary to add any further proofs towards this end. Therefore, it is manifest that this definition which we gave is that of the New Testament, and if Luther should contend that there's another use of this phrase in Luke's Gospel than there is in the other evangelists, I don't think he will persuade anyone of that; because although the words by which the evangelists narrate the Lord's Supper are distinct, we must confess that their sense nevertheless is necessarily in complete agreement, on which account the phrase "testament" does not signify something else in Luke than what it does in Matthew and Mark.

So because in all of these, as we have shown above, the New Testament is nothing besides the new law, it results that this word in Luke could signify nothing else but the new law, for which reason Luther's whole edifice comes crumbling completely down, as he had sought to establish it on that foundation. What manner then should we label Luther, or worthy of what epithet, since he attempted to dress up such a false foundation with citations from the Gospel? Will we call him a true prophet, he who created such a great and ghastly lie from Christ's words? Or a good shepherd of the Christian flock him who perniciously seduced so many souls? Or the corrector of the Sacred Books him who did not fear to corrupt the Gospel? What sort of subterfuge could there still be left for you, Luther? Which flip flop? By what arts or maneuvers will you fly now? Or did you not write these things: "Let this stand first of all — infallibly — that the Mass or the sacrament of the altar is Christ's testament?" And you try to prove this from the words which Christ spoke: "This chalice is the New Testament in my blood." You then double-down: "I say let this truth stand as an immovable foundation."

But now you see, Luther, I think, that these words of Christ in no way help your proposal because neither did he want the Mass to be understood by "new testament," but rather the new law, that is the Evangelical Law, which simultaneously contains precepts and promises as well as all of the sacraments. Oh, Germany, long ago noble, who could not be sullied hitherto by any Bohemian heresies, how long will you suffer this Lutheran pestilence to grow fat in your loins? And ye Lutherans, men who are otherwise both so learned and lofty, except that you glory in such a destructive teacher, may it bring you shame finally that you have been shamefully deluded up to this point. Just as he has at once horribly and harmfully fallen, none can doubt that he was thus able to fall even in the other things in which he contradicts the Catholic Church.

Although he has ruinously and repulsively fallen, he yet fails to blush when he insults the most illustrious king, saying that he had left the matter at hand untouched. He says, "He promises to leave intact that which ought to have been for him at the top of the list of those things to be refuted, what is my greatest strength and principal argument, wherein I prove from the words of Christ that the Mass is a testament and promise, and that therefore it cannot be called a work or sacrifice." Thus far are Luther's words.

But the king nowhere said that he would leave it intact, although he did say that he did not wish to contend upon many points on that subject, for he briefly and in few words indicated by which reasoning that error could be refuted and especially from the fact that the New Testament should be some promise made through the law of the gospel, just as the Old [Testament] was through the Mosaic law, because as in the Mosaic law earthly things were promised, so in the Evangelical law are heavenly things promised.

So since the New Testament is one, as we have taught above, it is clear that the Mass cannot be called the New Testament. Furthermore, the king himself showed convincingly that the remission of sins — which Luther said was named thus for the inheritance — was not the same thing as the kingdom of heaven, since it was rather the way to the kingdom and a certain aid upon the way, by which we might shortly after attain the inheritance itself, so long as we persevere in very purity. Nor does every single person who once attained the forgiveness of sins reach the heavenly inheritance, just as no one would rightly call "the endpoint" "the path," or "the means to an end" "the very end itself," so, too, the heavenly inheritance cannot be called the remission of sins. In these few words his Regal Highness clearly took down the Lutheran foundation upon which Luther sought to claim the Mass to be the New Testament. For this reason, since Luther called his primary strength and most important argument this very point, who does not clearly see upon what sort of fallen foundation he rests?

At this point, I know that he will seek many different allies in order to slither away, and this is why he is so variable in all places, more changeable than Proteus! You see, sometimes he calls the Mass the "sacrament of the altar"; at other times the "testament" or "covenant," at still other times "Christ's testament commended by or with the addition of the sign of the sacrament of his body and blood,"[10] and most often a "promise" — and nothing but a promise. He doubtless does this to such an extent so that whenever he is pressed more forcefully on any one of these single statements, he can quickly flee to another, and for this reason it will be necessary to refute his claims one by one.

To begin with, the following two statements do not fit with each other at all: "The Mass is the sacrament of the altar" and "it is nothing but a promise," because it is completely clear that the sacrament of the altar is something other than a promise, since the sacrament of the altar is nowhere if not under the species of bread and wine, and if these things did not exist in any locale, Christ's promise would still be present. Furthermore, the promise remains established even before the consecration of the bread and wine, but before that consecration itself, no one would be so foolish as to call it "the Mass." Therefore, the Mass is not a mere promise. On this matter, if after the consecration the sacrament of the body is reserved in a pyx or ciborium, as happens in many churches, the sacrament of the altar remains still; the promise itself even remains, but no one is so crazy that he would say that the Mass endures as long as the sacrament is reserved in a ciborium, or as long as the promise of Christ endures. For this reason, neither the sacrament of the altar nor the mere promise can be said to be "the Mass";

---

10 In Luther's English works, this is most often rendered: "promise with the sign added of bread and wine." —Editor.

but neither on this account is the Mass a "promise commended by the sacrament of Christ's body and blood," because the promise remains committed to the sacrament as long as the sacrament is preserved; for both the sacrament and the promise remain, yet no one will dare to say that the Mass will last just as long. Thus, the Mass is not a promise that is commended by the sacrament of the body and blood of Christ, because for Luther a testament is some sort of promise, but the Mass is not a promise.

If it were a promise, I should wish for him to consistently respond: a promise of what precisely? I ask this because he is so marvelously mutable on this point, since he sometimes writes that the Mass is the promise of Christ's death, whereas at other times the Mass is the promise of the remission of sins. Yet, he tries to establish this based on Christ's words, "this is my body which will be delivered for you" and "this is my blood which shall be shed for you." Luther claims "by these words, Christ testifies of his death." Since the one who testifies also promises it, by Luther's logic, then the promise of Christ's death should be the Mass. But this cannot stand as such, because the very death of Christ has passed: "Christ dies no more," says Paul, "death no longer has a hold over him." A promise, however, is of a future thing — not of what has passed — and for this reason, the Mass — which happens now — is not the promise of Christ's death.

Luther, on the other hand, will say that in the Mass, Christ's death is considered again: I, too, confess that if anyone were to say that the Mass is the representation of Christ's death through the sacrament of his body and blood, then he would be speaking correctly, in my judgment. Yet, it does not follow from this that the Mass is the promise of Christ's death; rather, at other times he writes that the Mass is the promise of the remission of sins, since Christ had said, "This is my blood which will be shed for you for the remission of sins." But this conclusion is no more valid than the previous, because if Christ — as Luther phrases it — testifies of his death when he says, "This is my blood which will be shed for you," and that it depends on the adjoined phrase, "for the remission of sins," it is clear that this is due to the shedding of that blood, and not to the drinking of it, that the Mass is a remission of sins.

Therefore, the Mass is not the promise of the remission of

sins, since it is not due to the reception of the body and blood at Mass, but rather to its shedding which happened long ago on the cross that the forgiveness of sins was promised. I think that this suffices to show that we should not believe the Mass to be the New Testament.

CHAPTER VI
The Mass Is Properly Called a Sacrifice and a Work by Those of Right Faith

OW, since it is abundantly clear that the Mass is not a testament, we will now show, as the sixth point, whether the Mass can be called a sacrifice and a work, because Luther pertinaciously and fully denies this, and if anyone could believe this man, he says that he is led to such by an invincible argument: "I have proven from the words of Christ that the Mass is the testament and promise, and that thus it cannot be called a work and a sacrifice." Luther has placed all his hope in this ram, such that he is not afraid to boast that it is his primary strength as well as his principal argument. Yet, I don't think that anyone will be able to miss how poor in principle this argument is, nor how shaky is his primary strength, at least if the person has not been asleep as we have covered his previous statements.

You see, from those arguments it is completely clear that one cannot draw from Christ's words that the Mass is a testament, because Christ nowhere called the Mass a testament. Nor has Luther shown from any words of Christ that such a thing is taught at all, therefore it is false to say that he has proved from Christ's words that the Mass is a testament and a promise. On this account, since we have completely overturned this foundational point, it is only fitting that we have no doubts that the rest of his structure will fall completely apart, so that there will be nothing left to pursue on the matter, given that Luther's sole confidence will have been completely cast aside. I think that all will see that his claim has not a bit of solid truth to it. From that point, no one will be able to rightfully demand anything more of us on the matter, since Luther's foundation will have been sufficiently and patently destroyed. On the other hand, we are not even forced to establish by argumentation against a heretic those things which the Church's common custom has approved for so many centuries; rather, it is incumbent upon the heretic to establish such valid reasons for his position — and publicly — that no one at all could overcome them, or otherwise instantly to submit to the orthodox believers.

So, it is more than enough for us to have taught that, from the beginning of the early Church, the Mass was received as a sacrifice, and that by the most ancient and surely saintly as well as most famous Fathers, it was held to be the Church's supreme sacrifice. I am convinced that we will amply demonstrate this, although we will not do this alone, but we will also show that the same belief is ably sustained by the Scriptures and most agreeable to right reason. To be sure, if nothing else stood on our side but long-standing tradition — and that from the very birth of the Church — it should suffice, since it is hardly likely that the Holy Spirit, who is given as the Church's perpetual teacher and guide, should have suffered the entire Church to err in such a serious matter and with such a serious risk for all souls.

What kind of strength does such an ancient tradition hold? That can be ascertained not only from those things which we have argued against Luther's articles, but also from that most ancient author Tertullian, who collected many such things in his book *De Corona Militis*, or On the Soldier's Garland/Chaplet: these were things that were held not from any scriptural reference, rather they had their strength from custom, and he affirms that this custom had come from apostolic tradition. But let us now demonstrate that the Mass was held to be a sacrifice from the earliest times of the Church.

Clement, who was a disciple and successor of Peter, in his letter to all orthodox believers, wrote thus: "It is not licit to sacrifice and celebrate masses in other places except in those which one's own bishop has commanded."[11] See here how Clement mentions the Mass and sacrifice, as well as in another letter to James: "We command

---

11 This is a mix of Ch. 41-42 of 1st Clement. —Editor.

that never should someone outside the Church or a layman be put over the fragments of the oblations at the mensa" (*Recognitions*). Here, too, Clement speaks of the sacrament as an oblation.

Paul's disciple, Dionysius, likewise says in Chapter 3 of *On the Ecclesiastical Hierarchy:* "We must, then, in my opinion, pass within the All Holy Mysteries, after we have laid bare the understanding of the first and principal offering, to behold its Godlike beauty, and view the hierarch augustly going with a sweet odor from the divine altar to the furthermost bounds of the holy place, and again returning to it to complete the sacrifice." For him, too, as you can see, the Mass is a sacrifice.

Ignatius as well, who was a contemporary of the Apostles, said in his letter to the Smyrnians: "Let that be deemed a proper Eucharist, which is allowed by the bishop. Wherever the bishop is, there let the people be gathered; just as wherever Jesus Christ is, there is the whole heavenly army present, as a military of the Lord's power is at attention to their ruler. And he himself is the dispenser of all intelligible nature. For this reason, it is not permissible to offer without the bishop, in order to emulate the sacrifice, nor to celebrate masses." He, too, understands that the Mass is a sacrifice.

Origen follows them, as one of the earliest ecclesiastical writers, in his commentary on Job: "Job demonstrates for all of us this form of piety and devotion: he arose in the morning and washed his sons clean by offering for them the host, according to the number of his sons. He first washed them, purified, sanctified, and then finally offered the host for them, so that he might show to all in perpetuity that sacrifices established and fit those who were already clean and chaste, as themselves sacrifices that were worthily emulated and in a holy manner, holy and worthy to be received by the holy. This is why the Apostle speaks in this manner: 'Let a man prove himself,' that is, let him clean himself and thus enjoy the most holy sacrifices of the Lord." This is how Origen treated the sacrificial sacrament of the body and blood of the Lord.

Chrysostom signs on in accord, as he said in his 17th *Homily on Hebrews:* "What then? Do we not offer every day? We offer indeed, but making a remembrance of his death, and this [remembrance] is one and not many. How is it one, and not many? Inasmuch as that sacrifice was once for all offered, [and] carried into the Holy of

Holies. This is a figure of that sacrifice and this remembrance of that. For we always offer the same, not one sheep now and tomorrow another, but always the same thing: so that the sacrifice is one. And yet by this reasoning, since the offering is made in many places, are there many Christs? But Christ is one everywhere, being complete here and complete there also, one body. As then while offered in many places, he is one body and not many bodies; so also he is one sacrifice. He is our high priest, who offered the sacrifice that cleanses us. That which we offer now, which was then offered, which cannot be exhausted. This is done in remembrance of what was then done. For he says, do this in remembrance of me (Luke 22:19). It is not another sacrifice, as the high priest, but we always offer the same, or rather we perform a remembrance of a sacrifice."

John Damascene agrees with these in Book 4 of his *On the Orthodox Faith*: "This surely is that pure and bloodless sacrifice which the Lord said, through the prophet, is offered to him from the rising to the setting of the sun (Malachi 1:11), that is, the body and blood of Christ are for the support of our soul and body."

Even the Sixth Ecumenical Council, of such great authority, testifies to what Basil had said about the celebration of Mass. This will suffice for the Greeks.

From the Latins, though, there is Tertullian, who was so close to the Apostles' times; in his book *On Women's Decorum and Dress*, he mentions this sacrifice. He says that there should be no cause for the woman to go out unless the cause were serious and necessary; he then gives three reasons: when some one of the brethren is ill, when the word of God is being preached to the people, or when the sacrifice is being offered to God in the temple. You see here that Tertullian notes that the sacrifice was offered in the temple, which sacrifice — for the Christians — could be none other than the sacrifice of the Mass.

Cyprian follows and imitates Tertullian in this when he writes to Caecilius: "In this part, we find that the chalice which the Lord offered was mixed, and that wine was there but was then called his blood; whence it is clear that the blood of Christ cannot be offered unless wine is in the chalice, nor can one have a legitimate celebration of the Lord's sacrifice unless the oblation and our sacrifice correspond to his Passion." You see that he clearly calls it a sacrifice. You can add Jerome to these, as he says in his letter to Hedibias: "The Lord Jesus himself is a diner and the dinner: he both eats and is eaten; we drink his blood and without him we cannot drink, and daily in his sacrifices, we express the red wine from the fruit of the true vine." Jerome is here clearly understanding the Mass by the word "sacrifices." Ambrose, likewise in his book on the sacraments, considers the words from the Canon, whereby he plainly confesses that the ancients considered the Mass a sacrifice: "The priest says: 'recalling, therefore, his most glorious passion, his resurrection from the dead and ascension into heaven, we offer to you this immaculate host, this reasonable host, and the chalice of eternal life, and we beseech and pray thee, that thou mayest receive this the oblation upon the sublime altar, through the hands of thine angels, just as thou deigned to receive the gifts of thy just servant, Able, and the sacrifice of our patriarch Abraham, which the great high priest Melchizedek offered to thee'." This was what Ambrose recalled from the Canon.

Finally, in book 17 of On the City of God, Augustine writes this: "But to be made partakers of this table is itself to begin to have life, because when he says in another book — which is called Ecclesiastes – 'There is no good for a man, except that he should eat and drink,' what should one believe him to mean, other than what belongs to the participation of this table which the mediator of the New Testament himself, the priest according to the order of Melchizedek, furnishes with his own body and blood? For that sacrifice has succeeded all the sacrifices of the Old Testament, which were immolated as a foreshadowing of that which was to come." This is how Augustine speaks.

Therefore, my dear reader, you see both from the Greek authors as well as from the Latins how the ancients all gave their assent to this belief, and what can Luther do when confronted with this, besides denying to them the faith, dissuading belief in them? Nothing at all. Nor on this matter, did they have any ambition, avarice, or the least suspicion of ill-will: no one can incriminate them in the least in these matters, because they were all noted for their learning and holiness of life, but they also all pronounced on this matter in unanimous consent. Who could have inspired such consent among sinners other than the Spirit of unity and harmony?

So, why should we not have much greater trust in so many Fathers, who were so ancient, so holy, so erudite, and asserted the same thing in one accord; compared to one Luther who, that I might omit so much else, was practically born yesterday, arrogantly disagrees with all of these men, has his foundation on no solid reason and on no Scripture — except such as is erroneously twisted by his own mind — and who yet relies on his own spirit alone? In Chapter 13 of the Prophet Ezekiel, we read the warning against such men: "Woe to the prophets who follow their own spirit." If Luther is not following his own spirit, no one ever has, since Luther does not hesitate to ignore even the most learned, most approved, and most received of the Fathers if they disagree with him; what is more, he at the same time rejects and ridicules all of them. But what led him to such mindless behavior if not that spirit of dissension and discord? You see, just as the Divine Spirit himself inspired those holy Fathers in their concord, there is likewise no doubt that the spirit of the devil — who is ever the author of dissent — inspired Luther to inflict this tragedy upon the Church.

Now, if what we have hitherto produced might seem insufficient for some, who should still desire some citations from the Apostles themselves, that could seem unjust, since it is completely believable that something which the Apostles had written on this manner might have perished throughout the ages; nevertheless, from their Acts — which have been reserved for us through the diligence of the great churchmen who precede us — what we seek is still abundantly clear. You see, in the *Acts of Andrew*, he is said to have responded thus to Egeas: "I sacrifice every day to the one, true, and omnipotent God — not by the smoke of incense, nor in the flesh of mooing cows, nor by the blood of many goats, but daily I sacrificed the Immaculate Lamb upon the altar of the cross, whose flesh the entire believing people thereafter consumes, as well as drinking that blood of the Lamb who was sacrificed and yet remains whole and alive." In the *Life of Matthew*, too, we read: "When Mass had been celebrated by the Apostle, each one went back to his own home, but the Apostle remained by the altar." The Sixth Council states that James, the Lord's brother, passed on a proper mode for celebrating the Mass. It is also common opinion that Peter celebrated the first Mass at Antioch.

The Mass Is a Sacrifice

However one might regard such, the matter is quite clear in the Acts of the Pontiffs, because in the decrees of Anacletus, who succeeded Clement, the second Canon has this: "The Bishop stands before God to sacrifice and he should have witnesses with him, more than another priest does, just as he enjoys a more honorable dignity in orders, so likewise he wants a more abundant witness. On greater solemnities, either seven, four, or three deacons — who are called his "eyes" — as well as subdeacons, and the other ministers should attend him on all sides when he is sacrificing, and priests should be at his right and left, with humble heart and contrite spirit, keeping custody of his eyes from malevolent men, and offering their harmonious accord to his sacrifice; at the close of the consecration, however, may all who wish to retain the Church's threshold commune. This is how the Apostles established it, and how the Holy Roman Church preserves it." Here you have the bishop sacrificing to God and calling the Mass a sacrifice.

So, too, Alexander, who followed Anacletus by one, thus writes in his decretal: "Truth itself instructed us to offer the chalice and bread in the sacrament when it says, 'Jesus took bread, blessed and gave it to his disciples saying, "take ye and drink from it, all of you, because this is the chalice of my blood which shall be shed for you unto the remission of sins".' Sins and faults are forgiven completely by the sacrifices that are offered to the Lord, and on this account his Passion is commemorated, by which we have been redeemed and which we so often recall, whenever we offer to the Lord. The Lord will be pleased and placated with such hosts, and he will remit great sins, for there can be nothing greater among sacrifices than the body and blood of Christ; nor is there any more potent oblation: this exceeds all: a pure conscience is to be offered to the Lord, and he is to be received with a pure mind." That is Alexander I.

We could call to mind so many other pontiffs whose decrees call the Mass a sacrifice, but we have decided to use those who were from the very beginning and so close in time to the Apostles. The first councils also agree with this truth, but we think that one should suffice, that is Nicaea, wherein there were 318 bishops. Here are the words of the Council: "It has come to the attention of this holy and great synod that in some places and cities deacons give the gift of Holy Communion to presbyters, although neither canon nor custom allows this, namely that those who have no authority to offer should give the body of Christ to those who do offer." Here this Council, which has always been of the greatest authority for orthodox believers, affirms that priests rightly offer the sacred Eucharist, which power it openly denies to deacons. I ask: what sort of oblation do priests offer other than the Mass? What good would be the signatures of so many bishops, or why would they give their faith to such a thing otherwise: therefore, the Mass — from the beginning of the nascent Church — has always been seen as a sacrifice, and it has seemed such to all the Fathers in all places and times.

Now let us show that it suits Scripture as well, that the Mass should be called a work and a sacrifice, and although Scripture should speak little about the matter, it nevertheless becomes clear from its few statements such as will abundantly suffice to clarify the matter.

Luther thus denies that the Mass is called a work and a sacrifice because it should be some promise, with the addition of the sign of bread and wine, both of which are given to us, that is: the word of promise and the sign in the bread and wine; for this reason, as Luther would have it, the use of each cannot be in offering or working, but only in receiving and in letting it be. But we will succinctly show from the Scriptures themselves that this is plainly false.

First of all, it is clear from Paul's words in 1 Corinthians 11 that not only is the Mass given to us, contrary to what Luther asserts, but something also occurs by our service, since Paul says: "As often as you eat this bread and drink this chalice you announce the Lord's death, until he comes." Note what he says, "you announce the Lord's death, until he comes," Paul did not mean for this to be understood of the reception by one person, but rather about those things that happen in a public gathering, because he had prefaced those words with these: "when you come together in one place." Therefore, it is in a public place where these most holy Mysteries are handled, and bread and wine are consecrated into the body and blood of Christ, and at that moment the Lord's death and sacrifice on the cross are represented and announced. For this reason, this sacrifice is given to us, but also because, manifestly, by this very sacrament Christ's death and sacrifice — the same which he offered on the cross to God the Father — is represented by us. What else is the representation of the sacrifice of the cross but the announcement of the Lord's death? It was in regard to this sacrifice that Paul said in Ephesians 5: "He delivered himself for us, an oblation and a sacrifice to God for an odor of sweetness." Of course he willed to represent to us, through this sacrament, this same oblation and very victim, so that just as he immolated himself to the Father upon the cross for us, so we likewise might perpetually immolate his body and blood in the sacrament. Therefore, this sacrament's utility consists not only in its bearing and reception, but also in its annunciation and representation of Christ's death and of the sacrifice on the cross. Additionally, if the Mass is nothing other than a promise, and it meanwhile includes no other work, then Paul in vain would have cried, "do this" in 1 Cor. 11. Christ, too, added just after the consecration of the bread, "Do this in memory of me," and once again after the consecration of the chalice, "Do this, as often as you drink, in memory of me." The evangelist Luke, at least, included "Do this in memory of me" after both: after the consecration of the bread and of the wine. What does this, "do this," inculcate, so often said — and said by Paul and Christ, if the Mass is only a promise and involves no other work? Can any other phrase suggest "operation" and "work" as much as "do this"? None at all. Therefore, since there is no Mass except that Christ has commanded that it be done, the priest has fulfilled this command in deed, by the working of it, as is clear and as could only be denied by the most senseless person: the substance of the Mass demands some work of ours. For it is so certain, that had no one consecrated after Christ, no one would have done what Christ did after Supper, clearly, since there would be no Mass or missive. Given that our work is patently demanded in the makeup of the Mass itself, it is clear that the Mass is not solely a promise. Therefore, it is evident from Paul's and Christ's words that the Mass cannot happen without our work or operation, since a promise would remain firm even without our cooperation, but the Mass cannot exist if we do not "do" it with Christ.

In addition, since Paul says, "Christ our Pasch is immolated," in 1 Cor. 5, is this not a clear distinction between our new and the old Passover, that is, that he differentiates the Christians' Pasch from that of the Jews? He is clearly teaching here that the Jewish Passover is related to the Christian Pasch just as a figure is related to the reality, and the body to its shadow. Wherefore, as their Passover was the Law's sacrifice of the lamb, so ours — the Christian Passover — is the sacrifice of the true Lamb, and all though this true Lamb was immolated for us upon the cross, yet it was not consumed upon the cross but only upon the altar. Likewise, this very true Lamb, Jesus Christ himself, who suffered on the cross, is also our Pasch upon the altar. There are not two Paschs or two sacrifices, but one Passover and one sacrifice, since one is representative of the other; for, the true and one and the same Lamb that is Jesus Christ is in both, he who was once immolated upon the cross by death, so now is he daily offered up, that is, as the memorial of Christ's death is renewed by us daily.

But when Paul speaks of the table of the Lord as well as the table of demons, it is quite evident that he is insinuating the same thing, as he writes in 1 Cor. 10: "Behold Israel according to the flesh. Are not they that eat of the sacrifices not partakers of the altar? What then? Do I say that what is offered in sacrifice to idols is anything? Or that the idol is anything? But the things which the heathens sacrifice, they sacrifice to devils and not to God. And I would not that you should be made partakers with devils. You cannot drink the chalice of the Lord and the chalice of devils: you cannot be partakers of the table of the Lord and of the table of devils." Paul's reasoning is there for this just as they who were of the old law did eat the emulated victims and were made partakers of the altar and entered a certain communion with him to whom those victims had been sacrificed, so, too wherever any such victims are offered to someone — be it to God or to demons. You see, as a pun the table of demons are their oblations to the demons, and whoever eats of them has a communion with the demons, so, too with what is offered to the Lord upon the Lord's mensa, and those who eat therefrom enter a communion with the Lord. For this reason, be very careful lest you taste anything of that which is offered to demons, because I would not have you be consorting with demons, since certainly if you were doing that, you would lack communion with the Lord, since you cannot simultaneously be partakers of the Lord's table as well as of the table of demons. Did Paul not clearly teach this, when he said that they become partakers of the demons from that table of demons, upon which there is an offering to demons, and they enter a communion with them; so, too, with those who commune with the victims offered on God's table, do they not enter into a communion with God?

If anyone should deny this meaning of the Pauline argument, then such a man clearly does not see what Paul is trying to accomplish with his argument, because Paul is trying to accomplish with words what we are all doing at the Lord's table when we take the Eucharist, as we commune both of his body and blood. You see, he had recently admonished the Corinthians, as much as they were fleeing a culture of idolatry, and he gives the reason just after this: because we communicate with Christ through the offering of his body and blood, which we eat at that table. And by what reasoning does he show this? Since he says as the victim which the carnal Jews offered made them participants of the altar, so, too, with the victim that is offered on the Lord's altar or on that of demons: it makes one in communion with one or the others. It is therefore clear from Paul that the Lord's body and blood is the victim and sacrifice that is offered upon the Lord's table.

To this may be added that in the Scriptures, for the most part, mention of the new priesthood has to do with the order of Melchizedek, and that Christ was a priest of this order is often asserted, which — if true — would make it necessary that Christ at some time sacrificed with bread and wine, just as Melchizedek, too, is reported to have done. Yet, we never read of Christ having done this besides at the Supper, when under the appearances of bread and wine, he instituted the sacraments of his body and blood. On this account, he truly sacrificed at the Supper, and he offered to the Father a true sacrifice. And because he commanded to the Apostles that they should perpetually do likewise thereafter, he also willed for them to sacrifice according to that ritual — and not that they alone should, but we believe that he wanted their successors to offer this sacrifice as well, as long as the Church should endure, since the Church has need of such a sacrifice just as much in our day as in the Apostles' times; and for this reason, it is clear that this very sacrifice exists now too.

Beyond this, in his letter to the Hebrews, because Paul says that the old Aaronic priesthood is now completely in the past, it is necessary to have successors of the Apostles who are priests of the new law, which might then have a sacrifice that corresponds to the order of Melchizedek, which order God the Father confirmed by an oath to be eternal. Yet, there's clearly nothing like this found in the Church — besides the august and adorable sacrifice of Christ's body and blood — which is continually offered by the hands of the priests and all the churches to almighty God. To be sure, it is abundantly clear that it is not only that oblation which Melchizedek offered, but rather re-presents the very sacrifice that is to be fully adored, which Christ offered upon the altar of the cross for our sins. For this reason, it is manifestly congruent with the Scriptures that the Mass should be called a work and a sacrifice.

Besides, we nowhere read of the law without its priests, or that the priests were ever without a sacrifice, because even in the old law — which is but a shadow of our new law — there were priests and sacrifices which, by their similarity, must correspond with those of the new. For example, Moses was commanded to do all things according to the exemplar which was shown to him upon the mountain, as we read in Ex. 15 and Hebrews 9, and although Christ our high priest entered once for all without blood into the temple that was not built by hands, we yet are inferior priests; it behooves us not to be lazy, but to be at these altars which are in the atrium: we must immolate some host that can satisfy for our sins and for the sins of others. Therefore, since no other can be so called except the host and sacrifice of Christ's body, it is certainly to be gathered that the Mass is for that very reason necessarily and especially to be called a sacrifice. You see, besides the Mass we have nothing which — according to Luther's designs — could be offered, because whatever is ours is too unclean and unworthy to be offered; but, whatever is God's is received by us and given by him to us; and if we are to believe Luther, its use consists in its passive reception, not in its offering and operation. Wherefore, since all things are either ours or God's, there's nothing at all left for us to offer to God. For as it seemed to Luther, we cannot even offer God's gifts; but there is not even any work of ours that we might offer, since whatever is of that sort is unclean and has become dirty, as Luther phrases it. Then, if we attempt to offer our very selves — since we do not lack the effects of sin (which Luther says is truly a sin) — our sacrifice must necessarily be impure; but the sacrifice that pleases God must lack all impurity, and since we have nothing like that amongst us — besides that most very venerable sacrifice of the Mass — it remains to declare that this same Mass is held by Christians to be most powerful in the place of sacrifice.

The corollary is that anyone who would attempt to remove this sacrifice from the Church would be intentionally aiming to inflict no less damage than one who sought to take the sun away from the world. Yet someone will say: for Luther there is no difference between the people and the priests. I confess that Luther does speak this way — but that Scripture does discriminate between the two, because what else was Paul describing in 1 Cor. 3, when he said, "We are God's coworkers, you are God's husbandry, you are God's building?" He calls the priests God's coadjutors, and the people he rather recognizes as the husbandry and building of God. Who would dare assert that there is no difference among these? The people are cultivated by enlivening sacraments after the manner of a field, and they are no less so when it comes to their edification, as the Savior's pattern shows. Although in this work Paul attributes the first place to God, he nevertheless makes himself and his fellow initiates — that is, the priests — to be God's cooperating workers. For this reason, since there are many lesser priests found under Christ the high priest, just as there were, under the high priest, many lesser priests who took care of the people in the old law, it is fitting that there should be a kind of sacrifice that is likewise suited to these new priests, whereby satisfaction would be made to God for their own sins and for the sins of others.

Here is the rationale: although that redemption upon the cross, offered once for all, has an eternal force, its power is nevertheless not applied to each and every sinner except by some means — which even Luther does not deny. For, although Christ died to abolish the sins of all, yet no one enjoys this abolition unless he believes and submits himself to the Church's sacred mysteries. Therefore, this is what it means to be a participant of that ever-valid redemption: to believe and to be initiated properly into the Church's sacraments.

But there must be some ministers of this initiation — whom we call priests — to whom it belongs to offer this sacrifice of the altar, and as often as they do this, they deliver again the very sacrifice of his cross and death.

In addition, sacrifice is nothing other than effecting the sacred,[12] where the sacred things happen, there, too, must be the sacrificing, and since the two are conjoined, it follows that there too must be the sacrifice. Yet, it is clear from the Scriptures that Christ mandated that we should do these same things which he himself had done at Supper. Now, since these things are certainly not profane but rather sacred, so we effect the sacred at his command. On this account and with Christ commanding it, as often as we consecrate the bread and wine, so often do we make the sacred effects, and we sacrifice, yes, we effect the sacrifice. Is there any man who ever heard of a priest doing the sacred things who did not immediately understand this same priest to have just offered the sacrifice of the Mass? It is manifestly suitable, both from the Scriptures as well as from reason, that the Mass should be called a work and a sacrifice.

But just as we had begun to say, Luther contends that the Mass is such a testament and promise that thereby he might make it understood that it is neither a work nor a sacrifice. Now, if Luther had been the first to have found this word "mass," he might have licitly interpreted it according to his good pleasure, and I would not have fought much about what he should wish to be understood by that word — if only he himself would clearly define it. Yet, since it is not just from yesterday or the day before — as they say — but rather from the very beginnings of the Church herself that we find this word to be used, it is completely rash and imprudent to apply another definition to it rather than the meaning and sense that was fitted to it by those who first used it long ago. Therefore, while our forefathers — whosoever spoke of the Mass — used the very word "mass" itself harmoniously to signify a work and sacrifice, it should be most wicked to fit to it another definition that signifies dissent from those Fathers' primary institutions.

---

12 *Facere sacra.* In English, the suffix "-fice" is added to a word to inculcate the sense of "effecting" from the Latin verb. This is important to keep in mind for Fisher's subsequent wordplay in the Latin which is lost in English. —Editor.

THE MASS IS A SACRIFICE

Moreover, it is abundantly clear from the Fathers' traditions themselves that the Mass is not one simple thing, but rather embraces within itself many things, because the Mass includes many sacred words — both those which Christ spoke after Supper, as well as others which were added later by the Apostles and other apostolic men to solemnize the decorum of this sacrifice; it also includes a theoretical reasoning regarding these very words, without which there would be nothing: that is, only through this Mass does the body of Christ come to be from the bread, as well as the blood from wine. For this reason, the exact recitation of these words is absolutely required for the very substance of the Mass. So, these words — when they are spoken by the appropriate minister over the bread and wine — confect the consecration of the body and blood. Wherefore the presence of bread and wine are necessary for this to happen at Mass. It also includes the representation of Christ's death, and through the sacrifice of the Mass there is the annunciation of just what Christ once offered upon the cross for us. It likewise encompasses prayers and the commending of the souls of both the living and the dead, just as one can clearly see from the most ancient traditions of the Fathers. Finally, it includes the mutual incorporation of Christ with us, and of us with Christ, which cannot happen so efficaciously by faith alone, but by the real reception of Christ's body and blood. I say that the Mass embraces all these things, so that it cannot be called one simple thing, but something manifold.

Therefore, it is right to describe the Mass in this way: the Mass is the ceremony or function of the priest, while the Eucharist is confected upon the altar, and which is simultaneously the annunciation of the crucified Christ's sacrifice; because just as the ceremony or religious rite of the Paschal Lamb — which certainly demanded many things — was called the Pasch, which is a "passover," so, too, the ceremony of the Eucharist's confection is called the Mass. Besides this, as regards the etymology, it matters little from what root you think the word "mass" comes — whether from an "emission," or "letting down" [demission], or a promise, or in the end, even a from a "transmission," about which we will speak more later. Meanwhile, it is pertinent to note here that just as the Pasch — although all interpret it as "the passover" — others still give other considerations for this Passover; for example, some would have it be understood of the people who passed over from Egypt to their Promised Land; while others prefer that it be used of the angel which passed over the homes of the Egyptians to strike them; in a similar manner, the word "mass" may have various origins. Why do I know this? In order to show how silly Luther's sophistry is regarding why the Mass could just not be a sacrifice, since he argues thus: "The Mass is a promise, but a sacrifice is a realization; therefore the Mass is not a sacrifice." Yet anyone could argue likewise about the Passover: the Pasch is a passing-over and movement, but not a realization, while the sacrifice of a lamb is a realization; therefore the Passover is not a sacrifice. But whoever would use such sophistry would be hissed out and driven away immediately by all, since the Pasch is openly called a sacrifice in Scripture — and not just once.

Paul, of course, says: "Christ our Pasch is immolated," and when do we eat this sacrifice, I pray ye, if not when we receive the Eucharist? For this reason, the consecration of the Eucharist is truly a sacrifice, since the Eucharist clearly references the sacrifice that took place on the cross long ago. Thus, this is pure sophistry: the Pasch is a Passover and movement, and a sacrifice is a realization; therefore the Pasch is not a sacrifice — and this is the sort of sophist that Luther shows himself to be when he argues in this manner, which he often does. The Mass is a promise, but the sacrifice is a realization, therefore the Mass is not a sacrifice; just as a promise that exists in words cannot be a realization. Yet, no one destroys this sophism more clearly than when anyone compares this new ceremony with the old, and thus also compares the new vocabulary with the old, because many things were required for that older ceremony — not simply the lamb that was to be offered up — but also the azyme breads as well as wild herbs, which were to be eaten with the lamb's meat after it had been roasted. Likewise, the door post of the houses had to be besmeared with the blood of the lamb. What is more, many things were forbidden: that one should not eat something raw or boiled, nor remove the head or feet from the body. But some things were also promised, such as that the Egyptians would be afflicted with plagues, while the eaters of the lamb would remain safe. Who misses how well on each particular point the old ceremony corresponds with the new, in which ceremony we emulate the true Lamb; and how the old was nothing but a shadow of the reality, and a figure of the clearest truth? For this reason, after even Christ had fulfilled that old law of the foreshadowing lamb at Supper, he promptly instituted another and new ceremony, by which he offered himself — the true and Immaculate Lamb. He offered after he had given thanks to the Father, and he forthwith ate the oblation together with his disciples, and he commanded that they should thus do this ceremony in memory of his death, by which his blood was shed for the remission of sins.

So, let Luther go now and blather on that the Mass is a promise, and that it cannot therefore be a sacrifice: we will listen to him no more than we would if he were arguing about the old ceremonies: the Pasch is a Passover and it cannot therefore be a sacrifice, since just as the word "Pasch" is from Passover and thus imposed on the ancient law, the word "mass" is from a mission. There were, of course, those who thought that the Mass was so-called because of an "emission," since the catechumens were "emitted" or sent out when the priest was approaching the consecration of the Sacred Mysteries. Yet others still thought it best named from "demission," since that very living host had been demitted or "sent down" from the Father from heaven; to others it seemed that it came from "transmission," since it is by the priest, who acts as a mediator between God and man, that our prayers and vows, as well as our oblations are transmitted to God. But some judge the Mass to be called what it is due to "remission," because once Mass is ended, the people are remitted or "sent back" their other matters.

Although there are many opinions about the etymology of the word, there is yet no one to be found who would deny that the Mass is a sacrifice, at least until Luther had come along, who — like an author of novelty — didn't see fit to imitate any one of the ancients, and makes the Mass a promise, because in it is promised the remission of sins. We do not deny that in the Mass there is mentioned the promise of the remission of sins, and that this is granted through the Mass, in as much as the Mass is the annunciation of the sacrifice of the cross, in which blood was poured forth for the remission of sins. What would stand in the way of calling the Mass accordingly because of the promised remission of sins? And yet, nothing would keep the Mass itself from being called a sacrifice. However it may be, this at least is doubtlessly clear to all: the Mass was unanimously held by the Fathers and believed to be the greatest sacrifice; yet, Luther arrogantly spurns these men, and on this point the king elegantly and intelligently pierces his acrimonious mendacity: "Luther alone clearly sees that the Mass is not a sacrifice nor an oblation: it is incredible that such a clear matter should have not been more clearly apprehended by so many holy Fathers, by so many eyes which read the same Gospels, and throughout so many centuries; what is more that all should be so blind still as to miss completely what Luther boasts of discerning in it — even while he demonstrates it! But is Luther not rather hallucinating, and seeing something which he does not actually see — and which is nowhere in reality — is nevertheless pointing it out with his finger?" That was the king's elegant and truthful rebuttal, as he clearly taught that one should not trust Luther — as opposed to so many and so holy and so learned Fathers — in this heresy whereby he believes that the Mass is not a sacrifice — unless he could prove this with the clearest of Scriptures, such that no one — not even the most pertinacious — could contradict him.

Thus, you see, dear reader, how great is the consensus that has been handed down from the Fathers, that the Mass is both a work and a sacrifice: from those Fathers, who shone like stars in the Church of God, both on account of their learning as well as their holiness. But also the consistent usage of so many centuries — really from the earliest beginnings of the Church — also proves it, just as its fittingness with Scripture and reason make plain. Yet, what has Luther brought to sustain his heresy beyond mere games and worthless lies, since he has violently twisted for his cause the very Scriptures that treat the Lord's Supper, such that no one misses the injury he causes to Christ's words in his great audacity.

Furthermore, because our dispute is over the word "mass," it would not be off topic to cite here what our friend John Capnion — a man most famous for his work on all literature — has written on the matter: in his introduction to the study of the sacred tongue, for the word מס — mas, he translates "personal office or duty, collect[ion], tribute, etc." and after a bit he adds: "Thence it comes about, from the addition of an 'ה — h', that we have 'מסה — masah', an oblation which is owed a personal duty to one's superior master, as in Deut. 16: the spontaneous oblation from your hand, which you will offer, according to the blessing of thy God — which name we Christians have retained for our sacrifice, just as we call up to this time, "mass", which the Greeks call λιτουργία - litourgia. Thus, note that the word "mass" is neither Greek nor Latin but Hebrew, just as the word "pasch" — which is neither Latin or Greek, but borrowed from Hebrew, and so we have "pascha."

You can here read how the word "mass" is neither Latin nor Greek but rather Hebrew, just as is the word "pascha," and you also are given to understand that the Hebrews also consider the same to be an oblation that is offered to one's superior lord, according to a personal and necessary duty or office. You will also note the passage cited from Deuteronomy whereby the Hebrew word masa, that is "mass," is interpreted as "spontaneous oblation." So, you see that this same word — borrowed from the Hebrew — is used by us Christians for the new sacrifice, that is, for that part of the new law that followed upon the antiquated sacrifices of the Mosaic Law. You finally hear that in Latin we say "mass," for which the Greeks have "liturgy," and clearly many of the ancient Hebrews (just as we established for the priesthood in our book against Luther on that subject) affirm that a messiah was coming and that in his day there would be a sacrifice of bread and wine according to the order of Melchizedek's priesthood. On this account, the same people strongly support our dear Capnion, as well as Scripture, in interpreting the Hebrew masah as "oblation." In my opinion, however, even Malachi taught this quite clearly, because just after he had rebuked the Jewish priests for having offered unclean bread upon the altar, he writes: "You offer polluted bread upon my altar," and shortly thereafter, "I have no pleasure in you, and I will not receive a gift of your hand." You see here that the gift of bread offered by the Jewish priests is what God is despising, but note, too, how he promises that he will receive what is offered by the Gentiles: "From the rising of the sun to its setting, my name is great among the Gentiles and in every place there is a sacrifice and clean oblation offered to my name." So I ask: what is this clean oblation, if not that of the very bread which came down from heaven, that is, the body of Christ, under the appearances of bread, in the Eucharist? If we trust Luther, then whatever else comes from us is impure, dirtier than the menstrual linens, precisely because of the sin — as Luther words it — which continually resides in us. And the result is — again, if we believe Luther — that no work of ours is without sin, wherefore whatever is from our works could be nothing other than impure. We are phrasing this according to Luther's opinion and heresy. Rather, this heavenly bread which we sacrifice to God, contains nothing of impurity, but is the immaculate sacrifice and the same which is perpetually offered throughout all Christendom in every church. Therefore, just like the oblation of bread which the priests of the Old Law offered upon the Mosaic altar — which is now completely cast aside and spurned by God — so upon our altars, the sacrifice of bread perpetually offered in the name of Christ by the priests of the New Law will be acceptable and most pleasing. Who does not see that this is plainly proven, that it all fits us, that is, that the Mass is truly called a sacrifice? What a pagan ethicist once said is completely truthful: "All things are fittingly in accord with the truth."[13] To be sure, all things are in a consensus with the truth, because the whole Church's most acceptable custom gives its assent to the ancient realities. Likewise, the judgment of all the most holy and learned Fathers proves this same reality, and the scriptural authorities demanded the exact same. But even the most inimical adversaries of the Christian name support this, since they openly confess in their own literature that, once all of the other ancient sacrifices were abrogated, there remains only the sacrifice of bread and wine according to the order of Melchizedek, which will be celebrated perpetually. But as we said, we covered this much more in depth in a book that was dedicated to that topic.

---

13 This is an adaptation of Aristotle's *Nicomachean Ethics* I, 8, 1098b 10-11. — Editor.

CHAPTER VII
Certain Quibbling Subterfuges and Lying Sophisms Are Laid Bare

O, in the seventh place, Luther tries to refute the king's arguments with subterfuge, sycophancy, and lies, as we will describe in detail. He first insinuates that the king brought forward only one argument, to wit: "If the Mass were not a good work, the laity would not reward the clergy with any temporal benefit in return for it." Not content with this maligning accusation, he adds: "Remember, reader, that no other argument is adduced by the royal defender for his mass, other than this." Yet, all of this is a complete lie, especially that the king had not proved the Mass to be a work with any other arguments besides the one mentioned. This first point is easily shown once we describe the context of the king's words, because he had first addressed Luther's other collaborators, who admittedly treat matters more succinctly and truthfully than Luther: one must include in the covenant not only those things which Christ did at Supper, but also what he suffered on the cross, as he says ironically: "So in this single matter, Luther's 'unequals' show themselves, in that they did not discover the marvelous and hitherto unheard of fruits of the Mass, whereby the clergy got all its fruit for the present life and the people lost the fruit of the life to come." The king immediately adds the reasoning for this claim when he says: "For not even the laity would confer any sort of temporal benefit upon the priest because of the Mass, since they were persuaded that no spiritual good accrued to them from the Mass." Here you have it, dear reader: the king is not trying to show by this one argument that the Mass is a work, but that the clergy would be on the verge of losing all fruit or enjoyment of any temporal gain if the laity did not expect themselves to be gaining spiritual fruit from the celebration of the Mass, operated by those same priests.

Thus, there is a lie here, as the reader can see, and you will now see another: Luther denies that the king provided any other argumentation besides that which Luther falsely fabricated — for the fabrication was false too. You see, the king shows from Luther's own principles that the Mass is both a work and a sacrifice, but since the king's reasoning is somewhat more involved and he waxes rather eloquent, we will abbreviate it into a succinct form: "I will grant him this foundational principle, which he begs to have immovable, yet I will show that the edifice which he has constructed can easily fall on its own. Let us grant that Christ established a testament at Supper; it is fitting, however, that he would establish a testament which could come into being as his memorial, after his death, and for this reason the principal part of the testament was that his disciples should do this in commemoration of him, for which reason he said: 'Do this in memory of me'. Yet he did not understand by this the commemoration of the one then dining, but of the Crucified One, and this is clear from Paul's words in 1 Cor. 11: 'As often as you eat this bread and drink this cup,' which is why thereafter he added, 'you will announce the Lord's death' — not 'you will announce the Supper of the Lord.'

Therefore, this is what is represented in the Mass: the sacrifice of the cross. Since the Mass itself clearly refers to this sacrifice, then this is quite justly termed a sacrifice." For this reason, the priests, too, offer and immolate the body apart from the blood, when they re-present his death in the Mass, because it is now carried out in memory of his death — that which he commanded to happen at Supper. And the testament involves death of the Testament-Maker, as Luther says, nor does it have any force or strength beforehand, and it is consummated in perfection only once the testifier has died. The king therefore concludes that if anyone considers and weighs these things diligently, he will see that Christ the eternal priest established this one thing in place of all the sacrifices that took place under Moses, and which bore the type of this sacrifice, so that it might be offered to God and might likewise be given as nourishment to the people. Therefore you understand, dear reader, how the argumentation is much different here than it was in the first part, so that Luther is now twice a liar.

So that we might additionally respond to the calumny which he aims at priests, who receive a temporal gift for masses, is it not found in Genesis 14, when we read how Melchizedek offered to God the sacrifice of bread and wine for Abraham's victory, that we find also how Abraham gave a tenth of all the spoils that he had acquired? Or is this not what Paul says in 1 Cor. 9: "If we sow spiritual goods, is it a great deal if we reap carnal goods?"

Let us now pass on to the king's other arguments, and since Luther did not ignore them, as he tried to refute them, it nevertheless did not shame him to impute to the king a different argumentation for "his mass," besides that initial one. Thus, the reader can now hear the king's second line of argument: "We will ask Luther whether Christ then did some work or not, when he consecrated bread and wine into his body and blood. If he denies it, we will be fully amazed, since the one who makes an image out of wood certainly doesn't work, but Christ did no work at all when he made his flesh from bread." Yet, Luther will respond to the king's argument in the most perverse manner imaginable: "The king so 'Thomisticates' when he says, 'the one who cuts wood does a work; therefore the one who consecrates does a work, thus the Mass is a work'." The reader sees here how Luther was definitely not ignorant of the king's other argument — besides the first — whereby he taught that the Mass was a work, yet Luther nevertheless shamelessly denied this above.

At this point let us see by what sort of twisting and turning Luther tries to evade the argument: he is consistently joking about the two-fold acceptance of "mass." For one, to use his own words, it means to consecrate or pronounce the words of consecration; for another, it is the word of promise, with the addition of the sign of bread and wine. According to the first meaning, he confesses that the Mass is a work, while he nevertheless denies that he could ever think of the Mass in this manner — whether by fever or frenzy. He also asserts in the same way that the Mass can be called many other things, because as he says, "If the Mass is the consecration, then it can also be called the acclamation, incantation, incensation, lighting of candles, cleaning of chalices, lifting of hosts, and maybe even sneezing and coughing up."

But who is so thick headed as to judge that there is no difference between the work of consecration and these other things? You see, without many of these things the Mass could still be fittingly celebrated, because even chant, loud speech, and incense are not required for the existence of the Mass. However, the consecration is such a part of the Mass's substance that without the consecration, there can be no mass. So, who has become so frenzied or feverishly insane as to think that there could be a Mass without the consecration of the body and blood? And if someone has the bread and wine, and the book in which Christ's very words are written, still: the words must be pronounced in order to consecrate the bread and wine; otherwise, there is no Mass. From this it is clear that not even according to the second manner — as Luther defined it above — can there be said to be a mass that is really and truly called Mass, and less that very Word of Promise is present with the added sign of bread and wine. We will demonstrate this succinctly, because as we have already said, if bread and wine are present and either in the mind or in a book are the words of promise, yet still there is no Mass unless someone who is found fitting should pronounce those very same words with the intent of consecrating. Therefore, Luther separates these things in vain, since these three parts are considered necessary for the substance of the Mass: because it is not the words alone, nor the signs alone, nor both of these without the enunciation of the words, that makes the consecration of bread and wine to be the Mass. That is, the priest's action or function is wholly necessary, just as Christ commanded at Supper, saying, "Do ye this in memory of me."

Let us now respond to what Luther scoffingly says as an objection to the king's argument: the king made it so that not only would the Mass be proven to be a work by his prior argument, but also that it would be shown to be a good work. He says, "If Christ did any work, it must have been good, as no one will doubt, I am sure, because if he did a good work in having anointed his head, then who would doubt that Christ did a good work when he offered his own body as food for men and established it as a sacrifice to be offered for God? If this cannot be denied — except by someone who would want to joke about a very serious matter — then it is also clear, and there is no denying that Christ did a good work and that in the Mass the priest does a good work, since he does nothing other than what Christ did at Supper and on the cross."

Luther offers this jeering response: "By this argument, the Mass will not be a good work unless the consecrator is a good man. For a wicked man does a wicked act in consecrating, that is to say, in celebrating Mass, according to what the king says. Therefore it should not be lawful for a bad priest to consecrate — or rather — he cannot consecrate because they require that the Mass must be a good work." Now the good reader can clearly see Luther's open mocking, as if no good work could come forth except from a good minister — which is plainly false. You see, even a bad priest who baptizes is the minister of a good work, even if he does not do it well; likewise a bad priest who absolves a sinner — who has actually confessed and has a firm purpose of amendment — does a good work, even if he does not do it well, because in either case he does something "not well" but in neither case does he do a "wicked work." And it goes in a similar manner for the one who consecrates, even if he himself were to be evil, he nevertheless does a work that is good, not only for the "work done" or "from the work performed," but also for the work of the agent, or "by work of the worker," just as the one who gives alms, although he might have no grace, is doubtless doing a good work, even if there is no belief that he is doing it well.

Thus Luther picks at the king in a puerile manner, although the king so occupied the many duties of his kingdom that he did not have the chance to call out the theological distinction between *ex opere operato* and *ex opere operantis* or the work done compared to the state of the one who did the work. In this matter Luther has clearly betrayed his own ignorance, since it has no place in this discussion, because here we are not disputing about the fruits of the Mass, which are always as abundant as any work ever done, whether the Mass should be done by a good man or a bad man. It does not, however, belong to the "work of the one doing the work" or *opus operantis*, whenever the one who offers the sacrifice is a bad man, because he is receiving no fruit for himself *ex opere operantis*, or thanks to his own state as the doer, since he does a good work — but in a bad state. A good man, to the contrary, bears great fruit both for himself as well as for others, and he not only does a good work but he also does it in a good way.

Therefore, Luther has spoken in an ignorant manner when he said that the great theology had perished when it stated that the Mass is always a good work, even if it belongs to a bad priest, by virtue of the work done or *opus operatum*. I say this due to the second part of the argument, which no theologian will ever assert, in my opinion: you see, the consecrating priest, if he be quite evil, and whether you understand the work as done or done by him, is still a good work from which he merits nothing, because the consecration as work done by a particular doer is still good, and what happens by that very consecration — the sacrament of the body and blood of Christ — is likewise a good work that is done. Yet Luther has erred, since theologians deny the fruit and merit from the work of a bad priest actually originates from the bad priest as doer, as Luther thinks that they would take away all goodness of the bad priest's work — which they most certainly do not think or say. And yet, this man's blindness or shamelessness is so great that he is not content to make this accusation once, but he repeats it to the king, as if he were a victor and insulting the defeated, when the complete contrary is the case. He throws this as an objection at the king, showing that he is ignorant of his own matters, that is the difference between the work done and the work of a particular doer; and Luther refutes himself when he so assails the king, when nevertheless the king himself is certainly knowledgeable of that distinction and how far it applies, while Luther struts around like a haughty blind man.

CHAPTER VIII
The Mass Is Not Solely a Promise

OW, we will not overlook the place wherein Luther tries to prove that the Mass is really and truly a word of promise: "If everything else fails, and you only believe these words of Christ: 'This is my body, which is given for you,' you have indeed the entire Mass. And then if you do but receive the sign with that same faith, you have received the use and fruit of the Mass."

You have just heard two things, dear reader: first, what the entire Mass is; second, how you can receive the fruit of the Mass. Let us first consider the first point: "For if everything else fail, and you only believe these words of Christ: 'This is My body, which is given for you,' you have indeed the entire Mass." Therefore, if I should anywhere give my faith to those words — either seen or heard — there will be an entire Mass, even if everything else fails — even if the bread and wine fail, even if the other words which pertain to the wine and blood fail — no one has ever thought such a thing! If the words alone are spoken, or if they are engraved upon a rock and thereupon recalled, or if they were pronounced by some woman or boy, should I only believe them and the Mass will be whole and entire? And if that were to happen 100 times in the same day, then the Mass should be entirely there just as many times. These instances would be quite incredible. But I would have Luther to tell us openly: "What if those words had not been pronounced by anyone anywhere, and had not even been considered, would there then be no Mass?" If he says that there is no longer any Mass, then that is curious, since the words still remain, since it is written, "my words shall not pass away." Faith, too, remains in the hearts of men, which Luther calls a living act and movement. Therefore, while this word perpetually remains and the act of faith is ever present, then according to Luther's dogma, the Mass will always exist at all times and moments — not only of the day but also at night — just as much while priests are sleeping, as well as when they are keeping vigil, or while they are celebrating the sacraments. You see, if nothing beyond the word and fate is required for the integrity of the Mass, and if these alone — even if everything else should fail — are what is needed for an entire Mass, who does not see that the Mass must then endure forever and be offered never-endingly? Yet, I see that Luther is urged to admit that some act beyond faith and the word is required for the integrity of the Mass, and without which we are without the Mass, and I think that he will say that it is the act of the recitation of those words, because, in order that the Mass might happen, those very words must be recalled in memory, otherwise we will not do what Christ himself did in the Supper, just as he commanded us to do: "Do ye this in memory of me." For he himself pronounced those very words over the bread which he had taken and consecrated in his sacred hands. For this reason, it is clear that something else is definitely necessary beyond faith and the word — as well as beyond the recitation of the words: the present of bread.

Thus, what Luther claimed is far from the truth, that is that if all else failed, you might only believe in these words of Christ — "This is my body which is given up for you" — and you would have a whole Mass, because the Mass can never be whole unless the priest does with Christ's words just what Christ commanded to be done; that is, that he should consecrate the bread and wine into Christ's body and blood. This action regarding the bread enters so much into the essence of the Mass that without it there can be no Mass at all. And if any priest does this — even if no one around him should believe — nevertheless there will be a Mass — not such that this act alone is required for the integrity of the Mass, but that without this act the Mass can simply not exist at all. So, as regards the refutation of Luther's prior assertion, which is sustained with no arguments from Scripture or reason — rather, they rest entirely upon his own audacity — that should suffice.

Now let us pick apart the second claim which he worded thus: "And then if you do but receive the sign with that same faith, you have received the use and fruit of the Mass." In this statement he wants it to be understood that the one who receives the use and fruit of the Mass is whoever has faith in Christ's words and accepts the consecrated bread — which latter he calls the "sign of the body."

Let the reader first note here that he said, "with the same faith," because just above he had said, "if you believe these words of Christ: 'This is my body which is given for you,'" and that if all else fails, you still have the Mass in its entirety. He then immediately adds: "Then if you do but receive the sign with faith, you have received the use and fruit of the Mass." Here the reader clearly sees, I think, what a grand assumption this is, because in order for the bread to be consecrated into the body of Christ, I do not think that he will say that a formed faith is necessary, but that an informed [faith] suffices; otherwise the people would be frequently committing idolatry, that is as they would be worshiping mere bread as Christ's body. Yet, this very same faith hardly suffices for the consumption of the body, that you might have the use and fruit of the Mass, rather to the contrary, you do eat judgment upon yourself, as St. Paul attests, and make yourself guilty of the Lord's body, because he approaches unworthily to consume the most holy nourishment, whosoever approach without a formed faith.

Additionally, one should note by what sort of subterfuge Luther has joined the use and fruit of the Mass, when he says: "If you receive the sign, you have received the use and fruit of the Mass" — which is plainly false, because the use of the Mass is the very function of the priest, which when it is finished, the Mass, too — as far as that goes — is also finished. Yet once the Mass is ended, some fruit of it nevertheless remains in the sacrament, so long as the sacrament itself remains after the end of the Mass; and the partaker of this fruit is the one who devoutly receives that very sacrament, even if no Mass should be taking place at that very moment. So, the one who receives in this manner is no longer using the Mass, although he is rightly believed to be making use of the sacrament.

Therefore, so that we might more easily examine the matter, it will be somewhat useful to include some examples: we will consider the Mass as if it were the function of an herbalist, who is producing a medicine which a rather experienced doctor had previously prescribed to restore some sick man to full health, because it sometimes happens that after the herbalist has made use of his art and has made the medication, he administers it immediately to the sick man, and yet some remains in the vial[14] for greater ease at the next time appointed for administering the medicine. Now, if the medicine is taken from the vial to some sick man, no one will call this carrying the "herbalist's art," since it may just as well be done by someone who is not an herbalist. From this example anyone can easily understand what a great difference there is between the administration of the Eucharist — which can be carried out by the deacon — and the function of the priest, at least as regards the confection of this sacred medicine, which is the only thing that is properly called "the Mass" by all. Therefore, the reader sees in this example that the doctor is Christ, the herbalist is the priest, and the minister the deacon: the function of the priest and the making of the medication is the Mass. Thus, the use of the Mass lasts just as long as the priest's function; the fruit, however, is great in this sacrament as soon as the Mass has begun, just as it is in the medicine which is still kept in the pyx.

Yet, I could not grant that the whole and entire fruit of the Mass remains in the sacrament, because when the sacrifices are offered at Mass for the health of the living and for the repose of the deceased, so many sacred prayers are also added, whereby the good intentions of the surrounding faithful are also commended to God; and it is beyond belief that one who remains at home — no matter how great his faith may be — receives this sacrament and gains as much fruit from it as one who, of like faith, devoutly assists at the Mass, and is likewise in that same place made a partaker of the holy prayers and Communion.

For these reasons, I don't think that the absurdity of Luther's position escapes anyone, since from that it would follow that as often as the Sacrament leaves the ciborium — for any sick or dying man's sake — that there would be a Mass just as many times. Who does not see how devoid of truth that is, since no one would be doing what Christ himself did at Supper — which very thing he commanded his priest to do? You see, in that case, no one is confecting Christ's body and blood from bread and wine, although he commanded his disciples to do that: "Do ye this in memory of

---

[14] Or "pyx," such as the Sacrament was once reserved — Editor.

me."

The conclusion from these points is clear: the Mass is not the reception of the signs or the promise that is added to the signs — therefore much less the sign alone.

Yet, Luther still continues with these prior points, and he adds the following: "Hence it is most clear that the Mass is not something of our work or word, but only of Christ who gives not only the word of promise, but also the sign of it in the bread and wine; and its use cannot be in offering or in working but only in receiving." I beg someone to tell me: whence is this "most clear"? Maybe to you, from your mere insanity, in your fever and frenzy — as you put it — it was dreamt up most clearly, but to us it is so far from clear from any Scripture that you have hitherto produced, such that it doesn't even seem to have any probability, since we have that most clear Scripture from Christ's mouth, whence he commanded that we do these things, that is that we consecrate the bread and wine into his body and blood — which can hardly happen without our labor. Could your shamelessness be any greater, since you would have us believe in your insanely silly propositions without any Scripture — my apologies, against the Scriptures — and to give our faith to dreams that are full of frenzy?

Further, because you insist on this word of promise so frequently, yet I do not understand what you mean by the word, because by it you show yourself to be greater than Proteus — making the word of promise now one thing, then another. I am thinking of what you noted above, that "this is my body which is given up for you" has nothing of a promise in it, since the things that are promised are those which are to come. Even if Christ was informing his then-present Apostles of the presence of his body under the appearance of bread, yet I beg you to tell me by what word of Scripture it is promised to us that, when we consecrate, the same thing is going to happen? You see, it is not written that "as often as the priest says my words over the bread, then immediately shall my body come from bread": this would indeed be a word of promise. For instance, we do read of promises being made in the Gospels regarding other sacraments: about Baptism we find it written, "whosoever believes and is baptized will be saved" (Mark 16), and again in regard to the sacrament of the Remission of Sins, "whose sins you forgive are forgiven them" (John 20). These are certainly words of a promise. On the other hand, in these very same sacraments, no one uses those very words, but rather other words which are not of the promise, such as, "I baptize you," and, "I absolve you," which are not written in Scripture.

Yet, Luther will say that all certainty on this entire matter depends upon that word: "Do ye this in memory of me." Therefore, this is more the word of promise than that which was cited above, and for that reason if there is such power in the word of promise, then this should be recited at the consecration of the body and blood rather than other words. Yet, plainly no one believes that, since all know that this word was announced and pronounced before the consecration, but such is the case even with the other sacraments, such as Baptism and Absolution, that the word of promise should be read, and yet no one ever does that, as we have just noted. For example, no one ever uses these words when he absolves: "Whose sins you forgive are forgiven them." Nor when someone is baptized, "Whosoever believes and is baptized will be saved." Rather, both the one who baptizes as well as the one who absolves must necessarily speak in his own person, such that he says: "I baptize you...I absolve you"; otherwise, nothing happens.

Furthermore, Luther calls the Mass the promise of the remission of sins in his Babylonian Captivity; and in this way he is never consistent, but always using such an ingeniously mutable versatility, so that he makes the word of promise now one thing, and now another. He puts it this way in the Babylonian Captivity: "You see then that the Mass—as we call it—is a promise of the remission of sins, made to us by God," and if I ask him where this promise is found written, I know what he will say in response: "It is written in these words: 'This is my blood of the new Covenant which will be shed for you for the remission of sins'." At this point we will certainly not dispute the expression of a promised remission of sins, but this promise does not occur thanks to the reception of the sacrament, as we have often said, but rather due to the shedding of blood while Christ offered himself upon the cross. One might add that, according to Luther's opinion, anyone consecrates equally, whether he pronounces it according to Matthew, according to Mark, according to Luke, or according to Paul; but, it is clear that neither Mark, nor Luke, nor Paul spoke of the remission of sins. For this reason, it is not necessary to have the promise of the forgiveness of sins in order to make a consecration.

Additionally, since he says at the end of that same bad book that the entire potency of the Mass consists in the promise of the forgiveness of sins, if such were true, then Paul was ignorant of the use and potency of the Mass itself when he wrote to the Corinthians to instruct them on this very thing and omitted completely those words, although he claims to have received from Christ himself what he taught to the Corinthians. For this reason, if so much importance depends on those words, so that the entire power of the Mass completely consists in them, then Paul — especially at that point in his letter — would have no way stayed silent about it, while he was teaching about that mystery. Therefore, the Mass is not the promise of the remission of sins.

Neither does the use of the Mass consist only in the reception and taking, such as Luther falsely tries to assert, but rather also in the offering and working, because it is not a single and simple thing, but it rather contains many things in itself, as we have said previously. For example, just as a pharmacist's function does not consist in just one work, but rather he now crushes, then mixes, and later cooks it all, so, too, does the priest's function remain varied, as he now consecrates, then offers, later prays, and finally commends both the living and the dead to God through the power of this very sacrifice.

Luther afterwards impugns another argument from the most illustrious king, after first having desecrated and destroyed it beyond all recognition as he described it in this way: "Next, in order to defend the Mass as a sacrifice, he speaks like a Thomist in this manner: let it be granted that the Mass is a promise: it does not therefore follow that it is not at the same time a sacrifice, since in the old law there were sacrifices which were at the same time promises." Yet, the king had not made his argument so poor and impoverished as Luther put it, but rather much more well-constructed, as you can see in his actual response: "I beg to see this proof, while he attempts to teach that the Mass is not a sacrifice precisely because it is a promise — as if promise and sacrifice were so mutually exclusive as were cold and heat. Yet Luther's reasoning is so lifelessly frigid that a response does not seem fitting, because the many sacrifices of the Mosaic Law — which were all but symbols of the things to come — were nevertheless themselves also promises. That is, they promised the things for which they took place — not only for the future things of which they were but figures, but also for the liberations, expiations, purgations and purifications of the people then present, and for whom they were solemnly offered year after year. This is so clear that truly no one could be ignorant of it, and so this is a simply ridiculous dissimulation by Luther when he argues that it is impossible, since both he himself and the people of that time knew how often it did happen." Such is how the king responded in truth.

You, the reader, see how the king proved that the sacrifices were promises in a twofold sense: on the one hand, because they certainly promised truths to come, of which they were the figure; on the other hand, because the freedom, deliverance, and purity of that people — for whom they were yearly offered — were likewise promised. It is not that the king thought that there was no difference between a sacrifice and a promise, but that promises were so frequently connected to those sacrifices, as we will presently show. Yet, Luther objects to this argument on two points; first, he claims that the king adduced no example on this matter: "I answer that the king ought to have produced at least one example of this Thomistic assertion."

What would it have mattered, had the king not brought forth a single example? Should the king's argument then have no weight? I ask because the king thought that he was countering someone who was familiar with these examples, given that the scriptural examples are so numerous and that Luther styles himself a master of the Scriptures: we now list some of the biblical examples: First, Levit. 4: Moses first describes how a calf is to be sacrificed for the sin of what the people ignored, as it is written: "And the priest praying for them, the Lord will be merciful unto them." You see here the promise that is adjoined to the sacrifice. Again, when the head of the people should have sinned through ignorance, Moses teaches that a goat must be sacrificed: "And the priest shall pray for him, and for his sin: and it shall be forgiven him." Here again the promise of sins to be forgiven is connected to the sacrifice. Additionally, if some single person happens to sin through ignorance, he teaches that a she-goat or sheep should be offered, and the promise of forgiveness of sin is attached to both sacrifices. It would take a long time to recount all examples of such sacrifices, such as are in Chapters 5 and 6 and following, and which demonstrate what other sins and faults are forgiven — wherein the sacrifice is found together with the promise of sin's forgiveness. You see therefore, dear reader, how many examples we have just produced — that is, of sacrifices in the old law which promised forgiveness of sins and how it is not against the custom of Scripture to call these promises as well.

Nor is Luther's sophistry of any account when says, in the second place: "A promise is a word, sacrifice is a thing, so that it is impossible for a promise to be a sacrifice." This is sophistry, plain and simple; nor does the king state that the sacrifice is a promise, since a promise is not sacrificed! Yet, he had called a promise a sacrifice at some point in the past, since by sacrifice the remission of sins is promised. You see, for the sake of purification and expiation, sacrifices were mandated in the law.

To this, Luther always responds that the Mass is not only called a promise, but a promise with added signs, such that the Mass involves not only a promise but, equally, signs — which signs contain true realities, that is, Christ's true flesh and his very own true blood; because of these very signs, the Mass is no less properly called a reality than it is called speech due to the promise, since, just as we said above in regard to the older ceremonies which the Hebrews call the Passover, not only is a promise involved, but also the sacrifice of a lamb. So, we do not hesitate to assert the same of the new ceremony, which — besides a promise and words, — comprehends the consecration of the Eucharist as well, that is, of the very body of Christ. For this reason and more besides, Luther's reasoning is childish when he says, "The mass is a promise and speech, whence it cannot be a reality," given that Luther himself has more than once admitted in his book against the king that the Mass is a promise that has signs added to it: and what else does that mean if not that the Mass is both words and realities?

He, however, often confuses these three things and takes one for the other. I mean: the Mass, the sacrament, and the covenant or testament, when he wrote of them in his Babylonian Captivity: "Let this first point stand infallibly, that the Mass or sacrament of the altar is a covenant." You can see here, if "covenant" can be said of either, that is, of the Mass or the sacrament of the altar, it is necessary that both of these can be mutually said of the other, and in this way, since the Mass is a sacrament for Luther, it will also be a reality as well.

Yet, he speaks of the promise very hesitantly, because he adds these words just shortly after: "Therefore, you see that what we call the Mass is the promise of the forgiveness of sins." Here he clearly makes the Mass the promise of the remission of sins, and a little further on he says: "Thus, I am right to say that the entire virtue of the Mass consists in the words of Christ whereby he promises that the forgiveness of sins is granted." Here again he would have the Mass to be the promise of the forgiveness of sins, but in his booklet against the king, he says: "We call that the promise in the Mass, that is, the very words of Christ, without which there would be but bread and wine, and not a sacrament nor the Mass." What he understands by these words is quite unclear, since if he were to understand some other promise than that of the remission of sins, then he would be speaking too properly and most confusedly — all the while, not consistently. Yet, the plain truth does not seek to be covered by such ambiguous wrapping: it seeks the light — not obscure darkness.

Furthermore, that the entire virtue of the Mass does not consist solely in the promise of the remission of sins, and that it is not the one thing without which the bread and wine would not become signs, sacraments, or the Mass, we will now show with abundant clarity. It could be most clear from this one thing, that the entire power of the Mass is not in the promised forgiveness of sins, since Paul did not say a word about it, and yet he was taught by Christ himself to hand on sufficiently a formula for consecrating the body and blood. What is more, given that only Matthew makes mention of the remission of sins, so if the bread and wine would not become a sign, sacrament, or the Mass without this phrase — as Luther suggests — then not only Paul, but also Mark and Luke would be in grave error — which is an impious belief. You see, none of them make any mention of the remission of sins, but Paul would have sinned most gravely of all, since he declares himself to be the teacher on this matter to the Corinthians, and by these words of consecrating the body and blood of Christ, he gave them a formula that did not include the phrase about the remission of sins. Wherefore, if the full power of the Mass consists in the promise of the forgiveness of sins, as Luther opines, Paul would have harmed the Corinthians greatly by defrauding them of that entire potency of the whole Mass. It is beyond belief that he would not have explained to the Corinthians that which Christ had previously taught him. From this, it seems most likely that Christ had not included that phrase in his interaction with Paul, and he would not have done that had the potency of the whole matter resided in the promise itself.

Additionally, since if the entire potency of the Mass did consist in the promise of the remission of sins, without it nothing at all would take place — and Luther himself will admit that this is not the case, because shortly thereafter in his little book against the king, he affirms that the consecration is just if one were to use Luke's, Mark's, or Paul's formula than if one were to use his falsely and impiously imposed canon. So, this shameless man dares to accuse the sacred canon of the Mass by calling it false and impious; yet, it is certain that in the form which Luke, Mark, and Paul passed down, there's not a single word of the promised remission of sins, and for that reason the entire virtue of the Mass does not consist of that promise, and neither can the Mass be said to be solely the promise of the forgiveness of sins — something which even Luther confirmed explicitly: if the Mass were solely the promise, nor should anything real happen besides it, then why does Luther so often call the Mass a "promise with signs added thereunto?" What need is there of signs if the Mass is only a promise?

Therefore, let him take the signs away completely — given that they are clearly things or realities — that is, the body and blood of the Lord. You see, outside of these realities, a promise remains a promise, and so if he can call the Mass a promise alone, then the promise exists even if the signs are taken away. In fact, he must admit that the Mass exists even if no signs remained, because even before the ceremony — which we do not hesitate to call "mass" — as well as after the ceremony, the same promise remains in force, since the promise itself never ceases to be, given that the word of the Lord remains forever (Ps. 118/119). For this reason, it is obvious that the Mass cannot be called solely a promise.

Although Luther engages in sophistry when he contends that the old sacrifices were not promises, and that a promise is not a thing or reality, he is still unable to deny that there is both a promise and a reality that is necessary for the fulfillment of the Mass. At this point, no one could have any doubts that the promise and even the signs — as Luther admits — are true things that are truly necessary.

Yet even beyond all this, since the very reality of the Mass — that is, the presence of the body and blood of Christ — cannot be had without the consecration of the bread into the body and of the wine into the blood, then there is no way of escaping the fact that this act is likewise required for the integrity of the Mass, and this is what we have so often said: that the Mass is not some simple thing, but that it includes many things within it. Nor does it matter much whence the name "mass" comes originally, as long as everything is clear about the reality itself, because just as we have shown that the ceremony which is called "Passover" did not receive its name due to any one part of the ceremony, but rather from the angel that passed over the Hebrews while the Egyptians were struck, and that thus was it called a "Pasch" or "Passover," so likewise with the Mass: it can be called what it is for some external reason, nor is it necessary that the word itself make evident every single matter that happens to be done or said in the Mass itself.

Therefore, Luther tries in vain to impose upon us with his trickery in his Babylonian Captivity, wherein he introduces this comparison of a poor man: "No one would be so audaciously foolish as to say that when a poor and needy man receives a benefit from the hand of a rich man, he is doing a good work. Now the Mass is the benefit of a divine promise, held forth to all men by the hand of the priest: it cannot be a work or a sacrifice." Luther is trying to trick us by this comparison, since there is otherwise a great deal of difference between a poor man who is receiving a gift from a rich man and the priest who is consecrating a gift to be distributed to the people, because the people would play the role of the poor man, while the priest takes the place of the rich man — that is of Christ himself. You see, Christ engaged in the office of priest at the Supper, as he consecrated the Eucharist, and when he was distributing, the disciples would have been the poor people of the comparison, because the disciples by only receiving and experiencing (to use Luther's words) offered themselves; but Christ was the one doing the work, the one who was consecrating, as well as the person doing the immolating or sacrificing: because what else could the evangelists have meant when they each mentioned that he gave thanks — which Paul did not say? But even that same ministry that he himself then exercised, he then handed on to his Apostles for them to do: "Do ye this in memory of me." By these words, even Luther admits that the power to consecrate the Eucharist had been granted to the Apostles: "To 'do this' is to imitate all that he himself did then." Therefore, when Christ was the operator, consecrator, and immolator, he also made them operators, consecrators, and immolators of this sacrifice. Thus, the priest does the Mass as often as he consecrates the bread and wine into the Eucharist; on the other hand, the people who receive the sacrament while these mysteries are transpiring are said to be present at the Mass, but not to preside or do the mass as if they were the handlers of the thing. On this account, the people would also be after the manner of the poor man who only receives, but the priest is like the hierarch who presides over the mysteries, since he is the mediator between Christ and the people, he represents something of both, because insofar as he consecrates and administers, he is compared to Christ who gives, but in so far as the priest receives, to that same extent he is in communion with the people or poor man.

So, I think that it is now clear to all that the Mass is something more than just the promise of the forgiveness of sins, that it requires many other things which pertain to the very substance of the Mass, and that it has much more importance than does any promise, because Paul explained the substance of the Mass without any mention of the remission of sins in 1 Cor. 11. Yet, even the remission of sins was promised by the old sacrifices as well, just as here the remission of sins is promised not — of course — for having received the sacrament, as we have said so many times, but in virtue of the sacrifice that is represented in the Mass, which is the sacrifice of the cross.

Of course, the species of bread in the Mass refers to Christ's body that hung lifeless upon the cross, just as the species of wine points to the blood that was spilled on the cross for the remission of sins, and that is why we read in these mystical words: "This is my blood of the new covenant which will be shed for many unto the remission of sins." In this way, too, the old corresponds with the new over and over again, just as it was commanded to Moses that he should do all things according to the exemplar that he had seen on the mountain. You see, just as the people offered certain things there, which very things the priest would then sacrifice, as he sprinkled the altar with blood and the fire would consume whatever remained upon the altar as fat, and to these things the priest would add prayers, and there was thus the promise of the remission of sins; so, too, in the new ceremony of bread and wine that were offered by the people, which would then be offered by the priest, as the fatty substance would be completely consumed by a heavenly fire — that is, the bread and wine, in their substance, would be consumed — and the bread and wine would be changed into the sacred Eucharist. The wine, however, is represented separately from the body, and what else could that suggest other than the killing and sacrificing? Meanwhile, the chalice is wet with the blood of Christ, so that although the altar may not be covered with it, there is yet no doubt that it receives its sanctity from the blood. Finally, there are prayers interspersed and thus by the true virtue of this sublime sacrifice, the forgiveness of sins is promised.

At this point, who does not see that those figures fit completely with this truth, and that likewise this truth corresponds to those shadows and figures? Yet, no one should believe from this comparison that just anyone could approach this sacrament unless he had previously been penitential, because if they approached even those ancient sacrifices, they confessed their sins to the Lord just as we see commanded in Numbers 5; so by an even greater reason are those who approach this sacrament held to a prior expiation and purgation so that they are worthily prepared, and it is for this very reason that the sacrament of Absolution was instituted. Therefore, it is not the case that just anyone can presume to approach the Eucharist should he be conscious of mortal sin, because those sorts of sins must be cleansed previously through the sacrament of Confession and Absolution. Nonetheless, the remnants of sin are taken away here, just as are those sins which we do not recall at the time of Confession, and yet this sacrament — as we have so often said — is not the sign of the remission of sins, but is rather the sacrament of union and incorporation into Christ — not the sacrament of the remission of sins, because it is one thing to grant the remission of sins, and it is another to be the sacrament of just such a remission.

CHAPTER IX
Some of Luther's False Accusations against the King Are Done Away With

THINK that we have now done quite enough to show that the Mass is not only a promise and that the whole power of the Mass itself does not consist in the promise of the forgiveness of sins. This is why Luther is far from the truth when he claims that the whole gospel and all consolation would be lost to us if we did not gain that the Mass is a promise or testament, which is what he boasts loudly to be the clear meaning of the words. For the whole truth of the entire gospel will remain in its integrity in any case, but Luther's fabrication will not be able to bring any consolation to men because it is not according to the common ritual and faith of the entire Church, all of which demonstrate something much more substantial than Luther's daydreams.

I should also add that if the Church's rite had not be approved by its centuries of use and likewise by the claims of the Fathers, neither Luther nor anyone else would yet be able to use the simple words of the gospel to disprove that the presence of Christ's body came about in this sacrament through any priest's consecration. And it would do us great damage to be deprived of this consolation, or to have even the slightest hesitation about the matter. Yet, we should fall into this hesitation without a doubt if — together with Luther — we decided not to defend the Fathers' interpretation, as well as that of custom. Yet, from the words of the gospel, together with the assertions of the Fathers, as well as by that uninterrupted and long-standing custom — especially in a matter of such importance — I do not doubt in the least that we should overcome against any and all in saying that the flesh and blood of Christ is truly consecrated at the Mass and that this is granted to the faithful. We will speak of these things more at length later on, and in the meanwhile we will make it clear that there is not a single word in all the gospel which Luther can use to boldly prove that the Mass is a sacrifice — just because he often and loudly yells it.

So let us now discuss how this shameless man is not ashamed to accuse the king of falsehood and self-contradiction, because he actually admitted how tedious it was to hear so often from preachers about covenants and promises, and yet when he afterwards speaks of the sacrament of Orders, he denies that there is any promise in the entire Lord's Supper! Luther is guilty of the greatest falsehood in and how he wished to interpret the king's words in his private reading. Here are the actual words: "Let someone read the Scripture on the Lord's Supper and he will not find among any of the evangelists that there is a grace promised upon the reception of the sacrament; we read that it was said by Christ, 'This is my blood of the New Testament which will be poured out for many unto the remission of sins,' and by those words he signified that he himself would redeem mankind by his Passion upon the cross. But when he said previously, 'Do ye this in memory of me,' he made no promise of a grace there to the priest who would consecrate, nor even to the one who would receive the Eucharist, and no promised forgiveness of sins." This is what the king really wrote. In these words it is clear that the king is denying that either grace or the remission of sins is promised in the Mass to the one who does the consecrating or to the one who receives the Eucharist — and this is so very true. Nevertheless, he does not deny that in the recitation of the words of the Mass there exists a promise of the remission of sins, which promise — as he says — was made on account of the spilling of blood upon the cross, and due to the Passion itself, whereby he redeemed the human race, not because of the eating of the Sacrament. Therefore, it is a most blatant lie to say that the king denied that there is a promise in the Mass.

But this, too, is still a lie, that the king would contradict himself since he conceded nothing that goes against what he said but only that he had heard from so many others about testaments and promises of this sort, and he only denies that there is any openly made promise of grace or remission of sins to the one who does the consecrating or to him who receives the Eucharist. The king is always consistent and in whatever he teaches he brings forward the most efficacious reasoning and scriptural citations; Luther either passes over these with a deaf ear, or he tries evasion by means of lies and sophistry, just as is clear in this matter that follows: you see, he says without any proof or evidence that the king asserted that the priests do not only what Christ did at Supper, but also what he did upon the cross. This is surely one of his most blatant lies, because the king brings forward two scriptural citations from Paul to prove it.

Here are the king's words: "If Luther is going to insist against us that the priest cannot offer [sacrifice] because Christ did not offer at Supper, then he should remember what he himself said: 'A testament or covenant involves the death of the one who is making it, nor does it have any strength, or validity, or perfect completion before the one who did the testifying actually dies.' In this way what belongs to the testament are not only those things which Christ did at Supper, but also his sacrifice upon the cross, because upon the cross he consummated the sacrifice which he had begun at Supper; it is to this point that the commemoration of the entire thing aims, that is, of the consecration at Supper and the oblation upon the cross — they are celebrated and represented by the one sacrament of the Mass, and to that extent death is more truly represented than a supper. The Apostle wrote this in 1 Cor. 11: 'As often as you eat this bread and drink this chalice, you announce,' and then he added not 'the Lord's Supper', but, 'the Lord's death'." That is what the king truly wrote.

By these words the reader can clearly see that the king made use of St. Paul's witness for what he said, that is, that in the Mass the death of Christ is more truly represented than the Lord's Supper: "You will announce the Lord's death until he comes," and we have amply treated this citation previously.

Now hear another scriptural reference from Luke, which the king produced to prove this same point: "It is impossible to deny that the priest at Mass is doing a good work — that is — he is doing in Mass nothing other than what Christ did at Supper and on the cross, and Christ's words declare the same thing: 'Do ye this in memory of me.' What else could he have meant by these words than that, at Mass, they would represent and do what he himself did at Supper and on the cross?" Despite these words of the king, Luther's depravity is such that he feels no shame in claiming that the king had only spoken and not proven, whereas the king had truly given two scriptural citations for the one claim, as we have just shown.

The reader can hear the lie for himself, as well as the sophistry that follows thereupon: "I say on the contrary: it is clear that the priests omit in the Mass what Christ did at Supper and that they do what the Jews did to Christ on the cross. Nor do I say this only, but I prove it, too, for he who perverts and extinguishes the word of God also truly crucifies the Son of God, and that is what they all do whosoever makes a work out of a promise, since this is indeed to change the truth of God into a lie." There are Luther's sayings.

Up to this point in my life, for sure, I have never heard that someone made a promise a work, nor that anyone had claimed that a promise was a work. I do not see how he changes the truth of God into a lie. Yet, I do know one thing: if "crucifying the Son of God" is perverting and even deleting the word of God, then Luther has so crucified Christ as no one prior to him, because he attempts to completely twist and remove the citations, "You will announce the Lord's death," and "Do ye this in memory of me."

Immediately after this — and no less shamelessly — he spurns the sacred canon of the Mass itself, which has been honorably reverenced throughout the centuries by the Fathers who were bestowed with great erudition as well as holiness, and yet Luther counts the canon as naught: "I have rejected and do reject the canon because it is quite openly against the gospel, and gives the name of sacrifices to what are signs of God added to his promises, and are given to us to be received — not to be offered up by us." First of all, the reader can see that Luther rejected the sacred canon, something which the true believers hold in highest esteem, after the Gospels. If this contempt were nothing else, it would abundantly show what sort of horrible monster Luther is, but he adds to the cause, because he openly says that sacrifices are against the gospel, such as are signs that are added to the promises; yet, this is patently a lie to claim that the canon goes against the Gospel calling God's signs sacrifices. I would like for Luther to offer even one citation from the Gospel which is an open contradiction to the canon, and I know that he will never do so. We, however, have produced an abundance of these, for why the true Lamb is Jesus Christ, truly under the appearances of bread and wine, upon the altar, to be sacrificed. And what is against calling the signs of God sacrifices? You see, even in the old law, whatever sacrifices were so called were likewise signs of Christ who was to be offered in his Passion; these were also adjoined to promises, just as we have shown above. Therefore, what wonder is there if the species of bread and wine are not only signs of that very Lamb's flesh and blood which was once offered upon the cross for us, but if they were also to truly announce that same presence, a repeated memorial of that same sacrifice. I wonder what wonder there would be if such signs were to be called sacrifices, especially since this Lamb is eaten nowhere else except from this sacrifice — although it must be eaten in order to obtain true life. Thus, this is a two-fold lie that Luther has pushed, as he is wont, since, on the one hand, he says that the signs themselves cannot be called sacrifices, but on the other hand he states that it is completely and openly against the Gospel.

When, however, he adds that these signs should not be offered since they were offered already so as to be received by us, is there anything more stupid, since we have nothing at all to offer which we have not first received from God? For so did David confess to God in 1 Paral. (1 Chr.) 29: "All things are thine, and from thy hands we have received whatsoever we give to thee." Paul says the same thing in 1 Cor. 4: "What do you have that you have not received?" For this reason, if we can offer to God nothing except what we have *not* received, then we can never offer anything, because in this way every offering would be precluded, and that is clearly against the Scriptures, since they frequently exhort us to offer some host to God. Now, if we can offer something to God which we have first received, then what would keep us from offering this Immaculate Lamb, so acceptable to the Father, and which was offered once for sins and given by God to us for our benefit? I ask again, what would prevent us from offering the very same to the Father as some perpetual sacrifice for the sins that we commit daily, so that they might daily be remitted? You see, even if Christ was offered once for the destruction of all sins, nevertheless the merit and fruit of that offering is not applied to all sinners except by appropriate means — otherwise no sinner would ever be saved but all would be damned.

Now, if Luther says that each person's faith should suffice for himself, I am not in opposition, if all else fails; yet, where other means might be obtained and sufficient diligence be used in the search, then I should think that such a faith does not suffice, but is rather quite deformed by its negligence, because otherwise not only would Baptism have been in vain, but even the sacraments of Absolution and the Eucharist would have been instituted in vain. Therefore, the fruits of that Passion are communicated to sinners by these sacraments. Therefore, nothing prohibits the offering of Christ the true Lamb under signs, since it is beyond thinking that there should be any other host that is purer, holier, or more acceptable to the Father.

At this point I will skip over his many insults, insanities, and childish ineptitude, as I come to that most serious lie about Sacred Writ, whereby Luther contends that there was no sacrifice in the law that was received and yet not completely burnt: "To me it is sufficient that in the Old Testament it is written: Whatever was offered to God was wholly consumed." You see, he thinks that nothing is offered that is not completely consumed by fire, while the Scriptures clearly say that not only did the people offer unto the hands of the priests, but also that the priests themselves sacrificed so many more things than were burnt up. But let us first use an example about the people from Leviticus 2: "When any one shall offer an oblation of sacrifice to the Lord, his offering shall be of fine flour." This offering is understood about anyone whatsoever, whether or not a layman. Furthermore, it was the priest's duty to take something of a memorial from that entire offering, so that it might be burnt by fire, as it is written: "And shall bring it to the sons of Aaron the priests. And one of them shall take a handful of the flour...and shall put it as a memorial upon the altar." Dear reader, you see here how that private person from the people would first offer something into the hands of the priest, and that then the priest himself would offer it anew. Again in that same chapter he says more clearly: "If the sacrifice be from the gridiron, in like manner the flour shall be tempered with oil. And when thou offerest it to the Lord, thou shalt deliver it to the hands of the priest." This is called an oblation, an oblation made to the Lord, just as it was written there: "thou offerest it to the Lord...deliver it to the hands of the priest." And then immediately in regard to the priest: "And when he hath offered it, he shall take a memorial out of the sacrifice, and burn it upon the altar." My dear reader, you here note that what was first taken as a memorial to be burnt, as a total sacrifice first offered by a layman, was called an oblation or offering, and that then once it was offered by the priest, it was called a sacrifice.

Moreover, none should feel scrupulous about the word "memorial," as to what Moses intends by this in Leviticus 5, because he explains the meaning clearly, since he afterward commanded the flour to be offered to the poor who did not have any wine to offer; he then immediately mandates that the priest take a handful of it and burn it upon the altar in memory of the one who had first offered it; whatever was then left, the priest would take for his own portion. So you now see what was consumed by fire, as a memorial or memory of the one who first offered, therefore, it was twice offered — once by a layman and again by the priest; thirdly, some of the oblation was burnt. Yet, in the same chapter, there is a fuller exposition not only of what offering was burned, but also of what was put in the hands of the priest, because there the poor man, who had no cattle, is commanded to offer two turtle doves or two young pigeons — one for sin, and the other as a holocaust. Therefore, both were offered, but only one was consumed by fire; however, we may be belaboring a clear point, but we are doing it to this extent so that it is crystal clear to anyone just how audacious Luther's lie is.

Although from what we have said it is quite clear that there were some sacrifices in the law that were received and not wholly consumed by fire, as is very clear from the turtle dove or pigeon, yet it will not be too weighty a matter for us to produce some more witnesses on this matter. I certainly marvel at the man who arrogates so much expertise to himself in matters biblical, so boldly states the contrary, while in the Bible there are so many occurrences of what he denies. For instance, in Leviticus 10, this is said to the priests: "Take the sacrifice that is remaining of the oblation of the Lord, and eat it without leaven beside the altar, because it is holy of holies." Here you have it where the remnants of what was offered to the Lord — that is, what was not consumed by fire — was a sacrifice that the priest took as his food; and although some portion of the whole was burned as a memorial, nevertheless the entirety was truly sacrificed to God. You see, whenever someone of the people offered anything to the hands of the priest, first of all, if the thing was inanimate — whether raw, or cooked, or fried — the priest soon offered that same thing as a sacrifice, as we have just noted, and then some portion of the sacrifice was consumed by fire upon the altar, and whatever was left over was eaten by the priests themselves, just as Moses plainly commanded it in Leviticus 2: "Whatsoever is left, shall be Aaron's, and his sons' holy of holies of the offerings of the Lord." If it was cattle that was offered by the people or by the prince of the people, or even by any private person, once it was first given to the priests, the priest then offered the cattle upon the altar by shedding its blood and sprinkling the blood upon the base of that same altar, and it was then called a host and a sacrifice. Finally, the priest would burn up some portion of it as a memorial of the gift, if it had been a peace offering or an offering for sin, but whatever was left over was turned over to the priests to eat: this is clear from Leviticus 3-5.

For this reason, even in Numbers 8, the Lord had said to Aaron: "Every offering, and sacrifice, and whatsoever is rendered to me for sin and for trespass, and becometh holy of holies, shall be for thee and thy sons. Thou shalt eat it in the sanctuary." Could it be phrased any more clearly than that? For this reason, Moses, too, just as is stated in Leviticus 10, was angry at the sons of Aaron, Eleazar and Ithamar, because they had not eaten the goat that had been offered for sin, rather they made it a complete holocaust: "Why did you not eat in the holy place the sacrifice for sin, which is most holy?" Now is it not clear from those words that what was eaten was both an offering and a sacrifice? But even in Exodus 29 you read: "The loaves also, that are in the basket, they shall eat in the entry of the tabernacle of the testimony, that it may be an atoning sacrifice, and the hands of the offerers may be sanctified." Here you have it that the very reception and eating of the bread

203

made a pleasing sacrifice, whereby even the hands of those who offered were sanctified. And it was written in Deuteronomy 18: "The priests and Levites, and all that are of the same tribe, shall have no part nor inheritance with the rest of Israel, because they shall eat the sacrifices of the Lord, and his oblations." Therefore, it is false to say that there was no sacrifice in the law that was received and not totally consumed by fire.

Further, let us prove from the Gospel this very claim: Christ calls the works of the priests a sacrifice in Matthew 12: "Have you not read in the law that on the Sabbath the priests in the temple break the Sabbath and are without blame?" Now, how can they profane or break the Sabbath except by doing sacrifice? You see, he also calls their work here a sacrifice when he adds: "I desire mercy and not sacrifice." Yet those things that were burned up were burned by the work of the fire alone and not by any sweaty labor of the priests. The priests' labor was especially in strangling and skinning the cattle — a work which was so sacred that it was permitted to no one to do this except the priests. For this reason, it is plain that this work is called a sacrifice by Christ, and therefore Luther's claim is a grave lie; that is, that whatever was offered to God in the law was wholly consumed by fire, because not only that which was burned by fire but also that which was eaten by the priest himself was truly a sacrifice — unless someone prefers to pervert the Scriptures together with Luther, rather than giving his assent to the truth.

Thus, I think that we have satisfied Luther's query, by which he arrogantly and repetitively sought to say that any sacrifice in the law that was received was also wholly burned up by fire. Therefore, it is patently plain from all this that there is nothing repugnant in calling Christ's body and blood in the Mass a sacrifice; and let us likewise confess that not only did God first give it to us, but also that we receive it in turn as food. For it was done thus among the typological examples, too, as we read in the old law, that the things given to God were then again offered to him, and finally offered to the priest as food to be consumed. From the statements the reader may presently learn just how great the ignorance or impudence of Luther really is: ignorance, first of all if one could be ignorant of so many Scriptures — a knowledge which he claims for himself as prince among many; but impudence in the sense that, if he were not ignorant, then he was faking such, or what is more, that he denies that such things could ever be found anywhere in the law.

But we have gone on for longer than was necessary in a matter that is already very clear; and yet if the insane accusations from Luther were anything other than infernal and drunken acts of fury, we should wish to continue in order to render the reader sure but not bored to death; so we shall leave these matters and proceed to those of even greater importance.

CHAPTER X

We Must Believe in the Fathers' United and Harmonious Scriptural Interpretation

HORTLY after this, Luther raises another controversy: whether or not we should give any trust to the Fathers' traditions, besides the Scriptures. Of course, the king does not engage this controversy at all — as Luther pretends — but Luther himself shrewdly instigates it, with the goal of more easily abusing the king's arguments, which arguments had been brought forward for another purpose. You see, when Luther tried to prove that the Mass was a promise with two principal points — that is, Christ's word and example — the king showed both by reason and Scripture that this was not the case, and he taught us rather how no word nor example of Christ proves Luther's assertion. Luther picked some of those arguments, and otherwise twisted what the king had claimed, as the reader will soon see for himself. Furthermore, because Luther introduced this dispute, we find it a most just and fitting occasion to grant now what we promised previously, that is, to show that the understanding of the Gospels is gained with more certainty from the Fathers' interpretation and from traditional usage, than from the bare words of the Gospel itself. It will simultaneously become clear that it is impossible from the Gospel itself to prove that the Mass is a promise.

Yet, let us first tackle and teach that, without the Fathers' interpretation and the testimony of traditional use that is handed down to us, no one can prove from the mere words of the Gospel that any priest is still consecrating today the true flesh and blood of Christ: it is not that the matter itself is ambiguously certain, but that it's certitude does not come from the words of the Gospel, but rather from the interpretation of the Fathers, as well as from so long a tradition of usage, as handed down by so many of the ancients.

First of all, if anyone should grant what Wycliffe completely denied, that at Supper, Christ truly made his body and blood from bread and wine, there is thence no inference that any priest will likewise change bread into the body and wine into the blood, because Christ surely did many things which no one — no matter how holy and wise one might be — could ever do. For this reason, unless it is plainly promised in his spoken words, that whatever layman or priest might attempt to do the same thing, that the same result would follow, then there will be no certitude about this matter. But nothing of the sort is promised in the Gospels, as will be made clear. Here is how Matthew puts it in Ch. 26: "Jesus took bread, and having given thanks, he broke and said: take ye, eat, this is my body; and taking the chalice, he gave thanks, gave to them and said: drink ye all of this, for this is my blood of the new covenant, which will be shed for many for the remission of sins." There is not a single word here by which it can be proved that in our Mass there is the true presence of the flesh and blood of Christ, because even if Christ made his flesh from bread and his blood from wine, it does not therefore follow that — in power of any word written there — we might do the same thing, no matter how often we attempt to do so.

So, Matthew offers no proof of this matter — much less according to Luther's fabrication, whereby he claims that the Mass is the New Testament — as we have often shown, nor did Matthew write: "This blood is the new covenant," but rather, "This is the blood of the new covenant."

Mark, likewise, does not help him, since he does not speak of the remission of sins, and in other matters he follows Matthew completely. For this reason, Mark does not support this claim or Luther's creation at all; but Luther claims that Luke and Mark state the matter plainly, so let us consider that immediately. First of all, they say nothing at all about the forgiveness of sins, and for that reason it is quite clear that — as far as the promised remission of sins is concerned — they do not help Luther one bit. Along the same lines, it is most clear that Luther cannot prove from the entire gospel that the Mass is the promise of the forgiveness of sins, but he will respond: "From both Luke and Paul it is clearly gathered that priests make from both bread and wine flesh and blood of Christ, because both of them narrate Christ's words: "Do ye this in memory of me." Yet, for one who will admit nothing outside Scripture, this will not prove his point at all, because although we grant that Christ spoke to his Apostles, it does not thereupon follow that he gave to all of their successors this same power, since to them it was also given to expel demons and cure maladies — which power did not pass on to their present replacements or vicars.

Furthermore, some things that were said to the Apostles and that are found in the Gospels do not suit them all, such as: "Do not go unto the way of the Gentiles." Therefore, since this promise is not read in the entire Gospel, there's plainly nothing by which we can prove that whatever was said to the Apostles at Supper is also said for all of their successors; and if this cannot be proven of the successors of the Apostles, much less so could one conclude this about any other Christian, because many things were granted to the Apostles and to their successors which do not belong to all Christians indiscriminately. Thus, it cannot be proven by any Scripture that a layman or priest would equally confect the body and blood of Christ from bread and wine, as often as he attempted to do so, just as Christ himself confected it, since this is nowhere contained in the Scriptures.

I think that from these considerations anyone will understand that the certainty of this matter does not depend upon the Gospels as much as it does on the consistent and traditional use throughout the centuries — and from the very first Fathers, because it seemed right to them, through the Holy Spirit's instruction, to interpret this part of the gospel for us. So, too, did they judge it necessary to be done during their times, so that now should anyone have another opinion or wish to introduce another usage, he will be fully fighting against the Holy Spirit, at whose suggestion our forefathers handed on this rite and ceremony in the consecration of the Eucharist, because it is most convincing to anyone who does not ignore or is ignorant of the gospel that the Holy Spirit, who was given to the church as a perpetual teacher, could never be allowed to err in such an important matter and through such a long period of time.

Moreover, so that we can confirm what we have said — that is, that one should have a greater faith in this long usage which we certainly trust to have been given to us by the very Fathers of the Church, beyond the bare words of the gospel — I shall add another example: in the words of the gospel which we have considered above, the two matters are what Christ did and what he commanded to be done, but I will now bring forward Christ's other words, wherein a third thing is added, beyond his doing and commanding: the promise, although nothing follows as necessary for our day from these three. I did say that I would reduce something from the Gospels that Christ himself once did, just as the evangelists narrate what Christ did as that work of the consecration; then, that he commanded the Apostles to do this very same work — just as Luke and Paul teach that Christ commanded to be done; and finally, that besides these things that are in the very words of Christ, I will show that Christ promised that some effect would plainly follow from the attempts of future Christians.

This is something which, among the words of the Lord's Supper, we find nowhere written as what Christ promised, and although all of these things are handed over to us in the gospel, and for the sake of a single result, nevertheless never — or extremely rarely — in our days did something like this result. Yet, I see that the reader is waiting for what sort of example I might produce, and here he has it: the Gospels teach that Christ cast out demons, gave sight to the blind, and healed the sick. That is the deed done. Furthermore, he commanded the Apostles to do those same works, for so did Luke write in Ch. 9: "When Jesus called the Twelve, he gave them power and authority over all demons and that they might heal infirmities." There is the command, because he commanded the Apostles that they should do these sorts of things, since that same power of doing those works was given to them by the Christ who had done them himself. But now note the third thing, that is the promise of what would follow — and for all of those who should believe in Christ: "These signs will follow those who believe: in my name they will cast out demons, speak new tongues, and take up serpents, and if they shall drink anything noxious, it will not hurt them; they will lay their hands upon the sick, and those same will get well." Such did Christ say, as Mark 16 has it. There you have the third given, this promise, from which we clearly see no similar work arising in our own days, since there is no one who is now casting out demons from bodies or healing the sick. Yet, we do not doubt in the least that today there are many who have the faith, and if there is no effect resulting from this promise that follows us to our own day, then where is the deed or command of Christ that preceded, from which verbal description we should have the certainty that he had not promised to the priests of posterity the power of consecration?

Yet someone may say: the promise of Christ is made in vain, then? Not at all! You see, Christ did not will this promise to have a perpetual efficacy, rather for the time of the nascent and early Church, although we do not learn this from the Gospels themselves, but from usage, as interpreted by the Fathers, because in the very beginning of the Church it was held by the true believers that these miracles took place in order to strengthen faith in the gospel; yet, after the teaching of the gospel had been diffused throughout the entire world, there was no longer any need for such miracles. Whatever, if we were to follow only the bare words of the gospel text, we would be convinced that no one truly believes today unless he is able to do these same signs, that is, to cast out demons and to heal the sick, which is what Christ so patently promised as the signs that would follow those who were to believe.

Thus, who does not clearly see from all this that we should have a greater trust in the usage and interpretation of the Scriptures that have been unanimously left for us by the Fathers themselves, rather than only in the mere words of the Gospel?

For the rest, let us consider ahead of time what Luther might here jeer in response: he could say that, today, this promise would have its effect if faith had not failed. But, I would like him to explain this more fully, because for a failure of the faith could be understood in at least three ways: in regard to the very substance of the faith itself, whence there would be no faith in the world at all; this might be understood for a greatness of faith, which is that there is not such a great faith in any man that might suffice for the completion of such miracles and such as the ancients did have; finally, this could stand for the quality of faith, and that due to the poverty or defect of a living and formed faith, that these things simply do not happen. Now, I do not think that anyone will uphold the first, unless he is completely insane, since it is clear that many believe and confess Christ. Nor can the second be affirmed, since it is beyond belief that today such faith would not be found in any single member of the entire Church, such as was found in each and every one then. For this was promised to each and every believer, that such signs would follow. But not even the third manner can be stated thus, unless someone wants to assert that Christ died in vain, since he endured death so that we might live by faith.

Moreover, and whatever way we understand this use of "faith" by Luther, if he himself cannot produce such miracles, then by his own judgment he confesses that faith is wanting in himself, a subject about which he has otherwise so often boasted in his assurance that he has it. Now, if Luther himself lacks such faith, then I should not doubt whether any man in the whole Church exists in whom there might be an equally true and living faith that is pleasing to God, even though this was the faith of some who had lived earlier and had carried out such miracles. I mean to say that an unformed faith was once sufficient to cast out demons, as is clear from the Gospels: "Many will say to me in that day, 'Lord, Lord, did we not prophesy in thy name, and in thy name did we not cast out demons, and in thy name did we not do many wonders?' and I shall say to them: 'I know you not'." Christ said that the faith of these men was not at all living and informed, and yet they cast out demons and did many other miracles besides. Therefore, whatever Luther may say, he will run the same risk, such as whether or not one might still confect the flesh and blood of Christ from bread and wine, just as we may not cast out demons, since it, too, is a great and arduous work, that is to make Christ from bread, just as to cast out a demon. For this reason, given that we see how Christ so clearly promised by those words of lesser import that a certain effect would follow and yet we see it now frustrated in its effect, much more so in a matter of greater importance, and about which no such promise was made, the fear can arise that this came about due to a lack of faith — but in that which was commanded and yet not promised.

I have stated these things in this manner lest anyone should unyieldingly attach himself to the mere words of the Gospel, while spurning the interpretation of the Fathers, just as Luther does, and considering the usage and interpretation that was handed over to the Church by the Fathers as worthless. Insisting upon the plain words here will not bring about what he intends to accomplish, because the custom which the Fathers unanimously approve is that which much more certainly teaches us what should be embraced, rather than the bear words of the gospel, and I think that in these examples this is abundantly clear.

You see, it is very clear that one can in no way draw from this previous example that either the successors of the Apostles or each and every Christian — or even a priest alone — could confect the Eucharist and consecrate the body and blood of Christ from bread and wine, because Wycliffe would never have admitted it from those words, nor would anyone else who is contentiously adhering to the mere words of the text.

Yet, from the example that followed, who would miss that if anyone embraces simple sense of the words, he should concede that no one in our day is equal to anyone who lived in the primitive Church in regard to having the faith, or it is plainly proven that Christ's promise was made in vain.

Luther, however, is especially unable to escape from this because he so openly denies that anything that was handed on from Paul or from the evangelists does not equally pertain to all Christians. If that ends up being the case, then it will pertain to those of us who live now to work the miracles that Christ promised, just as it pertained to those who lived in the early Church. For this reason, since no one any longer experiences such a fruit of his faith — either in himself or in anyone else — then it is clear that that promise of Christ either no longer holds, or if it holds, then such faith no longer exists in any man, such as it once existed in each and every Christian indiscriminately — and that is beyond belief.

Therefore, what we promised to demonstrate is manifestly true, that this long-standing usage and the Fathers' concordant interpretation — with none of them dissenting — gives a much greater certainty as to the manner in which any obscure spot in the Gospels should be understood, than the mere words themselves — which can be variously twisted by the contentious — each for his own part and as he prefers. This is why I do not doubt in the least that the *same one who* so fortified the Fathers in their pursuits and pronouncements that they should not fall or fail us in the discernment of the true gospels from the false and fake ones, that he also enlightened them so that through their use of those same gospels as well as their interpretation of them, all of us throughout the entire Church should not be led astray into unholy errors.

For what would it have benefited the Church to have discerned the true gospel from the false, unless a true understanding of that same gospel had been likewise made clear to us? This is why we have given our undoubting faith to the Gospels that were received by the unanimous consensus of the Fathers, just as it was fitting that we unhesitatingly trust in the usage and interpretation which they so harmoniously gave to the Church. Nor, since the Fathers gave it to us with none of them disputing it, should we have any less certainty that this is the right interpretation of the gospel than the certainty we have for the very same gospel which they offered to us: it should considered gospel-truth or the true gospel, because the very same spirit was in each case the one that suggested the truth of either matter to their souls, that is, both of what was the gospel and what was the proper usage and interpretation of that same gospel. Of course, one or another of the Fathers can err — that I do not dispute, since they are men — but that all of them should err together, so horribly hallucinate in matters which pertain to the faith? Neither the goodness of the Spirit — who is given as the Church's guardian — nor Christ's true promise that the faith should never fail would have allowed such a thing to occur throughout so many centuries.

Wherefore, just as it was made known to us with certainty through the Church and through the Fathers of the Church what was the true and which was the false gospel, so, too, through those same men will it become no less clear what is the true and proper use and the true and proper interpretation of the gospel, and the Holy Spirit by the same instruments — that is, through the tongues of the Fathers — both in the discriminating decision about the Gospels as well as in the interpretation of their meaning. Without a doubt I freely cry with Augustine: I would not believe the gospel unless I believed the Fathers of the Church.[15] But I would not have faith in the one or in the others if I were not certainly convinced that both they and the Church were governed by the Spirit. The Spirit thus certainly governs the Church to the point that, in her entirety, he could never allow her to be subject to error in matters that are necessary for the faith, and yet the Spirit himself did not instruct the Church if not by the words of the Fathers, and for that reason — since she was taught by them which gospel (among so many others) she should receive as authentic, then it is perfectly fitting that she likewise obediently received the proper interpretation of that same gospel from those same men.

---

[15] This is likely a reworking of: Truly, I would not believe the gospel unless the authority of the Catholic Church impressed me (*Contra epistolam Manichaei* , 5.6). —Editor.

CHAPTER XI
The Judgment of Doctrine Belongs to the Fathers Rather Than to the People

HERE is still an error that remains to be refuted in this matter about which Luther has bragged to a great extent, namely his claim that it belongs to the people to pass judgment on dogmas: "To know and judge concerning doctrine belongs to each and every Christian, so that, let him be anathema whosoever shall do one hair of harm to this prerogative." Look at how he captivates and adulates the people! Not even the most foolish judge ever turned all over to the people's favor, whereas Luther wholly relies upon it, because he shrewdly noted, skillful fox that he is, how to have the people applaud his own pestilential opinions, and thus he foolishly extols the people's judgment as some sort of oracle, and he tries to buttress this with Sacred Writ itself. But Seneca put it well when he spoke of popular favor: "Popular favor is sought by evil artifice." And of course it is by the worst of the arts that Luther tries to win the people over to himself, since he teaches that faith alone suffices, that satisfaction for even the most enormously serious sins is not necessary, but that simple absolution — so long as one believes — not only wipes out the fault but also all pain due to it, and he both shamelessly and damnably asserts all this. And whose soul — be it ever so wise in other respects — would not be easily perverted by such impunity for such serious sins and by such permissive license for every vice — as well as all that might pleasingly follow from these? Especially the souls of those in the crowd, that are accustomed at all times to be so inconstant and beset by levity, always prepared to do worse! Whatever might be the crowd's judgment, it is clear even from Gentile history that neither Lycurgus from the Spartans nor Solon from the Athenians would have suffered such ills had the crowd of citizens been possessed by a more upright and incorrupt judgment. I should not speak about the Gentiles only, but also about the people of God, whom God himself made his own: do we not read of the Hebrew people that, after they had been led from such miserable slavery, suffered at the hands of Pharaoh, and that after such great miracles were shown in their midst, as well as such great and good benefits as were given to them, that they nevertheless turned back to idolatry, and spurned the true God in order to adore a calf constructed by hands? Such was their remarkable and lofty judgment that, with God spurned — the one who had worked such prodigies to liberate them from the Egyptians — they understood a self-constructed calf to be their God!

But let us make our way to our own people and times: even the crowds that heard Christ's words and were drawn by his miracles to believe him worthy of all honor, even they went from that to being completely alienated from him, and to yelling their insane and rabid demand that he be lifted up and fastened to a cross — all within the space of one week. When Paul and Barnabas were at Lycaonia, as is described in the Acts of the Apostles, the crowds heard their sermons and saw their miracles, all of which they held in such great esteem, that they could hardly be held from sacrificing to them as to the gods; nevertheless, on the following day they were so changed that they would have stoned Paul and left him for dead. Yet, who is ignorant of how often even the Christian crowd has been deluded by heretical dogmas and thus led far away from the way of truth? Didn't the Donatists glory that they had gained the good pleasure of a much larger portion of the crowds than had the orthodox? Look, how often did even the Arians overcome the right-believing by sheer magnitude of their numbers? Without a doubt, the thickness of popular judgment has been so great that there would be popular acclaim for true dogmas of the faith at one moment and for the most blatant heresies the next moment. Could the undeniable be any clearer? You remember Athanasius' life, how he convinced the entire Alexandrian people to be against the Arian teachings, and how, while still alive and having suffered so much for the faith — but about to die, he commended the orthodox Peter as his successor as bishop, and they nevertheless took Lucius, Arian partisan though he was, as their bishop in a clear demonstration of such great fickleness; they would have never done that if they had been fortified by a true and orthodox judgment. You will, however, find many such examples if you peruse the histories of all times: there would have never been the insanity of Arius, Aetius, Eunomius, Sabellius, Photinus, Paul of Samosata, or even of Macedonius' poison, had not it been received by the Christians, had they not lacked such sound judgment.

Yet how can it be that the people could be discerning about such subtle dogmas, whereas even those who were long-trained in the Scriptures would hardly be able to judge accurately? For to forage on solid food is the property of the perfected — of whatever sort they may be — as Paul noted: they had to have their senses trained, as was wont, to be able to discern good from evil. Paul made it plain as can be by such statements that the discernment of dogmas did not belong to lay crowds of people, to know what teachings were sound and which were harmful. This duty has always belonged to the few and perfect — that is, to the spiritual — rather than to the multitudes that are rather nourished by milk than by solid food, just as Paul testified in Hebrews 5: you are in need of milk and not solid food. For not even all who believe are so spiritual that they are capable of judging immediately about the dogmas of the faith, because although Paul had praised the Corinthians as being abundantly gifted in all matters, in all speech and knowledge, such that no grace or charism was lacking to them, yet they still quickly became such as Paul would call carnal and in need of milk: "I could not speak to you as if to the spiritual but as to carnal men, such as to babes in Christ I have given you milk to drink and not meat, for you were not able then, nor are you able now, because you are carnal." You see here that those whom Paul had just previously called gifted, to the extent that nothing was lacking to them, he now calls carnal and says that they are not able to eat solid food.

But this is not to be understood of the Fathers, since there were some spiritual people in that crowd — among whom even Paul himself — and whom Paul called the perfected, to whom he spoke God's wisdom and spoke of God's hidden mysteries.

Besides, there were some who were carnal and crass, and they were far from perfect and spiritual; therefore, St. Paul was speaking of the perfect and spiritual when he said that the spiritual man judges all things; but about the carnal and imperfect when he said: "The natural man does not receive those things that belong to the spirit of God, nor can he know them because they are spiritually discerned." It is therefore clear from this that since the number of carnal and crass men is much greater than the number of spiritual and perfect, it does not pertain to the multitude to judge of dogmas, such as must be done spiritually and by the spiritual — and after a long habituation, or as Paul says, having one's senses exercised in the Scriptures for the discretion of good from evil.

You can also note that not even Luther himself attributes so much to the judgment of the crowd, except in so far as it does much to persuade people unto his position, because he elsewhere ridicules the crowd's judgment; as he said in *The Babylonian Captivity*: "What do I have to do with the multitude and great number of those who err? Strongest of all is the truth." You see that here he trusts only in the truth — as he judges it — and considers it of no account that the multitude might find itself against him. But he will say that he was here speaking of the great number of those who err and not about the flock that never errs in any way, as he contends. Yet how does he prove this? To be sure, in no other manner than Arius and his followers proved that they were free from error, because they, too, produced Scriptures which they erroneously interpreted according to their understanding.

If such Scriptures that are forcefully contorted deserve our faith, then Luther correctly teaches that the Lutherans do not err, but take away the Scriptures which he has so crookedly distorted, and what else will Luther be but the most poisonous heresiarch? What will the Lutheran flock be if not a people that has been seduced and let away from truth's path, while led to a precipice?

Otherwise, and this matter Luther has not rendered degenerate anything from his progenitors, given how Socrates writes in his history that peace had been restored to the church by the great ruler Theodosius' pursuits, when those who had left the errors of Novatian returned to the Church's bosom. Also, the greater part of the Arians, Eunomians and Macedonians had eschewed these heresies, save a few bishops who had contumaciously persisted in their insanity. So, although these bishops had once glory of the great multitude of their followers, now, however, they had been left by them, and they mutually consoled one another by that cry of Christ: "Many are called but few are chosen." But it will be worthwhile to cite the words of this very history: "The ruler wondered at the Novatians' unanimity in regard to the faith, and he ordered by law that they should have their own oratories and possess the privileges of their church and faith; however, the bishops of other regions — due to their own discord — as came to reprehend their own people, they left in sadness and embarrassment, while they consoled one another by letters, lest they should suffer too much that so many had left to go over to the faith of the *homoousios* [of the same substance], and they said, 'many are called but few are chosen'."

They certainly did not say this when they were gathering a great number of people and great power to themselves, but enough about that history: from those words it is abundantly clear that the Arian bishops would, at one moment, praise the judgment of the crowd, and then whenever it no longer suited, they would spurn and condemn it — just as Luther now does: when it suits him and as often as it fits his purposes, he approves the people's judgment; when it no longer suits him, he both ridicules and condemns it. So, now we return to the matter at hand.

If we must stand by the judgment of the people, then why do we not equally believe when the Arian, Eunomian, or Macedonian followers push for their dogmas, at least as much as anyone approves the true and orthodox teaching of the Fathers?

You see, I do not think that anyone is so silly as to think that whenever the people applaud heretical judgments that they are using right judgment, and that whenever they favor orthodox judgments they are betraying an evil judgment. That is why we consider it completely certain that the same people can judge at one moment for the right-believing, at another moment for the Arians, at another moment for the Macedonians, and even at some other moment for any other founders of heresies, so what wise men would ever establish that we must side with the people's judgment — and especially when no reason must be given why the faith could, at one moment in time, be judged in this manner, rather than more firmly establishing it by some other manner.

At this point it would be good as well to learn from Luther what he means to be understood by the word "judgment," since he says that the people have the right to pass judgment. If he understands this as a right of giving assent to God's word, I don't protest at all, because the people have such a right as to believe and assent. On the other hand, if he's saying that they likewise have the right of dissent, that is false since they are held to give assent such that it is not permitted to dissent.

For even Zachary was made mute on this account, since he did not give assent immediately to the word of God, conveyed to him by the angel; and the people are praised whenever they obey from the "hearing of the ear"; and even Christ in the Gospel says: "The scribes and the Pharisees sit upon the seat of Moses, therefore observe and do all whatsoever they tell you." Now, today it is not more permissible to the Christian people to dissent from those who have legitimately received a seat of teaching in the Church, as long as they labor under no suspicion of heresy or false teaching, but it is wholly obligatory that we should give an undoubting faith to those superiors who are rightly so-called. Otherwise, as is patently clear to all, how many hesitations, what sort of tumults, and what sort of confusion would follow from the opposite? I'm not speaking of those who have forced themselves in and are not legitimately called, or those who manifestly teach the opposite and interpret the Scriptures against the sense of the ancient Fathers, because one should understand of them what Ezekiel the prophet said in Ch. 13: "Woe to the foolish prophets who follow their own spirit." And as Jeremiah has it in Ch. 27: "I have not sent them, says the Lord, and they prophesy in my name deceitfully." And no one doubts who those false prophets are: they are those who inject themselves illegitimately to preach to the people, and who manifestly teach contrary to what has been handed down to us unanimously by the orthodox Fathers, nor can they object to us that "they said many things that are not contained in the Scriptures!" because the Arians had previously objected the same thing against the orthodox, that is that the word "consubstantial" was not found in all of Sacred Scripture. But the right believing considered it enough for their defense, just as Athanasius recounts in his history of the matter, that those orthodox men who preceded them had used the same word. At that point it is easy to see how the dishonest interpretation of the Scriptures, as done by the Arians, was something that was so far from the comprehension and judgment of the people that those matters were barely understandable to the most acute and astute minds of the time.

Further, let us see what the Fathers did in regard to either Testament, whether they took their judgment on dogmas from the people or not. It is certain that the Israelite people had their seventy elders, to whom they would have recourse and in whom they would have faith — as often as any ambiguity emerged — nor was it permissible to disobey them. As Numbers 11 has it, to them was granted the spirit that had been in Moses, insofar as they would be able to see more clearly regarding all dubious matters that needed to be judged. God also clearly showed them a certain image of himself in Exodus 24, which is something that he did not do for the entire people, as the Hebrew Old Testament clearly has it, and as the Hebrew teachers unanimously affirm. They also said that it belonged to those men what was written in Deuteronomy 17 about the priests from the tribe of Levi, that is, that they should uncover the truth of judgment in all ambiguous matters. Still, one was added to them in the place of Moses, so that the number of the entire college would be 71, and that is why when Moses had gone up to the mountain to God, he left for them Aaron and Hur, who would take his place during his absence. It is very clear from these things that in the difficult and ambiguous matters, no one expected a judgment from the people in the old law; but in the new law Christ designated twelve Apostles and 70 disciples, in whom he wanted the people to have faith — not that the people should be the judge of those things which were to be taught. This is because, in Luke 10, he said to them and not to all — just as we have taught here — that "whoever hears you, hears me; and whoever despises you, despises me." Now, you should understand the word "despise" to mean whoever does not give assent to their instruction.

Although Paul had received the same gospel from Christ as had the others, nevertheless, because he had not followed Christ while he was here on this earth, he was therefore commanded to compare his gospel with the Apostles, that it might be approved by them: "I went up according to revelation and communicated to them the gospel which I preach among the Gentiles: but apart to them who seemed to be something." So, you see that Paul solicited the judgment of the ecclesiastical leaders and not that of the people.

Besides that, when at Antioch some of the brethren had taught that circumcision was necessary, Paul and Barnabas — who taught the contrary — were sent to Jerusalem, to the Apostles and elders, to have a consultation about this question: as it is in the Acts of the Apostles, the Apostles and presbyters therefore came together so that they could look over the matter and, once having defined it, that they might write to those who were absent what they should believe. And it is certain that many Christians — and not only those who were at Antioch — but also many others throughout all parts of the world — were not called to that synod, and their opinion was not required on the matter, because it only belonged to the Apostles and elders to pass a sentence on this subject, just as it is written: "The Apostles and ancients assembled to consider of this matter." But someone will say: "Later on there is also mention of the brothers and of the whole Church, in whose name, too, letters were sent to Antioch." I do not dispute that, but this was something that came from the Apostles' humility rather than absolute necessity, that they should have written in such a manner, because it is clear that those who are mentioned later on had no greater say or authority in the matter than did those who were then in Antioch, or in Syria, or Cilicia, who were absent. Nor did they seek the agreement of those among the brethren or disciples who were then absent, and so it must follow that they did not have any right of dissent. Luke even describes the decree in the following chapter: "As they passed through the cities, they delivered unto them the decrees to keep, that were decreed by the Apostles and ancients who were at Jerusalem." Here you see, dear reader, that the decrees made by the Apostles and elders at Jerusalem bound all those who were absent. Likewise, we find it written in Chapter 21 that when Paul had come to Jerusalem for the final time to see James and the elders: "But, as touching the Gentiles that believe, we have written, decreeing that they should only refrain themselves from those things." You see that they speak of a decree, and that they had done this without any consultation of them, which they would have not done if it had been licit to ignore the decrees of the Apostles. Here, too, it is worth noting that the Apostles and presbyters did not fear to assert their decree as having proceeded from the Holy Spirit: "It seemed right to the Holy Ghost and to us that we should put no greater burden upon you."

In addition to this, when the Gospels were first received, there is no doubt that there were four read in the Church then, just as it is now, although there were others that had been suggested, such as the gospels of Peter, Thomas, Matthew, Nicodemus, as well as the one called "according to the Hebrews," and in this matter what did the judgment of the people bring forward in regard to rejection or acceptance? Nothing at all, and that is because — as was right and proper — it was based on the decisions of the Apostles and disciples that the people were required to believe in such things, since it was written in Psalm 71: "Let the mountains receive peace for the people, and the hills justice." Surely the mountains were those who were preeminent like princes in the church, just as much for their holiness as for their understanding of the Scriptures, and it was fitting for them to not only receive the gospel of peace but also to hand it over to be received by the people. Then, those lesser hills should be understood of those for whom it was proper to reverently receive and to believe unto justice whatsoever those very mountains had indicated to be worthy of belief.

Furthermore, if the people's judgment in this matter had been required, it is more believable that what is called the Gospel of the Hebrews would have been held up before all others, since the overwhelmingly greater portion of Christians were Hebrews, nor would they have lost all human respect for that. Otherwise, there would not have arisen any murmuring and complaint between the Greeks and Hebrews, that some widows were being overlooked in the daily rations, as in Acts 7. However it stands, it is clear to all that in the reception or rejection of the Gospels, the people's judgment was not sought out, but rather the approbation or repudiation of them belonged entirely to those princes in the Church and not to the plain people. Now, if the people's judgment was not sought in the reception of the Gospels, much less right should we stand by their judgment regarding the elucidation of obscure gospel passages, because when the question concerning "consubstantial" arose, what judgment of the people was sought, given how those who were very well and long trained in the Sacred Scriptures had hallucinated so much over this subtle question? For example, Eusebius of Caesarea — a great and learned man — as well as many others were for some time beset by error, whereas they later cast the error off, thanks to a greater illumination from the Scriptures. So since such great men were blind in this judgment on matters of the faith, who is so insane that he thinks that we should abide by the judgment of the unlearned masses?

In addition, if there is now a question of whether or not the Letter of James should be numbered among the Catholic Epistles or — as it seems to Luther — completely cast out, what people will be the judge in place of the flock? Will it be great and learned princes of the Church who are called "pastors" in the writings of the Apostles? Of course it is much more sensible to have these men as the judges on such an issue rather than the people, and that whatever they decide to decree should be received without contradiction by the others, because otherwise, if Luther ends up persuading his flock that this is not among the Universal or Catholic Epistles of Scripture and they decide to sign on to his sentence, then we will either have a manifest season, or we will all be bound by the judgment of the Lutherans, to cast out of our Bibles St. James. And although Origen — or if someone else might be found to be as diligent and circumspect in the examination of Scripture as Origen was — did say that this was truly a Catholic letter, will this not be considered against Luther? And why? Of course, because the Lutheran people think thus on the matter and so have judged it to stand by the judgment of the people. Who does not see here how Luther is trying to retreat? But what if some Christian group that is much more numerous than the Lutherans should end up judging differently, and decrees this letter to be replaced in the Bibles, asserts that it is fully Catholic — just as the most holy and learned Fathers commended it by name? Who will then be the judge between the two peoples? You see, it is not right that we to whom, by legitimate succession, the faith has flowed from the very first columns of the Church, through so many faithful and worthy intermediaries, should now despise and cast off their learning and diligence in order to join hands with the adversary, who has so ungratefully and impiously mutilated their life, doctrine, and learning. Yet this man will not suffer himself to be judged by us or by the writings of our great predecessors, whom he considers worthless. What, therefore, shall we say? Will we consider Christ who, on account of his great love for us, not only was born for us but also deigned to die and to nourish us by the sacraments of his flesh and blood, to promise us the Holy Ghost from heaven, that he should remain with us to teach us all truth? I am saying this: will we consider our ardent lover to have treated his flock — whom he redeemed at such a great price — that he would allow us to be cast down, to lie in the horrendous darkness of error (as Luther says to us), and that through so many centuries? And that he would have left us no judge to cast out this darkness — besides the one and only Luther? Does anyone who reads all this not see that he who writes with such fury against the most illustrious king must be moved by some demon that is quite alien from the Divine Spirit? Thus it was written ahead of time, against the judgment of Luther and the Lutherans, so that we might know how Luther has shown himself a carnal man, such as Paul would not permit to have any judgment over spiritual matters, but rather that we should have the doctrine of the Spirit through a most integral and upright conduit, through the sacred canals of the most learned and most holy Fathers, as derived from the fonts and sources themselves. Therefore, if Luther and his people have assumed the prerogative of passing judgment against the Letter of James or against any other Scripture, or against any other interpretation of Scripture that enjoys the unanimous consent of the Fathers, then this is clearly of no great importance to us, and we are not permitted in any way to admit their interpretation which goes against our much greater predecessors, unless we should wish to go against Paul, who strenuously warned that we should no longer be children who are moved and cared about by any sort of wind of doctrine through the wiles of men, and by the deceit which they use to rise up against us and impose themselves upon us.

To all of the preceding one might add that if popular judgment is of any account, there are so many litigious matters that plague us now that were already judged, because it is quite plain that throughout Church in the entire world, the truth which Luther condemns had already been approved long ago by the princes of all the churches, and received by the people without any contradiction. Therefore, why do we still contend about such a matter, since the judgment has been concluded — even by the judgment of the people — long ago? Is the judgment of such good and just people not of equal — not to say greater — authority, given that such a people was closer to the Apostles and martyrs than any people that now lives, and that they should be considered the pure wine compared to the dregs, if we are comparing people? So, if the people's judgment is worth anything in this case, then the matter is already decided and cannot be revoked by a lesser people, since it was approved by a much greater people — unless of course we want to imitate childish games and destroy today what was built yesterday. Yet, that would be the case of learning and yet never arriving at a knowledge of the truth, because by the same right that the people of the present should be allowed to cast doubt upon the judgment of that prior people, yes, by that very same right a future people will condemn the judgment of this present people.

Yet, what else would this be but to go against the doctrine of Paul, and to never grow up or mature, but rather to remain children and be moved and carried away by every wind of teaching, through the trickery and deceit of men? As we read in Ecclesiasticus (Sirach 34): "When one builds up, and another destroys, what profit have they but the labor?" Here Luther will respond: the people of that time had their liberty taken away. But this is completely false, because the Lutherans of today adhere to Luther no more constantly than did those prior people adhere to their ecclesiastical rulers. This matter is most manifest in Athanasius, Ambrose, Chrysostom, and so many others, because their hearers, too, were more prepared to suffer death than to suffer those men to be removed from their midst. I think that these points suffice such that any intelligent reader will see that the crowds of peoples do not have any right to dissent from the dogmas that are given by those who are legitimately constituted as preachers of the Divine Word, and interpreters of the Sacred Scripture — especially in those matters that pertain to the faith, and so long as the Fathers of old conformed themselves to these in harmony and unanimity.

On the Judgment of the People

Now, however, it is proper and right to put forth the reasons whereby Luther affirms the contrary.

First Reason

"Christ instituted this right by various and invincible statements, such as in Mt. 7: 'Beware of false prophets, who come to you in sheep's clothing.' This saying speaks to the people of their teachers, and commands them to avoid their false teachings, but how can they avoid them unless they know [them]? And how do they know unless they have the right to judge? And here Christ established not only the right, but the commandment to judge, so that this sole authority would suffice against the opinions of all the pontiffs, all the Fathers, all the councils, and all the schools, which reserve the right of judging and discerning for only bishops and ministers, and have thus impiously and sacrilegiously taken it away from the queen of the Church [the people]. For Christ stands saying: 'Beware of false prophets'."

Let the reader note first how forcefully Luther contorts this Scripture, since there is not a word mentioned here about dogmas or judgment, because Christ did not say here, "Beware of dogmas, so that you might discern from among them which are harmful and which bring Salvation"; nor did he say, "Beware of false dogmas, lest they harm you," but he said, "Beware of false prophets." And what else is this than as if he had said, "Flee the fellowship or society of false prophets, so that you do not listen to them?" For Christ does not suffer that such persons should be heard, that is, that their speech should not do harm straight away and easily take in the more simple people. This is why even Paul exhorted the Romans that they should move away from such seducers, since those were the people who spoke smoothly and flatteringly in order to deceive the hearts of the simple. It was this sort that Paul, too, called "pseudo-apostles" in 2 Cor. 11: "Such false apostles are deceitful workmen, transforming themselves into the apostles of Christ." Paul was fearful of these same, lest as the serpent had deceived Eve by his deceitfulness, so might these be corrupted in their senses away from that simplicity that is in Christ. Without a doubt, it is extremely dangerous that such men should be heard not only by those who are simple, but even by those who have a modicum of expertise in the Scriptures: this matter is well known enough that it will not require many words to explain. Who does not know about Novatus, Arius, Macedonius, and how many they corrupted, although the right-believing had warned them of the danger and that if they would flee and turn away from such men, they would not incur any harm? Thus, Christ here commanded us to be wary of false prophets who use as a pretext the name of Christianity, as if it were sheep's clothing, while on the inside they are hidden like ravaging wolves, just as Tertullian truly said, that is that their fallacious opinions and spirit are covered up so that they can infest Christ's flock; therefore, Christ is here forbidding that anyone should listen to such false prophets, but he is not commanding that these men's dogmas should be examined and judged by anyone and everyone, because that would be so much more dangerous, for sure.

But Luther will claim: "From this speech it clearly follows that all have the right to judge. You see, Christ said these words to the people, against the doctors, and commanded them to avoid their false dogmas: yet, how can they avoid whatever they do not know, and how will they ever know unless they have the right of judging?"

I respond: if a man should command his wife to be wary of strange men, will we think that it is now permissible for the wife to hear the perverse persuasion of the strange men, under the pretext of judging them? Of course not! Rather, the man is trying to make it so that his most beloved wife would not fall into danger, and that is why he forbade any conversation with them at all. This is the same sort of zeal that our spouse, Christ Jesus, has for us. He thus willed it not that we should be seduced by this sort of false prophet, and that is why he commanded that we should be wholly wary of them: "Beware all false prophets." False prophets are those about whom it is written in Apocalypse 2: "They call themselves apostles and they are not." That is, they say that they are sent and yet no one sent them. Christ also spoke of them elsewhere, saying that they would seduce many, as in Mark 13. It is for this reason that if one would not be seduced by them, then he ought to likewise avoid all and every common affair with them, because as Paul says in 1 Cor. 15: "Evil companionship corrupts gracious morals." Therefore, Christ did not mean by this phrase that each and every person should judge of their dogmas — which is something that could not take place without danger to the simple — but rather that they should not receive anyone who is even suspect of error or not legitimately sent, that they should refrain from them until their doctrines are more firmly approved by those to whom it belongs to examine doctrines.

My sincere reader, note here, too, by what sort of trickery Luther is trying to join Christ's words to the right of judging dogmas. In the beginning he cites the Scripture itself: "Beware of false prophets, who come to you in sheep's clothing," and then he adds a meaning to it: "Christ certainly said this to the people, against the doctors, and he commanded them to beware of their false doctrines." Then he adds a third part to this: "Yet how shall they avoid what they do not know?" Then, finally, he adds: "How will they know unless they have the right to judge?" In this manner he introduces the poison little by little and step by step. Now, although I could very easily undermine each of his points one by one, I will only respond to the final point, that the people — about whom Christ does not speak a single word here — could not only know the teachings, but the false prophets — and their note would be that they were not legitimately sent, although they would have usurped the teacher's seat or See, or that they would be held suspect by good men, or that their teaching was openly condemned, or finally even from other indications, which are found throughout Paul's letters everywhere. And just to give one citation from many, let us see Romans 16: "I beg you, brethren, to mark them who make dissensions and offences contrary to the doctrine which you have learned and avoid them." Certainly these words were not written only for the Romans, but without a doubt they are for all Christians, which Luther will not be able to deny, if he hopes to remain consistent. I should hope that all Lutherans would carefully weigh these words, but let us return to the matter at hand: certainly those are the indications by which a true prophet can be discerned from a false one, so that it does not become necessary for every single Christian to have the right of judging. Similarly, in regards to the third point I would say this: a false prophet can be avoided by the more simple-minded thanks to the admonition and warnings of others, although they may not be able to judge those dogmas, and I would say the same in regard to the second point, since they who flee the books and speeches of false doctors will also be able to avoid false doctrines, since the latter is impossible without the hearing of those doctrines.

At the end of it all, I am amazed by this man's shamelessness, that he would not be ashamed to introduce this Scripture — although the study of Scripture is his primary occupation, because this citation smites no one as much as it does Luther, for if he is not a false prophet, no one ever was. Who would not call "false-prophet" the one who so impiously calls God the author of evils, who takes away free will, who feels no fear in asserting that all things are led on by necessity, who goes so fully against the Scriptures by attributing everything to faith and nothing to works, who inflicts so much unseemly harm on the Scriptures by condemning some of them and by erroneously interpreting others, who completely disdains and defies the Fathers' holy councils and their most holy documents, and who finally leaves no stone unturned in the establishment of his own heresy? If only that very saintly Polycarp were still living, who, whenever he heard anything novel against the faith, was accustomed to shut his ears completely and to yell out: "O good God! What a time you reserved for me, that I should hear such things!" What would that most devout man do now, were he to hear so many and such pernicious heresies? But even that most upright father and bishop, Irenaeus, who so sharply reprimanded Florinus, the one who had stated that God was the author of evils, oh how he would immediately chase Luther with a flame, since he resurrected that ancient heresy! Anyone can read the battles of the orthodox against the heretics and he will find that there was no greater foundational principle upon which they were set than to say, "These are the things which we have received from our trustworthy predecessors, such that we cannot change this faith by any imposition of man or demon." That once sufficed to refute any heretic, and as Luther now incites people against that foundation, he is either a false prophet or else no one ever was.

ON THE JUDGMENT OF THE PEOPLE

Yet someone will still say, "Luther's followers hear him gladly, and a great fruit comes from his sermons, the sort of fruit that Christ used to distinguish pious prophets from the impious, 'from their fruits you shall know them'." I am not in amazement, however, that he is gladly heard, since he grants such license to all indiscriminately; for he permits Christians to be bound by no laws, nor does he allow bishops any faculty for establishing laws. This is how it comes about that he can remove from his subjects all obedience and subjection that they owe to their superiors, nor is that all, but he also levels any attempt to observe the laws of God, since he calls them "impossible for anyone," and says that no one can observe the divine mandates. He also cuts away all eagerness towards contrition for sins, since — as he says — contrition that does not come about in grace, only makes the sinner worse; he even takes away any diligent attention to Confession, at least that which is made to priests, because he states as a dogma that no one is required to do so; but he even contends that there is no necessary satisfaction and penalty that can be demanded for any sins which happen in secret, and rather that all of them are freely pardoned by faith. He cries that all tonsured priests are fakes, because — as he says — "every Christian is truly a priest." He denies that good works are necessary for salvation, since for him no work — howsoever good it may be — lacks sin. He widely and randomly preaches to the people all this, together with so many other claims that betray this libertine evil. What evil man would not gladly hear such things? As for what sort of fruits this gives rise to, they are the most bitter of all: schisms, quarrels, contentions, enmities, and the most rabid fury, shamelessness, a cornucopia of evil deeds, adulteries of the brides of Christ, breaking of vows, deflowering holy virginity, and what in return? The return of monks to the embrace of the world and women: giving what is holy to dogs and pearls to pigs.

You might suggest that in the midst of all this, there is still belief in God and that Christ is loved: even this is not true, unless the Scriptures themselves are false, because Christ says in John 14, "If you love me, keep my commands." And again, "He who has my commands and keeps them, he it is that loves me," and shortly thereafter, "If anyone loves me, he will keep my word." Paul, too, says, "Circumcision availeth nothing, but the keeping of the commands of God" in 1 Cor. 7, and in 1 John 2 likewise: "Whoever says 'I know Him' and does not keep his commands is a liar, and the truth is not in him." Thus, let them make believe all they wish that they believe and love: if they do not keep the commands, then what they are doing is nothing. Nor is it credible that they are busy about keeping the commands since they deny that it is possible that even the least of the commands could be observed and kept by anyone. Therefore, from his fruits, let Luther be abundantly known by you as just such a prophet, either as a good or evil one. That is why even Christ added, "From their fruits you will know them." If these are schisms, fights and furies, accusations and cursing, the adulteration of Sacred Scripture, impunity for every sort of crime, the breaking of vows, incestuous impurities with nuns, fornicating with monks, contempt for the praying of canonical hours, abominable violation of fasts, blasphemies against the images of Christ and the saints, horrible sayings against the most holy Mother of God, heinous abuse of the Sacred Eucharist — I repeat — if it is this and other innumerable disgraceful acts that should be called the "good fruits," then Luther will be a good prophet; if, on the other hand, these are the worst misdeeds and are execrable to all truly Christian ears, who would not flee in horror and denounce Luther as some terrifying virus?

Now, to return to what we had proposed: I think that is sufficiently clear now that Luther cannot gather from the words of Christ that the people should have a command or right to judge doctrines, but rather to flee and beware of false prophets, among whose number Luther shows himself to be principal by the clearest of indicators. That is because the judgment of doctrines is so difficult that, in such matters, even those who are much more learned are very often fooled, just as we showed in regard to Eusebius earlier; therefore, let Luther go ahead and boast that this sole authority should suffice against the opinions of all pontiffs, every Father, and the whole number of councils and schools, as he sacrilegiously and irreligiously cries that all of them took this right of judgment from the people. I'll say it again: let him go on pursuing them with such adulation, toying with a people that is rightfully seduced by such a prophet, while they decline to listen to the Christ who warns them to avoid this wolf's fraud and deceit. Christ indeed stands, saying, "Be attentive for false prophets who come to you in sheep's clothing, but who on the inside are ravaging wolves — from their fruits you will know them." There is no reason for Germans to think that the Romans are here called wolves, who would steal their gold from them, because wolves do not lust after a gold but after blood — which is what the heretics do, because they take that which is more precious than any gold, I mean souls, and they especially boast over that sort of prey. Luther has already shown himself to be just such a wolf in sheepskin, and although this sole authority seemed to him sufficient in this matter, he nevertheless wanted to render it a little more solid with quotes from the Old Testament, and I will now add those very words of his.

Luther's Second Reason

"Almost all the voices of the prophets agree with this, because what do the prophets do besides warn the people not to believe in false prophets? And what is this warning but a declaration and confirmation of the people having the right to judge and discern, admonishing them to do their very own work, and stirring them up against the doctrines of all their priests and teachers? Therefore, we here conclude that as often as Moses, Joshua, David, and all the prophets in the Old Testament call and admonish the people, just as many times do they shout, command, affirm, and stir up the right of the people to discern and judge all the dogmas of all teachers; and they do this in an infinite number of places. Has our Henry here — or any other impure Thomist — anything to bark against these arguments? Have we not stopped the mouths of those that speak wickedness?"

Here again he shows himself to be a false and fallacious prophet, as he tries studiously to deceive us by the polyvalent meaning of this word, because "prophet" is understood in a two-fold sense: for Paul, a prophet is one who speaks and explains the Scriptures to the people, and it is in this sense that Luther seems to have understood Christ's forgoing words, whereby he admonished the people to be wary of false doctors and — as he says it — false dogmas. Additionally, since we are warned in the Old Testament that we should take care for false prophets, that should be understood of those who falsely prophesy regarding future events, such as we read in Deuteronomy 18 an indication by which a true prophet can be discerned from a false one: "Thou shalt have this sign: Whatsoever that same prophet foretells in the name of the Lord, and it comes not to pass: that thing the Lord has not spoken." Yes, it is by that sign that a false prophet was judged among them, and although besides the prophets there were others who interpreted and taught the Scriptures, I do not read of them being called prophets anywhere else in the Old Testament. For this reason, Luther's second argument does not strengthen the first at all and has no affinity with it, because in the discernment of prophets it was necessary — as we said — to await the reality of future events to distinguish the truth, whereas there is no wait in discerning the truth of the judgment of those interpreters who have the grace of the Spirit and have their senses so very well exercised in the Scriptures. Thus are prophets distinguished in one manner and scriptural interpreters in another.

But Luther will say that those who were prophets also taught many things, and I do not deny this, but by the title of "teaching," they were not called prophets. Nor were there lacking among the Jews in the 300 years before Christ both teachers, or doctors, and interpreters, and yet it is an established fact that there were no prophets during that time until Zachary, John the Baptist's father. For this very reason, it is clearly false to assert that as many times as Moses, Joshua, and David or any other prophet in the old law called and admonished the people about false prophets, that just as frequently they also clamored and commanded all men, confirmed and raised up everyone to a right of discerning and judging doctrines. You see, even true prophets frequently warned the people that they should not listen to false prophets at all, just as you have Jeremiah saying: "Therefore hearken not to your prophets, and diviners, and dreamers, and soothsaying sorcerers, that say to you: You shall not serve the king of Babylon. For they prophesy lies to you." Shortly thereafter he says, "Thus says the Lord: Hearken

234

not to the words of your prophets that say to you: behold, the vessels of the Lord shall now in a short time be brought again from Babylon: for they prophesy a lie unto you; therefore hearken not to them." Does it seem to you that Jeremiah has just commanded the people to judge for themselves the dogmas of the false prophets, or rather that they should be against them and close their ears to them completely? But do you think that even Moses commanded the people to judge teachings when he said to them in Deut. 18: "Beware lest thou have a mind to imitate the abominations of those nations. Neither let there be found among you any one that shall expiate his son or daughter, making them to pass through the fire: or that consults soothsayers, or observes dreams and omens, neither let there be any wizard, nor charmer, nor any one that consults pythonic spirits, or fortune tellers, or that seeks the truth from the dead"? Did Moses not think that it was much safer for the people to necessarily ignore the teachings of those men, rather than to be investigators and judges of the teachings — to their own great peril? Now if Luther still tries to contest that there is just one received meaning of this word in both Testaments, I would like him to still notice how severe the warning about the false prophets is in every citation, as for instance in Deut. 18: "But the prophet, who being corrupted with pride, shall speak in my name things that I did not command him to say, or in the name of strange gods, shall be slain." If Luther attempts to excuse himself here again for the many errors and false doctrines that he has brought forth under the name of Christ — in the absence of any command given to him by Christ, rather corrupted by his own pride or inspired by some evil spirit — he will definitely hear himself condemned, nor can he in any way twist this Scripture back against the orthodox Fathers and their followers, since in the overwhelming majority of them there was not the smallest suspicion of arrogance, much less of interpretations of Scripture that received their impulse from an evil spirit, but on the contrary, from the Holy Spirit did such come, just as they did not doubt that the Spirit was sent for this very reason, so that he might faithfully instruct the Church. Who would be so lacking in shame as to say that these men were not legitimately called to teach the people, and that they were not instructed by that very same Spirit — unless he wants to suggest that the Holy Ghost had been sent in vain and had remained idle in the Church? But it is wicked to even think that. Now, if the previous interpreters were called to this task legitimately, then it is patently obvious that Luther is corrupted by pride and similarly pressed by the evil spirit, since he does not despise only one of those others but all of them without distinction. Or does he not show himself incredibly arrogant even in his frivolous disputes? I think that the reader now understands how his statements were nothing but blabber and whining, although he bragged that he had overcome by means of such, and with his words termed the most illustrious king an impure Thomist who had nothing to mutter back against his arguments, because he had shut up the mouths of those who spoke wicked things. If he did that, it would seem odd that he did not shut his own mouth first, since none has uttered anything more impiously and shamelessly than that mouth did. Now we will respond to his citations from the New Testament.

Luther's Third Reason

"Let us come to the New Testament. Christ says in John 10, 'My sheep hear my voice, and do not hear the voice of strangers, but flee from them.' Does he not here make the sheep judges, and give to those who hear the right of discernment?"

Let us note immediately what great license Luther takes in his citation of this Scripture: Christ certainly never spoke such about his own sheep: "My sheep do not hear the voice of strangers" — it is plainly false that Christ's sheep never hear the voice of strangers, but that they always flee from them. Christ's sheep have been found quite frequently to have followed the voice of strangers — especially when the Arian heresy vexed the Church of Christ, because at that time there were many who were seduced by false teaching, many of whom afterwards came to their good senses and returned to the Catholic faith, as we will show presently, and we do not even despair of Luther's followers, that the same should

likewise come about, although by his wiles many of them, Christ's
sheep, have strayed from the right path of truth for sure. Yet, I do
not deny that Christ spoke of the sheep in common, and in their
regard it is true that they do not follow the voice of strangers, but
rather the voice of their pastors with whom they have enjoyed
a long and lasting relationship; but, it is evident that some of
Christ's mystical sheep did follow another voice, that of strangers,
for some time, although they later returned to Christ, because it is
impossible that Christ's predestined sheep should not finally return
to Christ's voice when they hear it, as much as they may dabble
among heretical doctrines in the meanwhile. Christ gives witness
to the same truth in that very chapter: "I have other sheep that are
not of this flock, and I must bring them, too, and they shall hear
my voice: and they shall become one flock and one shepherd." You
see how he calls those sheep his own, which had not yet listened
or hearkened to his voice, but to one that was a stranger to Christ.

So, too, were many of the Jews, while Christ was here preaching
on earth, and who despised his voice, and yet after his Ascension,
they believed in his word, just as is very clear from the Acts of the
Apostles; for this reason it is plainly false that Christ's sheep would
never follow the voice of strangers, and this is nowhere to be found
in the Gospels. Now, if Luther is saying that this is contained in a
parable, I am not going to fight that, but it is not necessary that all
whatsoever is said in a parable should have an entirely mystical
truth, just as Chrysostom, Jerome, Augustine, and the other Fathers
say much more than once: those who labored longer sure murmured
in the parable against the master of the household, because those
who had come later were given the same recompense; likewise in a
parable, the elder son was indignant with his father because he had
slain the fatted calf for the return of the prodigal son, yet there is
not a single murmur heard from the mystical workers or brothers.
At this point, in order to demonstrate what we have in mind more
clearly, let us consider the example of Christ's words, "I and the
Father are one." All heretics as well as all orthodox give their assent
to this, but they do so precisely because it was said by Christ; and
yet from this very citation — because of the two-fold understanding
of these words — various different dogmas were born, with some
saying that the Father and the Son are one in substance, while

others denied that there was any unity of substance among them, but only a unity of harmony and of wills, as they taught it. Orthodox believers fully affirmed that the Son was consubstantial with the Father, but Arius and his followers disputed with them on all accounts, and while this contention went on, very many of Christ's sheep were in great danger. Nor am I speaking only of the more simple sheep, but also of the more potent rams, who — in addition to the light of faith — had a great amount of learning in the Scriptures. That same Eusebius of Caesarea, whom for his learning in the Scriptures Jerome calls the "key to the Scriptures" and "Guardian of the New Testament" in his Catalog, written for Desiderius, yes, this same great man heard Arius's interpretation and believed him and followed his partisans for some time; and yet who doubts that he was one of Christ's sheep, since he made his way back from there to the true faith of Christ? Now, if Eusebius was in such danger, and fell so in his judgment, then I would like to know what sort of certainty the rest of the people can have. Yet, you will say, Eusebius finally hearkened and believed that the Son was consubstantial to the Father: that is true and I do not dispute it: for me it suffices that he was misled by his own judgment while he was one of Christ's sheep, and that he then followed a voice that was a stranger to Christ, because if he had the right to judge, then he was within his right to do what he did, and that should have been perfectly permissible for him. No one, however, misses how horribly he acted by following his own judgment, since it did not escape him that his betters[16] held and taught the contrary, and when he repented and returned to the faith he admitted the same, as is clear in the history that he wrote.

This should convince anyone without reserve just what sort of right Christians have to judge dogmas, that is, that they have the right to assent — and not only to the gospel but also to the entirety of Catholic truth that is passed on to the Church by our great predecessors, in unanimous consensus, for us to believe, because in such matters there is no doubt that Christ himself speaks together with the Spirit of Christ.

---

[16] Editor's note: The Latin word *majores* here implies more than just better individuals, but predecessors in faith.

On the Judgment of the People

This is why all those who are truly Christ's sheep will hearken to this voice, and those who do not finally hearken to this voice clearly show that they were in no way the sheep of Christ. But every Christian does not have the right to dissent from this voice, because if every Christian had this right, then it would likewise be right to dissent from Christ's voice itself! And yet, this is manifestly false. You see, how do we know the voice of Christ except through the Fathers who pointed it out to us? I ask again: whence do we come to know which are the true Gospels — for instance, that of Matthew, or of Luke, or of John — if not through those greater men? For this very reason, as we have faith in them in the discernment of the true Gospels, it is just as fitting to trust their interpretation of them, handed down to us as it is, and especially when they are all in a consensus, because if any one of us should follow his own judgment and his own spirit, then there would surely be just as many opinions as there are people. On account of this, who does not plainly see that we should stand with our great superiors in their definitions? I do not deny that one or another of the Fathers might err, but that all should err in a serious matter that pertains to the faith, and when they have unanimously agreed upon it? I am so far from believing such, that I should much rather die in this faith. For it is unbelievable that the same Holy Spirit whom Christ called the Spirit of Truth and promised to send for this purpose — that is, to remain within the Church to teach us all truth — should allow it to happen that so many of our leaders who went before us should have all erred, through such a long period of time, and with such great damage and disastrous death for souls. I should also add that whoever decides to despise these predecessors and disdains to hold these prior Fathers as the leaders of his path and progress, but rather remains confidently reliant on his own judgment and follows his own spirit, such a person invades Christ's flock, and the indication is quite evident: the gatekeeper did not open unto him, nor did he enter through the true door, but like a thief and robber, he came upon the gate and the gatekeeper from another location. For who doubts that these Fathers of old legitimately entered the stable of the sheep and that they had the gatekeeper as a most familiar friend, as they took the direct path to the gate? So, since Luther so pridefully defies and disdains to follow the path traced by

them, who will ever believe that either the gatekeeper opened unto
him who was so against his fellows inside, or that a man of such
arrogant spirit could have ever entered by such a humble gate? Yet,
I fear that I might become tedious to my readers by prolixity of
speech, and thus I will succinctly respond to what follows.

Luther's Fourth Reason

"And when in 1 Cor. 14 Paul says, 'Let one speak, let the others
judge; but if anything should be revealed to one that is sitting, let
the former speaker hold his peace', does he not here desire that
judgment should rest with the hearer?"

I respond: he does desire that judgment should rest with some
hearers — but not with all — because Paul rightly knew that among
them there were many who were not able to judge, a fact that is
patently clear from the beginning of this epistle, where he writes:
"I, brethren, could not speak to you as unto spiritual, but as unto
carnal. As unto little ones in Christ. I gave you milk to drink, not
meat: for you were not able as yet. But neither indeed are you
now able: for you are yet carnal." Yet, whoever is carnal does not
perceive the things that belong to the spirit of God, since that
which is of the spirit of God is to be judged spiritually, just as
Paul said shortly before this. Therefore, it is incorrect to say that
he allowed for judgment among all the rest, but it was rather only
for those who were truly prophets and truly spiritual, since he had
even noted that among them there were some who seemed to be
spiritual and yet were not, as you see in Chapter 14: "If any seem
to be a prophet or spiritual, let him know the things that I write to
you, that they are the commandments of the Lord." It is thus clear
from these statements that nothing of the sort was given to all the
rest of the people, but rather only to those who truly were spiritual
and prophets — to them was granted judgment. Otherwise, you
can see, there would have been occasion for much confusion and
discord, had each and every one followed his own judgment and

spoken from his own sense. This is why even Paul prohibited this very thing when he said in 1 Cor. 14: "God is not the author of confusion but of peace, as it is in all congregations of the saints," just as if he had said: "All order would be very disturbed in this way, and there would be great confusion in the church, and that cannot come from God, from whom peace and the fullness of order flow forth." If Luther were to consider these words with precision, he would certainly know that this discord — which he has caused to arise in the Church against our foregone Fathers, with such great confusion and disturbance of all just order — does not proceed from God, who is not the author of confusion but of peace.

Luther's Fifth Reason

"If Christ, as in Mt. 24 and everywhere besides, says anything in his teaching about false teachers, and whatever Peter and Paul say of false apostles — who are teachers — and John about proving the spirits, it follows that the authority in judging, proving, and condemning must lie with the people, and it lies with them most rightly."

We will respond to each point. In Mt. 24, Christ says, "Take heed that no man seduce you. For many will come in my name saying, 'I am Christ.' And they will seduce many." He adds this in the same chapter: "There shall arise false Christs and false prophets and shall show great signs and wonders, insomuch as to deceive (if possible) even the elect. Behold, I have forewarned you." Is it not a great wonder that such a large part of Germany has been seduced by one little brother, such that they will no longer believe the numerous great princes of the Church who preceded us? And it is clear just as Christ laid out before them, because he commanded that no one should believe such false prophets: "Do not believe them," just as if he had stated: "Stand in the doctrine and teaching which you have received, nor must you leave it because of their new dogmas." Paul is likewise fearful in 2 Cor. 11 of the craftiness of these false apostles — whom he calls "workers of deceit" who transform themselves into apostles of Christ — and he fears, "lest, as the serpent seduced Eve by his subtlety, so your minds — O Corinthians — should be corrupted and fall from the simplicity that is in Christ." Here Paul is endeavoring to convince the Corinthians that they should abstain completely from even hearing such men, rather than suffering to hear out their doctrines. Peter, too, calls such pseudo-prophets "lying teachers" in 1 Peter, and those who secretly introduce pernicious sects; he also adds in that same place that these men follow the flesh and walk in the concupiscence of uncleanness, that they despise ruling authority, that they are audacious and inflexibly harsh, that they have no reverence for those who excel in glory, and that they attack with insults. If these descriptions do not fit Luther perfectly, then I do not know whom they fit.

Furthermore, the discernment of spirits is a particular gift that does not belong to each and every person, just as Paul clearly notes in 1 Cor. 12, and therefore when John, in 1 Jn. 4, speaks of proving the spirits, he says, "Dearly beloved, believe not every spirit, but try the spirits if they be of God: because many false prophets are gone out into the world." I am saying that, in this spot, John either orders that the spirits are not to be examined by every man, or he is demanding that sort of examination which requires great and subtle learning, because he wishes the pseudo prophet to be recognized by this sole indicator: that he tears apart the Church and introduces the thorns and thickets of schisms and heresies, because these are the fruits that give rise to such trees. But let us hear John himself: "By this will you know the Spirit of God. Every spirit which confesses that Jesus Christ is come in the flesh is of God." What shall we say here: did Arius not confess that Jesus Christ had come in the flesh? Or besides Arius, did not many other heretics, such as Eunomius and Macedonius? They doubtlessly confessed — but with their voice alone — as they nevertheless denied by their deeds, since Christ did come into flesh for the unity and charity which they were breaking asunder, wounding and destroying. For they were not gathering with Christ, rather they were scattering, or even worse they were dissolving Christ, which is to tear apart the oneness of his mystical body, and this is why

John added: "And every spirit that dissolves Jesus is not of God." Yes, that is the common translation that we here read and I think that it is the most accurate and truthful in this location, because as Bede noted (and he had learned from the Greek Theodorus and was most learned in the Scriptures), there were some among the heretics who wanted to erase this first from John's letter, especially among those who tried to separate the divinity of Christ from his Incarnation as man by their evil doctrine. Therefore, it is sure that every spirit that dissolves Jesus in any way is not from God, and thus who does not plainly see that Luther, the author of such a large schism, is so miserably dividing and lacerating the unity of the Church's body, and despising our Fathers who have gone before us, and that he is therefore truly a schismatic and by this very note a most manifest pseudo-prophet? I will not dispute that this right of judgment is granted to everyone among the people, by which I mean that as soon as they sense anyone to be under some suspicion of schism, that they should immediately and completely avoid his teachings and communion with him, until such a time as he should be legitimately cleared of that suspicion.

Otherwise, to judge the subtlety of dogmas is something that does not belong to the people, nor are there any Scriptures that demand this to be done by the people — at least not among those that we have up to this point. A little later in that same epistle, however, John adds a clear indicator whereby anyone could discern the spirit of error from the spirit of truth, and that this could be done without great erudition or some subtle adjudication of doctrines: "He that knoweth God heareth us; He that is not of God heareth us not. By this we know the spirit of truth and the spirit of error." Nor is it the case that, when he said "he that knows God hears us," he meant this to be understood only of the Apostles and disciples who were then living, but also for those who would legitimately succeed them within the Church, and who would keep and preserve the unity of the mystical body. Therefore, how can Luther's spirit be from God, since he considers all the successors of the Apostles and disciples to be worthless and completely defies them?

Is it not clearly established from all this that his spirit is the spirit of error and not of truth? Thus could Luther hardly make use of any other references that would more effectively show him to be a pseudo prophet, and yet he has not attained that which he strove to attain, which is that we would believe his doctrines to be Catholic since they are thought to be such by his sectarian followers, and because they are approved as truly orthodox dogmas by the popular judgment of the people.

Luther's Sixth Reason

"For every man, at his own peril, believes either rightly or wrongly; and therefore each must take care, on his own behalf, that he believe rightly, such that even common sense, and the need of salvation, urge the necessity of the hearer having the judgment."

We respond that just as it is with the purchase of goods, there is a danger for the buyer over whether he is purchasing rightly or not, and yet nevertheless not all are equally expert in the discernment of the goodness of the goods to be bought. This is why anyone who is not completely stupid consults those who are more expert, and they trust them in such matters rather than trusting in their own judgment, since they recognize that they can be easily deceived by their own lack of expertise. So, too, simple Christians who do not want to be deceived are required to do likewise — and with much greater reason since a much greater danger is imminent from an error in the faith than if one had made an error in the purchase of something. You see, one man simply loses some money, while this other loses even his soul. It is, therefore, more prudently discriminating for any man who might wish to follow his own thinking or judgment, to more safely follow the judgment of those whose goodness and uprightness is confidently trusted, and about whom he has never heard any sort of suspicion of false teaching. Now, if he cannot find living teachers of the sort, then he can have deceased ones whose faith, life and learning have never been in doubt to any good man: I am here speaking of those ancients upon whom the Holy Spirit fully and copiously descended. One would much more securely listen to them than to anyone who is now living, since we believe that they imbibed much more of the Spirit. Furthermore, when Luther claims that "common sense, and the need of salvation, urge the necessity of the hearer having the judgment," he is very clearly wrong — unless the hearer is wholly spiritual and well-exercised in the Scriptures himself: what is more, common experience and the need for salvation warn us that we should rather follow the judgment of others, whose learning and goodness we trust to be greater than our own. And now on to what Luther adds after this.

Luther's Seventh Reason

"Otherwise it would be useless to say, 'Prove all things; hold fast that which is good'."

We respond by saying that this was indicated to the entire body of the Church — not to each and every one of its individual members — just as if someone were to say to one man: "You go, listen, feel, run!" Each one of these commands was not said to each one of those members, but rather one thing belongs to the eyes, another to the ears, the third to the hands, and the fourth, finally, to the feet. So, too, when Paul says to the Church, "prove all things," he did not say this to every single one but to the spiritual, whose duty it is to be solicitous for the entire body and to pass right examination and judgment upon doctrines. Whatever they will have judged to be good, that same thing should be approved by the others without scruple, because just as the sense of taste in the human body judges for the rest of the members what is tasty against what is tasteless, so, too, in the entire body of the Church, the spiritual man takes a taste for the others, and these latter should unhesitatingly stand by the formers' judgment. Nor is this any less safe, as we have shown, but it is rather much safer than if one were to be confident in his own judgment and genius, which does not usually happen without significant danger and detestable arrogance. For the rest, I should hope that Luther would attend to what Paul immediately adds: "From all appearance of evil refrain yourselves." If he or his followers were to more diligently consider this statement, they would not leave behind the teachings of the Fathers who have gone before, nor would they scatter other new teachings that are completely contrary to the prior, especially since Paul commanded the Hebrews: "Be not led away with various and strange doctrines." If this is not the appearance of evil, then I have no clue what else could possibly be called the appearance of evil.

Luther's Eighth Reason

"And again: The spiritual man judges all things, and is judged by no man. And whoever is a Christian is spiritual — from 'having the spirit of Christ'."

In the very same place where Paul says that the spiritual man judges all things and is himself judged by no one, that is in 1 Cor. 2, he also states that there were many carnal Christians who were not spiritual, just as we have shown above, and that for this reason they could not judge the spiritual. You see, for St. Paul, it was not the case that everyone who had the Holy Spirit was thereby completely spiritual, but rather the one who clearly had his mind illuminated by the spirit and kept his affections inflamed by that same spirit, because there are various gradations according to the various gifts whereby the spirit comes upon men, and many who have the spirit do not enjoy a great insight and perspicacity, such that they could judge of all things. I have no doubt that this is clear to all, just as such a spiritual man who is thus enlightened and inspired knows to judge all things, nor ought or can he be judged by the more carnal and crass people, but this absolutely does not fit every single person among the entire people.

On the Judgment of the People

Luther's Ninth Reason

What he adds in the end from 1 Cor. 3: "All things are yours, whether Apollos, or Paul, or Cephas," does nothing for Luther's case, since Paul pursues this same fact everywhere, that it does not belong to others to judge of him in any way, just as when he previously testified that he was beholden to the mind of Christ, and that therefore he was spiritual and could not be judged by any man. He speaks similarly thereafter in Ch. 4, when he says, "But to me it is a very small thing to be judged by you or by man's day," and a while later, "He who judges me is the Lord." Therefore, the words that Luther reproduces here have nothing to do with the subject at hand, but it demonstrates clearly that he has brought forward another false interpretation, when he adds: "That is to say, you have the right of judging the sayings and doings of all men." You see, Paul later forbids these sorts of judgments when he says, "Judge ye not before the time, until the Lord comes." This is the proof that it is false to say that they have the right to judge all words and deeds. What follows from Luther is nothing but insult and arrogance, such as I shall not respond to, but I leave that to the judgment of the reader, whom I beseech to compare what Luther says with what we have written here; but whoever reads those insults will immediately perceive that they are not from the Holy Spirit, but proceed rather from some impure demon.

CHAPTER XII
Orders and Matrimony Are Sacraments and Efficaciously Confer Grace

IN conclusion, when Luther uses the end of his book to cast objections against the sacraments of Holy Orders and Marriage, we will respond to these briefly. Luther here contends that Orders is not a sacrament, because the reckoning of a sacrament that he thought up does not befit orders at all, as he puts it. "I have denied that the giving of Orders is a sacrament, that is, a promise with a sign of grace added, such as is Baptism and the Bread." So, it is no sacrament to Luther, unless it has a clear promise of grace in the Scriptures, to which a sensible sign is added. But what need was there for Luther to think up a new sort of reckoning of the sacraments for us? Understand here, dear reader, that he is here trying to enmesh us in a riddle so that he can more easily defend his erroneous conception of the faith, because this wickedly deceitful man has understood that if someone is able to obtain grace through the sacraments, then it must follow that we are not justified by faith alone, but also by the work of the sacraments. Now, as soon as he admits this, Luther's entire structure falls completely down, and yet we have shown frequently throughout our refutation of his articles just how suitable that truth is to the Scriptures, that we will add one more point here: if faith alone makes a man just and works add nothing at all to justice, then John did not correctly define the just man in 1 John 3 when he said, "The one who does justice is just," because if that is true — just as it is as true as can be — then the one who wishes to be just must necessarily do justice, and it does

248

not suffice for him that he should but believe. You see, however so much a man may believe, if he willingly sins, he is immediately made unjust, precisely as John adds in that same chapter: "He that commits sin is of the devil: for the devil sinneth from the beginning." Therefore, how will the one who sins whenever he does any work — just as Luther sustains at every opportunity — not be thus of the devil? But John even adds to this: "For this purpose the son of God appeared, that he might destroy the works of the devil." So therefore, the son of God came not so that we might believe, but so that we might walk in his commands and that we might not sin of our own accord; yet, whoever does that, does justice and is just, and faith alone does not render him just, but his works in addition to that faith. Paul also exhorts Timothy in 1 Tim 1, to the extent that he should have a good conscience in addition to his faith: "Having faith and a good conscience, which some rejecting have made shipwreck concerning the faith."

Therefore, faith does not suffice by itself, but it must be buttressed in addition by a good conscience, which only that man obtains who is first truly sorry for his previous sins and has a firm purpose of doing right henceforth. Whoever is not conscious of having both of these things is certainly not in possession of a good conscience, nor will it be possible to call such a man just. We have said all this so that you might understand, oh good reader, that the foundation upon which Luther rests is not solid but so easily falls, since he teaches that faith suffices without works, and that the works of justice add nothing at all to the faith. It is just on this sort of basis or foundation that the man is attempting to build this edifice, such that no grace would be conferred by the sacraments, but that we obtain grace by faith alone, as he phrases it. We, on the other hand, do not deny that the first grace of justification is acquired by faith alone, whenever and wherever that faith is alive and valid, and likewise we do not doubt that among those in whom faith is rather weak, grace is conferred by the sacraments, and that can be strengthened further through good works. Luther, on the other hand, in his attempt to more easily construct his heresy, has imagined up a new reckoning and rationale for the sacraments, such that should we admit it, barely one of the seven sacraments would remain for us, while many other new sacraments would be granted to us, such as have not been thought up yet.

But let us first teach about the first part: the Eucharist has no open promise of grace, and especially if one were to deny that Chapter 6 of John's Gospel treats the Eucharist, as Luther does. For the promise of the forgiveness of sins which is there mentioned is without a doubt thanks to the spilling of blood upon the cross, and not because of the reception from the chalice, just as we made abundantly clear before. The Eucharist would, therefore, not be considered a sacrament according to this reckoning, and Baptism, too, if one wanted to be even more contentious about the matter — and, together with Luther, admit nothing — unless there is some clear mention in Sacred Writ, but nowhere do we read of a patent promise of grace by that same and express name. And thus not a single one of the seven sacraments will remain.

Now, what if he claims that one can prove it by an inductive argument, that grace is promised for the reception of either — and that would certainly be true — but to gather something by an inductive argument is certainly not to be convinced by the clear and explicit expression of the same thing, because there are many things that can be gained by inductive arguments, but which, at first sight, are quite obscure. Then it could also be proven by an inductive argument that grace was promised for each one of the sacraments, because if the one who is properly prepared receives some sacrament and thus receives grace — which could not come about without the promise of God making it happen for us — then it follows that God would have promised this to be the case. So, there you have the inductive argument for the promise of grace for every single sacrament, and if Luther were to deny that it could be proven from the Scriptures that grace is given for other sacraments besides Baptism and Eucharist, then he ought to teach us first that which happens in the Eucharist and in Baptism, and then we will teach him the same with equal facility about the other sacraments. Yet, I am rather sure that unless he asks for assistance from John 6 — which he openly refuses — then he will never show this in regard to the Eucharist.

Yet now, let us demonstrate the other point which we promised to show, that according to the reason and reckoning imagined by Luther, many other sacraments would exist which have yet to be imagined: for example, alms will be a sacrament, as well as forgiveness for injuries done by a brother, prayer, too, and so many things of the sort. First of all for almsgiving, there is a clear promise from Christ when he says, "Give alms: and behold, all things are clean unto you" (Lk. 11). Yet, without sin the soul is not cleansed, which is why grace is promised here, which is hidden and invisible; nor does it lack a certain sensible sign, which is the thing that is given in alms: it immediately follows that alms is a sacrament for Luther. Forgiveness of a wrong done by another will also be a sacrament, because Christ promised, "Forgive and you shall be forgiven," in Lk. 6, but forgiveness of sins does not come about except through grace: there you have it! There is thus the promise of grace, and the sensible sign is when anyone forgives his brother by word or expression. So, too, there is a promise for prayer: "Ask and you shall receive." The sensible sign is the gesture and words of the one who is praying. Now since there is a promise in each of these, as well as an additional sign of grace, who would deny that — according to Luther's tradition — these would have to be true sacraments? Nor am I here affirming that these are sacraments or that I had anywhere prior to this affirmed such — as Martin Bucer was silly enough to jest in objections posed to me. I only said and am saying that according to the rationale and reckoning that Luther has handed on, it necessarily follows that these should be called sacraments. Therefore, there was no need to think up this new reasoning for the sacraments, but rather to demonstrate that what all men commonly take to be the reason and reckoning of the sacraments does not fit at all that which the right believers consider in regard to the sacraments. If he has not done this, then he has accomplished nothing, because it is hardly rhetoric that we get from Luther when he says, "Such things are not sacraments according to the reckoning of sacraments, but rather dreams, and therefore not sacraments." The reason for this is that the orthodox consider sufficient that those things are called sacraments which the school of theologians has hitherto approved according to the rationale of a sacrament, and that is, that they are signs of sacred realities and certain visible forms of invisible grace. Therefore, since these seven which the Church has numbered among the sacraments fit that description and are sacraments, Luther strove in vain to invent a new reckoning of the sacraments. Moreover, although the most illustrious king has showed by many and clear testimonies from the Scriptures that Orders is numbered among the sacraments in this manner, Luther nevertheless disdains to recognize anything — as it fitting for that man's impudent attitude — except the one citation from Paul's letter to Titus, about which he says: "They bring forth nothing worthy of reply in all that they write of the six sacraments — except that one thing which is adduced concerning the sacrament of Holy Orders, when Paul of course orders Titus to ordain presbyters in all the churches, because by this passage he wishes the sacrament of orders to be instituted." Yet, the king himself never actually used these words, nor did he claim that the sacrament of Orders was instituted in that instance; rather he brought forward many more citations from Paul and even ones that were much more evident, whereby he satisfactorily showed that grace is given by the imposition of hands at the ordination of presbyters. Is this not the very thing that Paul precisely indicates when he writes in 1 Timothy 4: "Neglect not the grace that is in thee, which was given thee by prophecy, with imposition of the hands of the priesthood?" And again in 2 Timothy: "For which cause I admonish thee that thou stir up the grace of God which is in thee by the imposition of my hands." And even again when he forbids that anyone should abuse the authority and power given to him: "Impose not hands lightly upon any man." Is it not clear from these references that the laying on of hands in the ordinations of priests comes about with the gift of that very same grace from above? Therefore, the imposition of hands that happens at ordination is a sensible sign of invisible grace, and is thus a true sacrament.

Luther, however, elsewhere contends that Timothy received this grace from Paul when he was baptized and not when he was instituted as bishop. But he should have first shown that Timothy was indeed baptized by Paul, if we are to believe him, and let him show that from the Scriptures — and yet I know that he will never show this. Unless he brings forward the Scriptures, his proof will be in vain. But he will say, "Paul calls Timothy his son in each epistle," — granted. He also calls the Corinthians his sons in 1 Cor. 4, when he says, "I write not these things to confound you: but I admonish you as my dearest children. For if you have ten thousand instructors in Christ, yet not many fathers. For in Christ Jesus, by the gospel, I have begotten you." There you have how Paul boasts of himself to the Corinthians as their father through the gospel, as you heard when he called them his beloved sons, and he probably called himself their father; nevertheless, they clearly were not baptized by Paul: "I give God thanks, that I baptized none of you but Crispus and Gaius," and he adds shortly thereafter, "For Christ sent me not to baptize, but to preach the gospel." Therefore, he does not prove that Timothy was baptized by Paul, simply because Paul calls him his son; yet, Luther says, Timothy was at Lystra when the people there were converted by Paul and Barnabas. Well, even if we were to grant you this, it would not thereby follow that Paul baptized him, because when the Corinthians first believed in the gospel and were baptized, there were many other Corinthians besides Crispus, Gaius, and the family of Stephanas, and yet they were not baptized by Paul, as we have already said; therefore, Luther has lost all ability to show from Holy Writ that Timothy was baptized by Paul, and thus his subterfuge serves him not a bit.

This twisting and turning snake, however, does have another deviating retreat up his sleeve: that the imposition of hands does not belong properly to the sacrament of Orders, as he says shortly thereafter: "But as to what he alleges concerning the laying on of hands at ordination, even boys see that this has nothing to do with the sacrament of Orders. He does just as his papist manners dictate and takes from Scripture whatever seems good to him. The laying on of hands, according to what he says, was the visible giving of the Holy Spirit." Yet, we can see that the Holy Spirit was given visibly by the laying on of hands, such that those to whom it was given immediately received the gift of tongues, and that they even spoke those whichsoever they willed, but this in no way prohibits that the gift of that same Spirit could be reiterated invisibly with the laying on of hands and with other effects. The reason is this: the same Spirit is conferred for various effects and likewise in various manners: on the 50th day, it was given without the laying on of hands, such as when he sat upon the heads of all and filled those who were there present with his presence — among whom were Stephen and Philip, who would have likewise received the spirit, doubtless, and yet the same two men were afterwards set up as deacons, and they received the spirit anew in the laying on of hands — but for a different effect than that they should speak in tongues, to wit, that they might promptly, willingly and efficaciously fulfill the role and duty of deacons, as had been conferred upon them by the Apostles. For they previously received the gift of tongues, but at this moment it was another invisible grace, such as happened to Paul: at the Spirit's command, Ananias laid hands upon him and he received the gift of tongues, but afterwards when he was ordered by that same spirit to be set apart for the Apostleship, he once again received the spirit of the prophets and teachers, through the laying on of hands, and for what was certainly another effect, because the prophets and teachers who were then at Antioch and who had received the Spirit's command to set apart Barnabas and Paul while fasting and offering sacrifice, indeed laid hands upon them — and they likewise did this while fasting and praying, as is very clearly stated in Acts 13. Nor is it believed that Paul and Barnabas received the Spirit in a visible manner again at that time, but rather his invisible grace, by which they were rendered suitable to worthily carry out the office and duties of Apostles. Likewise, when Paul and Barnabas later made priests by laying their hands upon them, as is evident from Acts 14, that such men received the Spirit twice is beyond doubt: for sure, they received it once when they were confirmed — which was common to all Christians at that time — and then again when they were ordained priests, just as Luke hands on to us in regard to that ordination: "χειροτονήσαντες δὲ αὐτοῖς πρεσβυτέρους (ordaining priests for them)" (Acts. 14:22). And although the verb χειροτονέω — to ordain or lay hands on — pertains to the people in some other places, such as when they raise their hands to select magistrates, at this point however, it is clearly not used in regard to the people but about the very Apostles Paul and Barnabas, that they should, by their imposition of hands or laying on of hands, create and establish priests for the people, that they might pray and fast: there you have fasting, prayer and the laying on of hands.

Now, dear reader, apply some judgment: which of the two — the king or Luther — more truthfully and fittingly makes use of the Scriptures? I think that you already see how clear it is that not only were deacons created by the laying on of hands, but so were Apostles and priests. Yet Luther will say: "Why wasn't Matthias ordained in this way?" If he says that this is not given to us in the Scriptures, then this is merely a negative argument that cannot prove anything, but this is just the sort of logical distinction that often fools Luther. Nevertheless, even from Acts we can see that Matthias was made an Apostle by the laying on of hands, because it is there written: "and he was numbered with the eleven Apostles," and it is beyond belief that this numbering was carried out by the Apostles in any manner other than the imposition of hands. But let us grant for a moment that there was no laying on of hands: the cause might have been that the Spirit had not yet come, who was to teach the Apostles that this grace should be given by a sign, but that after this revelation of the Spirit had made the matter clear, thence forward and in all places, they would lay their hands among those who were to be confirmed and ordained; you see, it is certain that unless the Spirit had inspired this in the Apostles, never should such an incredible thing have come about, nor would they have attempted such, otherwise how could they believe and hope that such an effect would infallibly come about? This certainty of a confident hope — which possessed the Apostles at that time and in this matter — plainly indicates that the Spirit was promised to come upon them whenever this happened, and that is to say that he would both be present as well as presenting the gift of grace to those who were being confirmed and ordained, upon whom the Apostles would lay hands for these very reasons. It is easily gathered from this — besides for Luther's obstinate opinions — that there are many things that we must believe, yet which are not contained within the Sacred Scriptures.

I think that it is clear from these statements that deacons and priests were ordained by the imposition of hands, that by the same act grace was conferred upon them, and that this all happened as stipulated by divine inspiration, for this reason there is nothing more to be demanded from the particular reckoning of the sacraments, than that it should be a sensible sign and that grace is promised: who could thereafter doubt whether Ordination — which is the conferral of grace promised through a sensible sign — is truly a sacrament? For the rest of Luther's argument, by which he insists that this election should happen with the people's supporting suffrage, just as it happened with the institution of the seven deacons, I would not fight back if the people could agree on any one matter without any contentions and disturbances, and after having set aside all emotion, but this is so near impossible that even for those noble and celebrated men of the Church there were disputes as well as insurrections — even planned murders happened upon such elections at various times — while one faction or another was firmly and obstinately attached to one person or another, such that those men were forced to handle the situation by their own authority and without having first consulted the people.

Furthermore, if the election were to be carried out by the people, this confers nothing of the presbyterate or episcopate upon them, since it is nevertheless necessary that whoever was elected should also be ordained rightly and in a rite by one who enjoys that authority and privilege. This is even evident in the seven deacons themselves, about whose ordination we read in Acts 6: "And in those days, with the number of the disciples increasing, there arose a murmuring of the Greeks against the Hebrews, that their widows were neglected in the daily ministration. Then the Twelve, calling together the multitude of the disciples, said: It is not reasonable that we should leave the word of God and serve tables. Wherefore, brethren, look ye out among you seven men of good reputation, full of the Holy Ghost and wisdom, whom we may appoint over this business." You see here, dear reader, that there was first need of the Apostles to choose the deacons whom they would send to be over the multitude, because they would have otherwise had great difficulty in calming the murmuring that had arisen unless the people would accept the ministers as a sort of sentence for their own souls. You also see how the Apostles granted this to them, such that the Apostles still retained the delegation of the duty itself: "Whom we may appoint over this business." Moreover, it is very clear from the words that follow just what sort of ceremony the Apostles used to set up the diaconate: "And they praying, imposed hands upon them." Luke had already spoken previously about the fasting, for the Apostles used all three in any and every ordination: fasting, prayer, and laying on hands. Therefore, there is nothing in the Acts of the Apostles that contradicts what happened with Titus, who enjoyed the authority given to him by Paul and ordained priests in the churches, because in every location the priests were ordained by the hands of other priests.

Nor do Paul's words differ in the least from the example of the Apostles, since it was the Apostles and not the people that delegated this duty to the deacons, and who, after having prayed, laid their hands upon them. "But," he will say, "the people nominated those seven and set them up in the sight of the Apostles!" I do not dispute, but this nomination did not make them deacons, because it was only afterwards that they were established as deacons, once the Apostles had laid their hands on them, just as we have shown. Therefore, it is very clear that the Apostles laid their hands both on priests as well as deacons to ordain them, and since in this manner grace is infallibly conferred by the Ordination — unless the one who is being ordained were to fight against it — it is clear that Ordination is truly a sacrament, since the peculiar rationale and reason for sacrament truly befits it: that is, there is the visible form of invisible grace, such that it exists as the cause and retains the image. A certain invisible grace accompanies that Ordination that is like a certain sign. For the rest, since we have otherwise spoken copiously about the priesthood and the sacrifice of the Mass, this will mark the end of what pertains to the sacrament of Orders.

Regarding Matrimony, too, that it is a sacrament in the identical manner, we shall now attempt to show succinctly, although one will grasp this much more easily by faith than by any arguments. That saying from Augustine proves it well and is very well approved by me: "Faith should be applied to the divine sacraments more than to worded arguments."[17] This of course should wholly suffice for any good Christian, because the Church herself gave to us seven sacraments, and she commands that we apply our faith to them, because if truth should be found anywhere upon earth, it will nowhere be found more infallibly than inside the Church. This matter can be completely clear to anyone on account of the numerous references that exist, but especially thanks to three: first, that Christ, who called himself the truth, promised to be with the

---

[17] Editor's note: From the *De visit. infirm*, which subsequent to Fisher's time has been agreed to be of questionable attribution to Augustine.

Church for all time unto the consummation of the age. If Christ, who is truth itself, will never leave the Church destitute, it is certain that she will never be destitute of the truth either. The second point is that Christ himself promised that the Holy Spirit would be perpetually within the Church, and that he would lead her into all truth: "I will ask the father and he will give you another comforter, that he might remain with you forever, the Spirit of Truth," as in John 14; and just a little later he says: "When he who is the Spirit of Truth comes, he will lead you into all truth." If the Spirit of Truth will never be absent from the Church and will lead her into all truth, what would he be to suffer us to receive false sacraments in place of true ones? Third, as it is written in 1 Tim. 3: "That thou mayest know how thou ought to behave thyself in the house of God, which is the church of the living God, the pillar and ground of the truth." If the house of God that is the Church of the living God is the column and foundation of the truth, then he cannot go wrong who relies upon the doctrine handed on consistently by her. These points so completely move me that I do not hesitate in the least to adhere to those things that I know have been approved by the Church's definition.

For this reason, since it was defined at the Ecumenical Council of Florence — at which both the Greeks and the Latins convened — that the Church has seven sacraments which confer grace to those who worthily receive them, and among which Matrimony was also numbered as the seventh, thenceforth no right-believing person can doubt within himself the truth of this declaration.

Furthermore, lest the council be thought to have decreed such without the use of the Scriptures and sufficient reasons, we will display some of the evidence on account of which all believe that it acted rightly. The primary and most impressive point is John's martyrdom, when he confronted death for his rebuke of that violated marriage: there were of course many sins and crimes that were more serious in kind and appearance, for the review of which he would have gladly suffered, but the friend of the Bridegroom would not have more fittingly shed his blood than on account of this adultery and violation of marriage, since this especially did such harm to Christ the Bridegroom. Moreover, the Baptist testifies that Christ was the bridegroom when he says: "He that hath the bride is the bridegroom: but the friend of the bridegroom, who stands and hears him, rejoices with joy because of the bridegroom's voice. This my joy therefore is fulfilled." That is how John the Baptist put the matter: Christ is the bridegroom, you see, and the Church is the bride of Christ; John is the friend of the bridegroom. Therefore, just as John, the friend of the bridegroom, greatly rejoiced at the union of the bride and bridegroom — that is of Christ and the Church – so, too, was he unable to consider it anything but most grievous that there was this public harm inflicted upon matrimony, which he held to be a sure sign of that very union. At this point Luther will say, "I know that we are begging the question which is first incumbent upon us: that we should prove that Marriage is the sacrament of this union." Unless I am mistaken, we will do this in a moment, but at this first opportunity I want the reader to consider how incumbent it was upon John, the friend of the bridegroom, to vindicate that very evil, since this necessarily caused harm to the spouse, whenever that sign of Christ's union with the Church — Matrimony — should itself suffer any damage. You see, anyone can very easily gather that the violation of Marriage would redound unto the abrogation of this sacred union itself, and that John fittingly and properly suffered such a martyrdom for that marriage that had been dishonored.

Otherwise, that Matrimony or Marriage is the sign of that most sacred union itself, the most illustrious king illustrates so copiously from Paul's words in Eph. 5, that I barely see anything to add, or by what backward retreat Luther can evade admitting this fully — although unwillingly. You see, no one but the one who likewise loses his mind with Luther can possibly deny that these words were used about those first spouses, when even Christ in Mt. 19 and Mk. 10 attests to the same, because he there teaches from those same words that the bond of a husband with a wife is indissoluble: "But from the beginning of the creation, God made them male and female. For this cause, a man shall leave his father and mother and shall cleave to his wife. And the two shall be in one flesh. Therefore now they are not two, but one flesh. What therefore God hath joined together, let no man put asunder." Therefore, it is evident that these words pertain to husbands and wives, and if these phrases about spouses signify that union of Christ with the Church, who does not clearly see that what bound those first spouses is so similar to that which we confess between Christ and the Church? For example, by those words Paul is fully constructing a great mystery, and although it otherwise pertains there to Christ and the Church, nevertheless it sprouts forth from that same matrimonial union as if from its basis and figure. Thus, the marriage between husband and wife signifies the bonds between Christ and the Church — otherwise Paul would not compare the husband to Christ and the wife to the Church in Eph. 5, when he says that the husband is the head of the wife just as Christ is the head of the Church, and as he commands the husbands to love their wives as Christ loves the Church. He also adds that just as the members of the Church are formed from the flesh and bones of Christ, so, too, did that first woman have her origin, and by these descriptions of the first couple, he joins it all together: "For this reason a man will leave his mother and father, and be joined to his wife, and there will be two in one flesh." And at length, Paul introduces it in this way, "This is a great mystery or sacrament," that is, "a man shall leave his parents and be joined to his wife" and that "they shall be one flesh." Truly, this is a great mystery and sacrament, insofar as it represents the bond between Christ and his Church. Nor will I dispute that, should you investigate this matter some more, you find the union of man and woman in one flesh to be something of modest amount, while if you look to that joining of Christ with the Church — to which Matrimony refers — you will understand that this latter is a great mystery or sacrament.

Though all of these things are as clear as day, Luther still obstinately persists in denying that marriage is a sacrament, and he phrases it thus: "And what shall I say? He has not even wished to understand the meaning of the word 'sacrament,' which he plainly shows when he handles the passage from Paul in Eph. 5 concerning matrimony, in which Paul refers to Christ and the Church saying, 'This is a great sacrament, but I speak of Christ and the Church,' because Scripture does not permit that matrimony be called a sacrament." At this point, the reader will note by what necessity Luther is forced — with such intensity and focus — to try to do damage to this sacrament, since he will bitingly state that there is sin in any good work whatsoever, and that the *fomes [peccati]* or "kindling [of sin]" is sin even in the most holy men; for that reason, he completely denies that the conjugal act can be without sin, and it thereby follows that he can do away with the sacrament of Matrimony — the primary necessity of which sacrament was so that the conjugal act could be engaged in without sin between husband and wife, and that there would be no offense to God in mutually rendering the debt — a debt of benevolence or good will. You see, I cannot be led to believe that this act is essentially evil, such that it can in no way be good to do, since otherwise God would not have commanded our very first parents to act so, and yet it is patently clear that he did command this, in Gen. 1. And lest anyone should say that it could have then happened without sin because our flesh had not yet become resistant and rebellious to the spirit, see how the very same thing is commanded in Genesis 9:7, for our fallen nature: "Be fruitful and multiply" — which cannot come about without the conjugal act. Yet, whatever God commanded, it is thereby made — by his command of it — necessary that it be a good, just as is clear of the plundered Egyptians: it would not have been licit for the Hebrews to do so, had not God commanded them beforehand to do that very thing. Therefore, since God commanded that this act should be done, it is certain that it is not an essentially evil thing, but that by its circumstances it can be a good act — and even done well, for the good, and without any sin: otherwise Paul would not have said, "If thou marry, thou hast not sinned; and if a virgin marry, she hath not sinned." You see here that Paul clearly states that they do not sin, and once again a little thereafter: "But if any man think that he seems dishonored with regard to his virgin, for that she is above the age, and it must so be: let him do what he will. He sinneth not if she marry." Here again Paul has affirmed that they do not sin who are joined in matrimony, just as he will say later in the same chapter: "Therefore he that gives his virgin in marriage does well." There you have it. Paul here teaches not only that this act is good but that it is done well: "He does well." Therefore, in order that spouses might exercise this act without sin, the sacrament of Matrimony was instituted. So that this matter might appear further apparent, we will strive to establish certain truths from the Scriptures, from which we will gather that Marriage is a true sacrament and that it is so according to the precise definition of a sacrament.

The First Truth
A perfect marriage is also indissoluble.

The truth of this matter is clear from Matthew 5: "I say to you, that whosoever shall put away his wife, excepting the cause of fornication, makes her an adulterer: and he that shall marry her that is put away, commits adultery." He confirms this with nearly those exact words in Chapter 19, as well as in Mark 10: "Whosoever shall put away his wife and marry another commits adultery against her. And if the wife shall put away her husband and be married to another, she commits adultery." Just as in Luke 16: "Whosoever puts away his wife, and marries another, commits adultery: and whosoever marries her that is put away from her husband commits adultery." Paul, too, in 1 Cor. 7: "To them that are married, not I, but the Lord, commands that the wife depart not from her husband. And if she depart, that she remain unmarried or be reconciled to her husband. And let not the husband put away his wife." There you clearly have it from all of these: the matrimony that is contracted between a man and a woman by mutual consent cannot be dissolved by mutual consent, but as long as both of the contracting parties are alive, then as far as man is concerned, it is indissoluble.

Second Truth
This bond is indissolubly forged — not by men but by God into the souls of the spouses

So, too, the truth of this statement is evident from Matthew and Mark, for it is written in Mt. 19: "Is it lawful for a man to put away his wife for every cause? Who answering, said to them: Have ye not read, that he who made man from the beginning, made them male and female? And he said: For this cause shall a man leave father and mother, and shall cleave to his wife, and they two shall be in one flesh. Therefore now they are not two, but one flesh. What therefore God hath joined together, let no man put asunder." You see how Christ clearly stated that this indissoluble union of the spouses comes from God, and in Mark 10 we find the complete agreement of the evangelist, and thus it is clear that the spouses are mutually joined by God's authority, and bound by him through some link that is indissoluble as far as man is concerned.

THIRD TRUTH
This indissolubility is not found in its absolute fullness except through the faith of Christ, and at the time of the fullness of grace

Marriage does not receive its full and absolute perfection until both parties have received Christianity, because if one of the spouses accepts the faith of Christ and is made a Christian, but the other spouse completely rejects the faith and — due to hatred for the Christian name — repudiates the other (either the husband his wife, or the wife her husband), then that party which converted to Christ has full rights, nor is confined and bound to follow the other, but may be joined to another, if that party so wills. This is what Paul teaches in 1 Corinthians 7: "But if the unbeliever depart, let him depart. For a brother or sister is not under servitude in such cases." You see here that both for the man as well as for the woman, if that person should have come into a union before coming to Christianity, and the unbelieving party leaves from hatred for Christ, Paul declares the other free to leave and not be bound to follow the departed party. Thus, it is also clear that that very marriage that existed previously, contracted among the Jews, did not have its full and absolute indissolubility. Nor is this thwarted by what was quoted above, that what God has joined, man may not separate, because this divorce or separation does not come from man, but is rather from the authority of God, who granted to Christians such a freedom that they should not be forced to follow the unbelieving party and have their faith put in danger. From this it becomes evident to all that matrimony had not previously received its complete and most absolute perfection until Christ had joined the Church to himself, and this at the time of the "fullness of grace."

Fourth Truth

As often as God thus binds the spouses, he likewise confers grace, by which the parties may more easily keep their intertwined course of life unseparated

I understand this to be the case as long as the spouses themselves do nothing to oppose this acceptance of grace, because not even from Baptism or the Eucharist — or any other sacrament — is grace conferred upon those who, during its very reception, oppose and bar it by a mortal sin. This is because, as far as it pertains to the spouses who are to be joined together, they must remove and put away any obstacles beforehand, and they must prepare their souls, just as Solomon says in Proverbs 16: "It is the part of man to prepare the soul," and as in Mt. 3, as it is quoted from Isaias: "Prepare ye the way of the Lord." If the spouses thus prepare their souls, there is no doubt that God will pour out grace upon the two who are contracting Matrimony: we will here consider first how reasonable this is, and immediately thereafter we shall show the same from the Scriptures. It is certain that this obliging bond that connects husband and wife — if anyone should consider it attentively — encompasses great difficulty, such as that one would not be allowed to separate from another who was irascible, argumentative or scurrilously foul-mouthed, beset by bad habits, a drunk, glutton, or even a wandering vagrant. This is why the Apostles said to Christ in Mt. 19: "If the case of a man with his wife be so, it is not expedient to marry." Thus, it would hardly befit God's largess — he who is so rich in mercy — if he were to bind the married together with such a tight link and yet was not equally giving them the grace whereby they could peacefully persevere in that very obligating bound, in order to render service to those three goods: offspring, the faith, and the sacrament. For it is difficult — not to say impossible — that any spouses might live without some help of grace, so that the good of children might be taken care of zealously, that the faith of both parties might be integrally preserved, and finally that the sign of that most excellent union of Christ and the Church might be in no way damaged. Yet someone will say: "These things do not even transpire now among all those who otherwise legitimately entered into marriage." To this I respond: such does not happen because grace is failing the sacrament of Matrimony, but rather because they who are so joined show themselves to be failing the grace, such as when it was written of Rehoboam in 2 Par. 12 [2 Chr.], that they had not prepared their hearts to seek the Lord. Otherwise, for those who are properly prepared, there is not the least doubt that grace is conferred, because God — especially at this time of the plenitude of grace — never gives anyone a duty to do something upon whom he does not also confer the grace to fulfill that very duty. This is why, given that God indissolubly joined man and woman in this duty and covenant, no one should waver with the least uncertainty that God constantly and habitually gives the grace necessary to worthily exercise the acts of that duty and role. But now let us prove this from the Scriptures.

At this point we note, besides what we have cited earlier, that we read how God did so "from the beginning." That is, when he joined our first parents, he blessed them and said, "Increase and multiply." Nor was this blessing just some bodily benefit, but it was also spiritual, because God's blessing blesses according to the capacity of each one. You see, although the other creatures that were blessed did not receive thereby any grace of the spirit, since they were not capable of grace, nothing yet kept rational man from the reception of grace when he was blessed: for, who would not know for sure that the children whom Christ blessed in Mark 10 indeed received grace from that very blessing, since they were capable of grace? Again in Genesis 9, when God blessed Noah and his sons at once and all together, commanding them to increase and multiply, not only did a certain virtue strengthen their bodies, but grace was also divinely impressed upon their spirits. Now, as time has passed for our tainted nature, and while the sacrament of Marriage was not yet fully concluded and perfected, and yet God so blessed those patriarchs for the sake of that conjugal duty, and now at the moment of the plenitude or fullness of grace, when the sacraments are fully completed and fulfilled, would God join the spouses with a completely indissoluble bond and not sprinkle them with the grace of his blessing?

Then, in support of this we have what is written in Tobias 6, that those who come together to receive matrimony but to cast God from themselves and their minds, and thus to live for lust, are like the horse and the mule, and the demon has power over them; on the other hand, it happens in a contrary manner for those who are joined by a love for children rather than by lust, because they are safe from the demons and received the blessing upon the offspring in Abraham's seed side-by-side with them. This is the manner in which God so greatly encouraged piously contracted marriages, such that he granted such a grace to the spouses, even when that great mystery of Christ and the Church had yet to be referenced, and when marriage had yet to be made wholly indissoluble. Now, since Christ as true bridegroom has joined to himself his bride, the Church, and decorated marriage with such wondrous praise, will he not give any grace to those who are joined in a holy way? Yet now let us come to the New Law.

In 1 Th. 4, Paul put it this way: "This is the will of God, your sanctification, that you should abstain from fornication, and that every one of you should know how to possess his vessel in sanctification and honor, not in the passion of lust, like the Gentiles that know not God." It is certain from these verses that Paul was not striving to make all of the Thessalonians live a celibate life, or forcing the married among them to completely abstain from their spouses, just as he testified in 1 Cor. 7 to what he had established on the matter in all the other churches, that is, that they should each have their own spouses in order to avoid fornication, and that each spouse should benevolently render the debt to the other. He also says that the spouses do not have complete rights over their own bodies, but one and the other: the wife has rights over the husband's body, and the husband has rights over the wife's. Therefore, there is no way that Paul is here forbidding the enjoyment of the conjugal act to the Thessalonians, just as the conjugal act does not stand in the way of the honor and sanctity of these vessels, or bodies, of the two spouses, as you might understand the word. Now, since Paul says that it is God's will for them to be sanctified, and that each one should know how to possess his vessel in sanctification and honor, who could still doubt whether God did grant grace to the married, who were led to enter marriage not by any attachment to concupiscence but for the sake of avoiding fornication and procreating children, so that they might be able to keep themselves holy in their conjugal work, both in mind and body?

This is what Paul is describing in Hebrews 13:4: "Marriage is honorable in all, and the bed undefiled." You see that Paul calls marriage honorable, and asserts that the bed is undefiled, and for this very reason mutual benevolence among the spouses is rendered one to the other in such a holy manner, so that not even the conjugal act profanes or pollutes them in any way, since if any stain of sin or any dishonor were to affect their souls or bodies, then marriage should no longer be honorable, nor should the bed be considered undefiled. But who does not comprehend that this cannot be had without some gift of grace? The reference to 1 Cor. 7 shows Paul's support, too: "The unbelieving husband is sanctified by the wife who believes, and the unbelieving wife is made holy through the husband who believes." I think that such words should be understood to mean that the unbelieving man may mix with his right-believing wife and no mortal fault will be imputed thereby, rather this very act is protected from mortal sin by the wife's faith, and by the grace through which she meanwhile conjoined with her husband, as long as she wills not to depart from him. Now, if this can happen to the completely unfaithful husband, on account of the faith and grace of the bond, by which he is not totally indissolubly bound to the wife, then what might we expect where there is a totally indissoluble bond, and an integral faith in Christ within both?

Additionally, you have what is in 1 Timothy 2, where Paul attributes such greatness to holy Matrimony that he says that spouses even merit through the generation of children: "She shall be saved through child bearing; if she continue in faith," that is, if the woman births them so that they may be entered into Christ. Yet, who doubts that this generation is the work of Matrimony? For this reason, too, the woman who lays out a holy and sincere education of the children in Christ, is able to merit for herself eternal salvation, which could not be the case were it not for grace. Finally, as we said above, in 1 Cor. 7 Paul confirms that they who are joined in a holy manner do not sin: "If you take a wife, you have not sinned, and if a virgin should marry, she does not sin," and just after that, "The one who gives his virgin to be married, does well." Yet, if the conjugal act could not happen without sin, how will the one who consents to it not also sin? Or how could one do well who is conscious of the fact that, by that very act in which he is engaging, he is simultaneously sinning and perpetrating a bad act? Now, if this is a good act and he does well when he does it — and since that could not happen without grace – who does not see how clearly it follows that God has thereunto affixed an indissoluble bond and likewise infuses grace thereupon? This should suffice for the fourth point.

Fifth Truth

These things are not lacking a sensible sign, whereby it is certain that the grace of this unbreakable bond is given to the spouses themselves

The truth of this is likewise distinctly evident, because if any unmarried man were to have relations with a similarly unmarried woman, unless they had made it clear either verbally or by other manifest indicators that they were making a mutual contract among themselves and were mutually promising themselves one to the other, then we are not dealing with a matrimony, nor of a bond by which they are bound such that it cannot be easily broken; rather, it would be within the freedom of both, as soon as they might wish, to leave the other. Yet, if both were within their rights, and completely free from any other contract, nor had any legitimate impediment, if they were to communicate by words or indications that they were clearly witnessing the mutual communication of their bodies, and if they prepared for this sacrament in a holy way, then this bond will doubtless be unbreakable, and grace will likewise be infused into their souls from God above. Therefore, the sensible sign both of this indivisible union, as well as the graces that will flow into the souls of the spouses, is the words themselves, as well as any other indicators whereby the contract comes about between the two, because if the contract is defective on the part of either party, nothing transpires; no matrimony is confirmed.

Furthermore, as it pertains to these visible signs, Luther does not oppose very much, because not far from that same spot of his that we just opposed, he speaks of marriage in this way: "Matrimony is not such a hidden thing, nor is it perceived by faith, since unless it is done openly and in front of men's eyes, it cannot be matrimony. For matrimony is the outward joining together of a man and a woman, confirmed by a public profession and by the exchange of vows." By what he says in these words — at least in the latter portion — he plainly teaches that there is no ratified matrimony where there are not manifest and evident signs and indications, which transpire openly and before everyone's eyes. Now, for what regards the first part of that quotation and from what we have said previously, who does not see the patent error and falsity of it, that is, that matrimony is not some hidden thing, or perceived by the faith? You see, if nothing else is happening within their souls, except that which happens patently in front of their eyes, no grace is given to the spouses, and they are not bound by God above in any indissoluble bond. Yet, if this bond is lacking, who will still affirm the contract is a marriage? This is why, seeing that this bond is a certain hidden thing, and would not be perceived other than by faith, and likewise, since the grace which only exists through the spouses is equally infused with this bond, it will have been invisible, known only by faith.

In summary, since, both an invisible bond and grace accompany the very contract which, in the same way, is a kind of sensible sign carried out in the public forum, who does not clearly perceive that the marriage which is made up of these three things is something hidden and perceived by faith — and rightfully called a sacrament? Marriage is, you see, according to the proper reckoning of a sacrament, endowed with a visible image of the invisible grace, such that it bears the image and is the cause of it, just as it is clear from what we have said that the very contract that is entered into externally is the sign and cause of the interior bond and grace that come from God. If anyone objects to this, that a contract could take place without grace, we have shown above and respond that the sacraments of Baptism and the Eucharist could likewise be conferred without grace, and nevertheless they remain the signs of grace and, to be sure, are infallibly efficacious, as long as one receives them without presenting any barrier to it and rather has rightly prepared himself for reception. Thus must we say likewise about the sacrament of Matrimony, because we do not doubt at all that God bestows grace upon those who contract it, as long as their hearts are worthily prepared, and if no grace should accompany the contract, that should not be God's fault, but most certainly comes from the fault of those who are contracting it. Since this is so very clear from the Scriptures, who could still be in doubt that God has once given such a promise, although the promise itself might be nowhere openly mentioned in the Scriptures, just as we nowhere read of it being openly promised, with explicit words, that grace is given upon the reception of the Eucharist?

Therefore, dear reader, you discern how the Council of Florence was hardly audacious in decreeing that Matrimony was one of the seven sacraments that conferred grace, and that this council that represented the gathering of the Universal Church — both of the Greeks and the Latins — is justly and rightly to be believed besides the Scriptures, both because of the truth of the Spirit who ever resides with us, as well as on account of the Church herself, being represented as the column and foundation of the truth, as Paul did not hesitate to call her. Moreover, since the entire matter itself is additionally illustrated by so many Scriptures, who but the completely mad and obstinately-minded could hereafter hesitate on this matter and call it into doubt in any way?

Orders and Matrimony Are Sacraments

At this point, I think, there is nothing of importance left untouched or ignored in that cursed and cursing little book by Luther, and to which we have not abundantly responded in kind — except to his insults, which exceed all measure and even all meanness — and which we willingly allow to most justly fall right upon the head of their very author. For I do not doubt in the least that the equitable and judicious reader, who fairly and worthily weighs and considers the defense of Catholic truth taken up by the most illustrious king, and then the very poisonously offensive assault and attack against this very truth, launched by this impious heresiarch, will end up judging one of them to be much more worthy of all those insults — and many more besides. On the contrary, I am certain that it will be far from such a gracious and good reader that he would judge the great king to be in any way harmed by any of Luther's insults and invective, but that he would much rather consider him to be all the more wondrous, splendid, and illustrious on their account. Fare thee well for now, my dear reader.